LANGUAGE AT HOME AND AT SCHOOL
Volume 1

Learning through interaction
The study of language development

LANGUAGE AT HOME AND AT SCHOOL
Edited by Gordon Wells

Forthcoming titles

GORDON WELLS *Language development in the pre-school years*
BRIDIE RABAN *Children learning to read*

Learning through interaction

The study of language development

GORDON WELLS
Research Director, Centre for the Study of
Language and Communication, University of
Bristol

With contributions by

Allayne Bridges
Lecturer in Psychology, University of
Birmingham

Peter French
College of Ripon and York
St John

Margaret MacLure
National Foundation for
Educational Research in
England and Wales

Chris Sinha
Avery Hill College of Education

Valerie Walkerdine
Research Fellow, University of London
Institute of Education

Bencie Woll
Centre for the Study of Language and
Communication, University of Bristol

Cambridge University Press

Cambridge
London   New York   New Rochelle
Melbourne   Sydney

Published by the Press Syndicate of the University of Cambridge
The Pitt Building, Trumpington Street, Cambridge CB2 1RP
32 East 57th Street, New York, NY 10022, USA
296 Beaconsfield Parade, Middle Park, Melbourne 3206, Australia

First published 1981
Reprinted 1983

Printed and bound in Great Britain at The Pitman Press, Bath

British Library Cataloguing in Publication Data
Wells, Gordon
Learning through interaction. – (Language
at home and at school; vol. 1).
1. Children – Language
I. Title II. Series
401'.9   LB1139.L3   80-41113

ISBN 0 521 23774 2 hard covers
ISBN 0 521 28219 5 paperback

Contents

Acknowledgments   *page* vii

Introduction   1

1 Language as interaction   22
  Gordon Wells

2 Becoming a communicator   73
  Gordon Wells

3 The development of comprehension   116
  Allayne Bridges, Chris Sinha and Valerie Walkerdine

4 Context, meaning and strategy in parent–child
  conversation   157
  Peter French and Bencie Woll

5 Developing linguistic strategies in young school children   183
  Valerie Walkerdine and Chris Sinha

6 A comparison of talk at home and at school   205
  Margaret MacLure and Peter French

7 Language, literacy and education   240
  Gordon Wells

  Appendix. Bristol language development study:
  transcripts   277

  References   283

  Index   299

Acknowledgments

With a research programme that has lasted so long and involved so many people it is impossible to mention them all by name. Our greatest debt of course is to the children and their families who have provided the material on which the research is based. Their cooperation has been generous to an extent that far exceeded our expectation and was most deeply appreciated when equipment failed and other arrangements went awry. We are equally indebted to the head and class teachers in the schools that the children attended, who found themselves caught up in a project that made demands which it was difficult for them to refuse. We also wish to acknowledge the help of the Medical Officer of Health for the Bristol Area in making the initial contacts with the children and the Local Education Authority in allowing us to carry out observations and collect data in the schools.

The many people who have worked at transcribing and coding the recordings of conversation and interviewing the families are also too numerous to mention by name. For their loyal and painstaking efforts we are extremely grateful; without them the research could never have been undertaken, let alone brought so far along the road to a successful conclusion. To colleagues in the Research Unit of the School of Education we also owe an immense debt of gratitude: Professor Alan Brimer for setting the whole research programme going and advising on the design of the earliest phase; Linda Ferrier, who contributed substantially to the development of the coding scheme and, between 1973 and 1976, trained and supervised the coders who used it; Dr Bernard Chapman, who designed the recording equipment, and Ivan Colhoun, who built and serviced the actual kits; Chris Amos and Frank Maddix, who wrote the computer programs for processing the coded data; and the research programme secretaries and other secretarial staff, who organised the observational schedules, typed the transcripts and carried out all those other tasks which are such an essential, though taken-for granted, part of large-scale research.

Funding for the research has come from a variety of sources. The Nuffield Foundation provided a small grant for the initial feasibility study and subsequently made a substantial grant towards the cost of carrying out the study of the 'Transition from home to school'. This phase of the research also benefited from donations from Boots Charitable Trust and from James Robertson & Sons Ltd. By far the greatest part of the financial resources, however, has been provided by the Social Science Research Council, whose officers have been most understanding of the difficulties encountered in keeping to the schedules laid out in the original proposals. We have also been generously supported by the University of Bristol, and particularly by the staff of the Computer Centre and the Audio-Visual Aids Unit. We are grateful to all these organisations for their support and assistance.

Finally we should like to express our gratitude to those who have helped in the preparation of this volume: Jean Aitchison, Tony Edwards, Mary Gutfreund, Barry Kroll, John Nicholls and Bridie Raban for their constructive comments on earlier drafts of the various chapters, and Maureen Devoy and Dickie Cannell for their labours in typing and retyping the manuscript. To all our sincere thanks.

Introduction

It is easy to understand why language has been and continues to be a subject of such widespread interest. From the infant's first interaction with his mother, speech permeates almost all human activity, directing actions, enlarging and modifying knowledge and arousing and communicating emotions. In literate cultures writing adds a further dimension, allowing experience to be recorded in a permanent form and so communicated to others who are removed in time and space. It also provides a means for reflecting upon experience – for working out ideas and feelings away from the pressure of face-to-face communication. Above all, writing is the medium of literature. Through language in its many forms, therefore, we are able to enter into the thoughts, feelings and intentions of others and to discover more about our own.

Although language provides the means for personal development and interpersonal cooperation, its influence is not always so beneficent. Where words can enlighten and unite, they can also be used to conceal and deceive, to spread false information and to stir up hatred and distrust. As well as bringing people closer together, language can also be an instrument of social divisiveness, its various forms and different usages being treated as indicators of relative status and prestige and as a way of controlling access to information and power. In addition to studying language as a universal human phenomenon and its acquisition as an integral part of human development, therefore, it is also necessary to study differences between speakers and between groups of speakers that can contribute to inequality and oppression.

Nowhere in our own society have differences of language use and language ability aroused such controversy as in Education. Given the central role of communication (both spoken and written) in the transmission of knowledge and in the assessment of the success with which that knowledge has been mastered and retained, it is to be expected that differences between individual pupils in their linguistic abilities will be related to their academic performance and leaving qualifications. But do differences of accent or patterns of language use have anything to do with the social distribution of academic attainment? And if so, why does this occur and what can be done to remedy the situation?

The scope of language studies is thus extremely broad. And questions such as those outlined above call for interdisciplinary collaboration if the answers that are offered are to have worthwhile practical applications. The research of the Bristol language development study to be reported in the series Language at Home and at School, of which this is the first volume, has attempted to keep these objectives to the fore. Although its central focus is on language development, it attempts to situate that development within the broader context of social interaction and, although the subjects selected for study are children, the total research has involved collaboration of many kinds: with the children's parents and teachers, with students attending courses at Bristol University and, not least, among the members of the research team, who have varying academic backgrounds and intellectual commitments.

To take part in an interdisciplinary longitudinal research programme is a challenging experience. There are inevitably many difficulties to be overcome, including personal differences about priorities amongst the questions to be tackled and about the best ways of attempting to answer them. At the same time, the recordings of the children's spontaneous conversation with their parents, with their siblings and peers, and later with their teachers, have given a continuity to the work which has led to a coming together of perspectives that would be unlikely to emerge in a series of separate studies.

The Bristol language development study: language development in pre-school children

In 1972, when our research began, fifteen years had elapsed since the last major survey of language development (Templin, 1957) and that survey, like those of the 1930s (cf. McCarthy, 1954 for a review), had been based on a sample of American children. In the meantime, a number of detailed studies of small groups of English-speaking children had been carried out in the United States, strongly influenced by the theory of language proposed by Chomsky (1957, 1965). From these studies (Brown, Cazden & Bellugi, 1969; Klima & Bellugi, 1966; Miller & Ervin, 1964) had emerged an account of the acquisition of English grammar, cast in the form of 'rule-learning', which suggested that, in spite of variation in the rate at which children mastered the various grammatical systems, there was substantial similarity in the sequence in which learning took place. The first aim of the Bristol study, therefore, was to attempt to replicate the detailed studies of American children, but with a representative sample large enough to provide normative data on the acquisition of English by children born and growing up in an urban environment in Britain.

However, whilst the research was in the planning stage, theory was developing apace in the field of child language, as will be described in chapter 2. In another detailed investigation of a trio of children, Bloom (1970) had shown the possibility of systematically studying the meanings expressed in children's speech, even in the earliest stages, provided that careful attention was paid to the situational context in which that speech occurred. However, as Halliday was shortly to show in the study of his own child (Halliday, 1975), the earliest meanings to occur were functional, or pragmatic, in origin and depended as much on the dynamics of interpersonal interaction as on the articulation, from within, of the complex structure of a transformational grammar.

In fact it was Halliday, rather than Chomsky, who provided the theoretical basis for the descriptive framework that we gradually constructed, though this was supplemented by 'case grammar' as developed by Fillmore (1968) and Chafe (1970). As an indication of our intentions, the coding manual that was developed for use in the research (Wells, 1973) was entitled *Coding Manual for the Description of Child Speech in its Conversational Context*.

Another important development during the 1960s, which had far-reaching implications for educational thinking was the elaboration of Bernstein's theory of the role of language in primary socialisation (Bernstein, 1971). The theory attempted to explain class-related orientations to meaning first learned by children in their earliest years, as a result of their differing experience of parental language use in the critical socialising contexts of the home. Empirical validation for the association between classes and codes had been sought through various interviews with groups of mothers, and through the administration of linguistic tasks to children after they had started school; but no systematic observations had been made of the conversations that actually occurred between children and their parents in their pre-school years. In similar vein, differences between children in the functions for which they used language in a play situation were attributed by Tough (1973, 1977) to different experiences of conversation with their parents, depending on whether they came from 'enabling' or 'non-enabling' homes. However, the conversations that were assumed to have such different educational outcomes were never actually observed.

It seemed imperative, therefore, if a study was to be made of the language development of pre-school children, that the data recorded should be truly representative – both of the full range of social background and of the many kinds of spontaneously occurring conversation that make up children's experience of language in use in the years before they go to school.

This was an extremely ambitious undertaking (indeed it proved to be far more demanding in practice than we had originally envisaged). However, in the end the project was carried through essentially as it had originally been planned, although at the time of writing there are still some analyses that remain to be completed. More importantly, however, new areas for investigation opened up as the research progressed and the original project has grown into a many-sided programme with far wider objectives than those of the original normative survey.

Before going on to outline these developments, a brief account will be given of the way in which the children were selected, and of the methods used to obtain and analyse the samples of conversation. In fact, these two aspects of the design of the study were closely connected as, with limited resources, a balance had to be struck between the number of children studied, the frequency with which observations were made, and the amount of speech to be analysed from each observation. Good arguments could be, and were, presented for studying a much larger number of children, for recording at much more frequent intervals and for obtaining and analysing a much larger corpus of speech on each occasion of recording. If with hindsight we have wished that we had done things differently, as indeed we have, those wishes have changed with each new avenue that has opened, and no ideal solution has revealed itself with blinding clarity. Broad-based research such as this seems fated to have to settle for compromise – at least until the day arrives when theoretical developments have ceased and there is no limit to the resources, both human and financial, on which ambitious researchers can call!

The solution finally adopted was to aim for a target sample of 128 children, divided between two ages. This division was suggested by other researchers, who had attempted to carry out longitudinal studies and had experienced a high degree of 'attrition' as subjects had, one by one, withdrawn from the research, either because they moved from the area or because personal circumstances made it difficult for them to continue. We therefore decided to cover the pre-school period with two parallel, but overlapping studies: the first covering the range from 15 to 42 months and the second the range from 39 to 66 months. Within each group, there were to be an equal number of boys and girls, an equal number from each season of the year for date of birth and an equal number from each of four classes of family background. These classes were defined in terms of parental occupation and education, and covered the full range occurring in the population.

Approximately 1000 names were drawn at random from the record of births held by the City Medical Officer, and the families of all these children were approached initially by health visitors and subsequently by members of the research team. Details relevant to the classification of family background were obtained from all families, including a small minority who declined to take part in the study. At the same time, information was obtained which allowed us to exclude a number of categories of children: multiple births, children with known handicaps, those in full-time day care and those whose parents did not speak English as their native language.

These categories were excluded, not out of any lack of interest in the problems that such children might be expected to encounter, but because their numbers in a sample of this size could not be expected to be large enough to permit meaningful comparisons to be made with the 'normal' population.

Then, finally, names of those children whose families had agreed to take part were picked at random to fill the cells in the sample design, and a number of reserves were picked in a similar manner. During the following four years several families withdrew from the study, but when the schedule of recordings was finally completed, the sample still numbered 129 children.

Each child was observed a total of ten times at three-monthly intervals, each observation consisting of a recording in the child's home and the administration of a number of tests at the Research Unit in the university. In addition, the parents of each child were interviewed when he or she was aged $3\frac{1}{2}$ years, to obtain information about the long-term environment provided by the home and about the parents' beliefs and practices concerning their role in the up-bringing of their children.

The recording of spontaneously occurring conversation was the main part of each observation. The decision was made at the outset to obtain recordings in conditions that reduced to the minimum the possibly distorting effect of the actual observation process. To this end, special equipment was constructed which could be delivered to the child's home on the day before the observation was to be made and left there to work quite automatically until after the observation was completed. In the morning, when the child was being dressed for the day, a lightweight 'harness' containing a radio microphone was put under the child's top garment. This transmitted continuously all speech produced by the child and any speech by others that was loud enough for him to hear. It also, of course, picked up and transmitted a large range of other noises, such as doors shutting, footsteps, and even the bubbles of goldfish in an aquarium. Because the microphone was linked to the tape recorder by radio, it caused no impediment to the child's freedom to move around, and reception remained good up to a range of 100 metres.

At the other end of the radio link in an out-of-the-way room or cupboard was a box containing the rest of the equipment: a radio receiver, a tape recorder and a rather complex timing mechanism which was programmed to record 24 samples of 90 seconds' duration at approximately 20-minute intervals between 9 a.m. and 6 p.m. The intervals between samples were irregular so that parents would not be tempted to plan activities in regular 20-minute cycles. In fact, they were completely unaware of the precise times at which recordings were to be made, and the programme was changed for each observation. The result was that, as far as is humanly possible within the limits set by ethical considerations, we recorded samples of these families' normal spontaneous conversation without their being aware that they were being observed.

There was, of course, a price to be paid. By choosing to give priority to naturalness, we had to forego the making of on-the-spot notes about the context in which the conversations occurred. To a considerable extent we were able to compensate for this by playing the recording back to the parents in the evening and asking them to recall, in as much detail as possible, the location, participants and activity for each of the recorded 90-second samples. An experiment subsequently carried out to compare this procedure with the more traditional procedure of a researcher being present during the recording revealed little difference in terms of the amount of contextual information that could be recovered; in some cases the mother was able to make more sense of an episode when she listened to it in the evening than the observer had been able to do while it was actually occurring.

Once the observation had been made, the recording was transcribed and checked and then each child utterance was analysed using the coding framework briefly described above. Coding was carried out by part-time assistants under the direction of Linda Ferrier and Bencie Woll, the project linguists. Each utterance involved making anything from 30 to 150 coding decisions, depending on its length and complexity. The resulting codings were entered on computer cards so that, when errors had been spotted and corrected, the information could be read directly into computer store. The whole operation took rather more than four years; when it was completed, an average of 110 utterances had been coded for each of over 1200 recordings.

In addition to the recordings of conversation, each observation also included various kinds of test. These were intended to fulfil two functions: firstly, to yield information about the children's linguistic abilities in a relatively standardised situation and, secondly, to provide an opportunity for a more exploratory study of children's comprehension and of the situational factors that influence the way in which children respond to items presented in the 'decontextualised' settings of a test. (The results of some of these latter investigations by Allayne Bridges, Chris Sinha and Valerie Walkerdine are described in chapters 3 and 5.) Finally, as already mentioned, the parents of each child were interviewed, and information obtained about the social organisation of the family and about the parents' beliefs about their role in the child's linguistic development. Information from tests and interviews was then added to the coded speech data in computer store and the overall analyses begun. At the time of writing, some aspects of this analysis still have to be finished, but the major part of the work has already been completed and is being prepared for publication as volume 2 of this series.

However, before the end of this large-scale operation had been reached, it had become apparent that there were a number of further investigations that would benefit enormously from being able to capitalise on the longitudinal information already obtained. These are briefly described in the following section.

The Bristol study: further developments
Children learning to read
At the time when the older group of children were about to start going to school, Bridie Raban was studying for a higher degree in the Bristol School of Education. As tutor responsible for work with children with reading problems in North Bristol, she was naturally interested in the opportunity of following the early development of reading in a sample of children whose oral language development had been so systematically monitored. On the basis of pilot work that she carried out in the early part of 1975, a proposal was prepared to carry out a small study of twenty of the older children during the first two years of schooling, starting in September 1975.

A great deal of previous research on reading had concentrated on different methods of teaching and on what were considered to be prerequisite skills of visual and auditory perception and of hand–eye coordination. Some work had also been carried out on the relationship between oral language and reading, although not on oral language development in the years immediately preceding school entry; studies had also been made of the relationship between home environment and success in learning to read. These previous studies had typically investigated only one of these topics. However, we believed that learning to read involves an interaction between all of these and still other factors, such as the nature of children's individual encounters with print, and the relative emphasis given to different activities in school that are considered to contribute to mastery of the written language.

The project accordingly had three strands: a gathering together of information about each child's pre-school experience, judged to be relevant to reading, drawing upon a further interview with the parents as well as on information available from the recordings from the earlier phase; interviews with the head and class teachers to discover the nature of the schools' provisions for the teaching of reading, including the methods and materials used in the first two years' curriculum; and regular observations of each child in his or her own classroom for the whole of one morning each month. Tests were also administered at the beginning of the study and after one and two years in school. During the second year it was also decided to ask the teachers to complete an assessment of the child's attainment in reading and writing at the end of the sixth term, and to interview the parents again to discover what part, if any, they had played in helping their children learn to read.

Language in the transition from home to school

One finding from the previous study was that even the most careful observation and written recording of children's activities failed to capture differences in the quality of what they were doing. This was particularly so where speech was concerned. Even though each child's every encounter with the teacher was timed to the nearest second, the written record gave no indication of how the teacher's instructions and comments were phrased, and of what contribution the child made to the transaction. It seemed, therefore, that to discover how the one-to-one interaction between child and teacher was contributing to the child's learning, it would be necessary to obtain a verbatim recording.

There was a second reason for wishing to record speech in the classroom. One of the explanations put forward for the relative underachievement in school of working class children was a supposed mismatch for these children between the language of home and the language of the classroom. No reliable evidence was available, however, that could be brought to bear on this claim or on related counter-claims. Since we had already obtained recordings of spontaneous conversation in a sample of children's homes, a continuation of the study in the classroom would provide an opportunity to put the competing theories to an empirical test.

Recording in an infant school classroom is not easy, as anyone who has attempted it will know. Apart from certain times of the day, such as when a story is being read, there is a busy hum as children talk to each other about the task in hand or about any other topic that comes to mind. Identifying the teacher's voice is simple, but it is extremely difficult to separate out the voices of individual children, and even more difficult to identify them. However, after modification, the radio microphone used for the home recordings proved capable of picking up the speech of individual children and, with the addition of a dictated commentary and a 'bleeper' which was pressed each time the target child spoke, it proved possible to identify at least the one particular child we were trying to record.

These procedures clearly required the presence of a researcher in the classroom and so, having once decided to have an observer, it seemed sensible to go one stage further and to obtain a video recording of what was observed. A special mobile recording unit was therefore designed, capable of being taken from school to school, assembled quickly, and used unobtrusively so as to cause the minimum of disruption to normal classroom routines. The resulting package was based on a collapsible trolley with the camera mounted on one of the corners; a mass of wires connected the various components: a video recorder and monitor, two radio receivers, two stereo tape recorders and an equaliser to cut out irrelevant low and high frequency sounds – not to mention the camera operator's headset for monitoring the speech signal and dictating the commentary on the child's activities.

The pictures and sounds recorded with this equipment are of remarkably high quality. But keeping the total package in working order was a nightmare – particularly for Peter French, the researcher charged with this unenviable responsibility. Nevertheless, with the help of the School of Education's technician, Mike George, and of members of the Audio-Visual Aids Unit, all the scheduled observations were made. These have now been transcribed and provide the basis for a number of investigations, some in progress and others still at the planning stage. Excerpts from some of these observations are discussed in chapter 6.

We were also successful in remaining unobtrusive – in spite of the unusual spectacle that the trolley with its operator must have provided. Part of the explanation of this success lies in the practice of demonstrating the equipment to the whole class at the beginning of each recording session. The TV monitor was turned so that the children could see it and then the camera picked out each child one at a time and an opportunity was given to wave, pull funny faces and generally enjoy the experience of being 'on TV'. At the end of the performance the children were asked to pretend that the equipment and its operator were invisible, and to carry on just as usual. To our surprise, this is exactly what they did. Whether the teachers were as unselfconscious is another question but, almost without exception, they willingly cooperated not only in allowing us to make the observation but also in completing assessments on the project children and on a 'control group' picked from amongst the project children's age peers.

The sample for this second study following children into school was selected from the younger age group who had been recorded at home between 15 and 42 months. In fact, exactly half of the original group were selected, although the distribution of the thirty-two children on the scale of family background was biased towards the two extremes. In order to bring the longitudinal records up to date, a further recording was made of each child just before he or she reached their fifth birthday. In this case a smaller number of longer samples were recorded, and exactly the same procedure was followed in the first school recording, made after six weeks in school. These two recordings form the basis for a direct comparison between the language demands of home and school. As in the first study involving children in school, tests were administered at the beginning and end of the two-year study, and the parents were interviewed at approximately the same time.

The project also involved a more experimental component: a comparison between the 'teaching styles' of the mother and first teacher of each child as each helped the child to complete two tasks. The first involved sorting a stack of picture cards into groups that went together; the second involved making up a story about a sequence of picture cards. This investigation, which was carried out by Jan Adams, a research student, was particularly concerned with the style of interaction adopted by the adults and the manner in which they solicited and responded to initiations by the child.

As a result of financial cuts affecting schools, several of the children were one term later in starting school than was originally anticipated. As a result the final observations were not made until December 1979 and analysis of the material collected is still in progress.

The development of conversation

The importance of conversation, both as the context within which the child experiences language in use and as part of what he has to learn, was fully recognised right at the beginning of the research programme. But in 1972 there was very little guidance from published research on how to set about a systematic analysis of conversation. The initial coding framework concentrated, therefore, on the children's utterances considered one at a time, although both the child's utterances and those that immediately preceded and followed were categorised in terms of a taxonomy of interpersonal functions which was derived from Austin's (1962) and Searle's (1969) work on speech acts.

However, conversation involves more than a simple succession of functionally defined, independent, utterances. For conversation to be coherent and mutually rewarding, each turn must also be shaped to take account of the content of the previous turn and to indicate what is expected in the turn that follows. It also involves more than vocabulary, and grammer. For, in each turn, the speaker also makes choices concerning intonation, and these play a vital part in signalling how the present turn is to be heard in relation to the conversational context that has already been established.

The fourth phase of the research, begun at the same time as the 'Transition from home to school' study, attempted to take account of this broader view of language in use by reconsidering some of the pre-school recordings as examples of conversation. We set ourselves three main questions, each a substantial topic of research in its own right:

1. What are the guiding principles that enable participants to achieve coherence across conversational turns?
2. What are the sequential stages through which a child progresses towards competence in participating in conversation?
3. How does experience of conversation with others contribute to the child's developing mastery of the language system?

In attempting to answer each of these questions, we have also been particularly concerned to discover more about the role of intonation.

With more than a thousand recordings of adult–child conversation, there has been no shortage of material to work upon. Even after deciding to concentrate on the longitudinal recordings of the 32 children in the study of the 'Transition from home to school', we have still felt overwhelmed by the range and variety of data. Given the background and interests of the members of the research team, there has been some tendency for investigation to proceed on three fronts independently: Martin Montgomery developing and applying a system for describing intonation; Margaret MacLure wrestling with the complexities of discourse and conversational analyses; and Gordon Wells attempting to find ways of identifying the potentially facilitating features of adults' conversation with children. But there has also been a strong commitment to uniting these separate endeavours, which has resulted in several jointly published papers. In these, a model of conversation is developed and applied to the description of particular sequences of adult–child conversation (Wells, Montgomery & MacLure, 1979; Wells, MacLure & Montgomery, 1979), including one which examines material from the same child at home and at school (Wells & Montgomery, in press). Chapter 1 of this volume, although written by one of the members of the team, owes a great deal to these earlier collaborative endeavours.

In September 1979, Martin Montgomery took up a permanent post at the Polytechnic of Wales and Margaret MacLure joined Peter French in the analysis of the recordings of classroom interaction. For the moment, therefore, active work on the analysis of the pre-school data from the point of view of the development of conversation has ceased. This, we hope, is only temporary, for we plan to pick up the threads at some time in the future: learning through conversation still seems to us to be one of the most important and challenging topics in the study of child language.

A scale of language development

One of the most striking findings from the earliest phase of the research is the high degree of uniformity across the sample as a whole in the sequence in which different linguistic systems and sub-systems are learned. Although there is very considerable variation in rate of learning, certain categories of meaning and formal structure reliably appear before others in the children's speech. This is not to say that there are not individual variations of strategy or emphasis – and indeed it has been suggested that there may be important differences recognisable as distinct styles (cf. chapter 2). But even when allowances are made for such differences, there are impressive regularities.

The aim of this phase, begun in 1979, is to establish the sequence of development, where evidence for such a sequence exists, for as many linguistic systems as possible, and then to pick out clusters of categories which, whilst tending to appear more or less simultaneously, are reliably ordered with respect to categories in the clusters which immediately precede or follow in the sequence of development. If this aim can be achieved, it will be possible to produce a developmental 'scale' which will fulfil two important functions. Firstly, it will provide an instrument which can be used in the assessment and diagnosis of children suspected of delayed or disturbed language development. Here it will complement a similar instrument developed by Crystal and colleagues, which is based on data obtained from predominantly 'linguistically disabled' children (Crystal, Fletcher & Garman, 1976). Secondly, it will provide a more precise measure than 'mean length of utterance' (Brown, 1973) for researchers who wish to equate children for stage of language development, to measure progress over a period of time, or to assess the results of some form of intervention.

Figure 1 shows the relationship in time and in children studied between all five phases of the research so far undertaken. However, the potential of the longitudinal material that has been collected is far from being exhausted. By its nature, such material is more appropriate for description than for explanation of the course of language development. But careful description can provide a rich source for the development of explanatory hypotheses, which can then be tested in further investigations. Our hope is that our efforts will be fruitful in just this way.

Learning through interaction: the study of language development
As will be clear from the preceding overview, the research programme has been concerned with a wide range of topics within the field of child language studies, and the publication of the findings will inevitably take several years. In the meantime, however, it is possible to consider in a more general way some of the major issues

with which the research has been concerned. These are linked not only by a continuing involvement with the language development of the same group of children, but also by a concern with language as interaction: people collaborating in the negotiation of meaning; talk as a form of social action; the reciprocal influence of language and context. At the same time there is also a common interest in development: development of mastery of the various language systems and development of skill in using these resources in order to communicate with others for different purposes in different contexts. The following chapters attempt to explore these issues.

No attempt has been made to impose an artificial uniformity of approach. The various chapters express the individual points of view of their authors. However, we hope that the differences of disciplinal affiliation and preferred focus of attention represented here will lead to a more rounded interpretation of the evidence to be considered.

Figure 1. The successive phases of the Bristol language development research programme

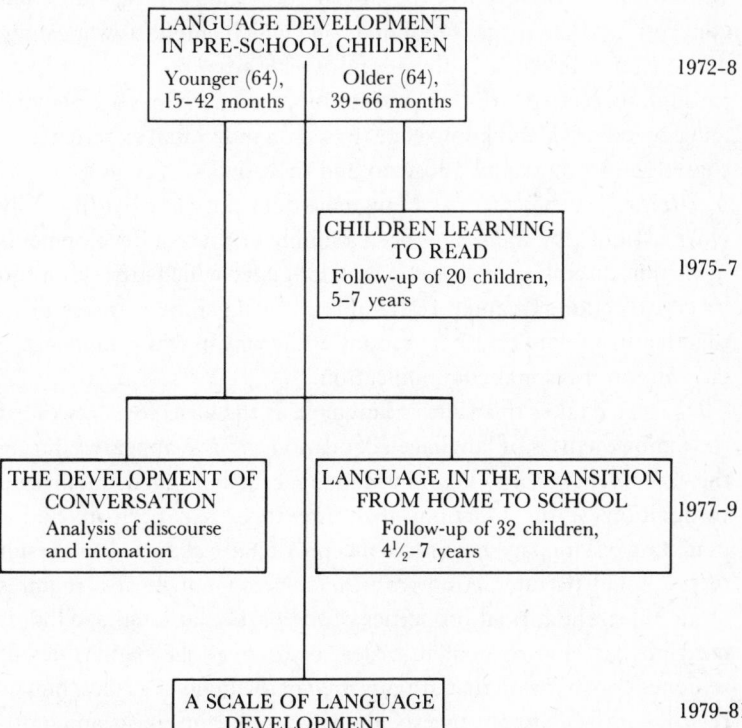

They are offered, therefore, as perspectives on the central theme of children's linguistic development in the interactional contexts of home and school.

The first chapter presents a general account of language seen as a means of communication. During the last twenty years many introductory textbooks on language have been published, most of them strongly influenced by the work of Chomsky and his associates on transformational-generative grammar. There is no doubt that their investigations have greatly increased our understanding of the internal organisation of the language system and provided a powerful and elegant apparatus for the description of the formal structure of actual texts. But the emphasis on abstract knowledge of linguistic form has been at the expense of an interest in the way in which people actually communicate through language and of the relationship between linguistic messages and the contexts in which they occur.

If, as we believe, language is acquired in the course of human development as a means of interacting with those 'significant others' who are most involved in the life of the child, a rather different conception of language is required: one which emphasises meaning and purpose as much as form; and which attempts to show how, through successive turns in conversation, joint activities are planned and coordinated, and knowledge (based on individual experience) is shared with others and added to and modified.

Although such a theory of language does not yet exist in a fully worked out form, there have been a number of recent developments in various disciplines concerned with language which are relevant to its construction. Chapter 1 attempts to bring some of these ideas together in a relatively brief account of the way in which language is used in interpersonal communication.

Chapter 2 takes this view of language as the basis for a review of the major theories of language acquisition to have appeared during the last twenty years. Learning language, it is argued, involves a recognition of the functions that utterances can perform and a matching of language forms to concepts that are acquired as a result of pre-linguistic interaction with the environment. It also requires attention to the formal properties of the particular language that is used in that environment in order to discover the regularities of sentence construction that are captured in the linguist's rules. But, as the title of the chapter suggests, the most important basis and motivation for the child's way in to language is to be found in communication with others, and this is seen to become established in the first weeks of life, long before the infant is capable of producing or even responding to linguistically organised messages.

Conversation is thus the all-important context of language development. Although the child's earliest contributions are extremely rudimentary, they permit the adult participant to build around them; and thus to provide the framework within which the child can learn by taking part in the interaction. Several examples of conversation between child and parent are presented in order to illustrate this process of learning through interaction, and the chapter concludes with a discussion of individual differences in language learning and their possible relation to differences in style of interaction.

Chapter 3 examines in greater detail the development of comprehension. In the past, comprehension has often been viewed as a rather passive process – the listener merely reacting to the incoming speech signal. Recent investigations have shown, however, that this is far from being the case: the task of comprehending speech involves the listener in actively searching for cues to guide his interpretation, in the situational context and in past experience as well as in the signal itself. At the same time, his success in constructing an appropriate interpretation is monitored by the speaker, who adjusts both his verbal and nonverbal behaviour to facilitate the listener's task.

What is true of adult interaction is even more true of interaction where one of the participants is still in the process of learning how meaning is communicated through speech. Chapter 3 considers some of the factors that are involved in the gradual development of adult-like comprehension, in which the relative importance of the various types of cue is determined by the purpose and context of the communication. The first main section considers the role of the adult and the way in which he or she progressively modifies the range of nonverbal cues as the child shows himself more able to attend to the information contained in the speech signal itself. The second section examines the relationship between words and experience: the progressive restructuring of conceptual categories so that they mesh with the semantic organisation of the lexicon of the language to be learned. The final section focuses on the influence of context, showing how, from using it as a support for the interpretation of the speech signal, the child has to learn to separate the meanings derived from message and context and eventually to be able, when necessary, to interpret messages independently of the particular contexts in which they are received.

Chapter 4 continues with the theme of language and context, focusing on their reciprocal relationship. The first part of the chapter is devoted to showing how social settings and relationships not only form a background which is drawn upon to interpret what is said but, at one and the same time, are themselves given form and substance through the saying of what is said. For the language learner the relationship is also two-way: on the one hand it is through entering into relationships with competent speakers of the language that the child learns to express in conventional forms the meanings he wishes to communicate with respect to the shared context and, on the other, the meanings themselves are discovered and the relationships embodied and managed by means of linguistic interaction.

The second part of the chapter concentrates on one specific and highly important social relationship for language development – that of the child with his parents – and considers in some detail the conversational expectations and restrictions which parents set up for their children. The child's part in this relationship is not, however, seen as one of passively conforming to his parents' wishes, for children are extremely resourceful at devising interactional strategies which, at the same time as appearing to fulfil their parents' expectations of them, also allow them to get round many of the restrictions that stem from their inferior status. These strategies are described in some detail and illustrated by transcribed extracts from the Bristol data.

The relationship between language and context is one of the aspects of the child's experience which tends to change rather dramatically when he goes to school. Whereas most talk – and most learning – in the home arises out of contexts of practical activity, often ones which the child himself has initiated, a great deal of learning in school, and the talk associated with the tasks through which that learning is planned to take place, is largely teacher-initiated and involves contexts which are unfamiliar to the child and ones which, in many cases, are also relatively abstract. The result is that, for many children, strategies that have proved effective for interpreting and learning from the very varied situations that occur in the home are less effective at school and in some cases are even counter-productive.

Chapter 5 examines some examples of the ways in which children interpret problems in a variety of contexts at home and at school. The authors show that, although the solutions that children arrive at may be incorrect from an adult point of view, they are rarely arbitrary or stupid. Children, just like adults, constantly strive to make sense of their experience. If the sense they make is misguided or illogical in adult terms, this is typically because they are inadequately informed or because the criteria they are operating with are different from those of an adult.

Recognition of this view of children as active seekers after meaning has important implications for those who teach them. For it calls for a much more thorough-going attempt to achieve continuity between home and school: capitalising on the child's existing strategies for learning and contextualising learning tasks in terms which make sense from the point of view of his coherent but limited understanding of the world. And this, in turn, means making a greater effort, through observation, listening and sensitive questioning, to discover what form that understanding takes. This, it is suggested, is what is meant by the slogan 'Start where the child is'.

Chapter 6 focuses more specifically on talk in the two contexts of home and school. One of the explanations that has been suggested for the underachievement of so many working class children is a mismatch between the language of home and school. This chapter examines recordings made of the same children at home and at school for evidence of such a mismatch, concentrating particularly on the asking and answering of questions, since this form of interaction plays such a central role in the implementation of the school curriculum.

Little evidence is found of systematic differences between the two contexts in the sequential patterns of interaction through which questions are posed, answered, and acknowledged. However, there are differences in the relative frequencies of the different structures in the two contexts and in the distribution of speaking rights, in particular the right to initiate a question exchange. These differences are seen to derive from and constitute the different social relationships that obtain in the two settings of home and school, as a result of the differences in ratio of children to adults and of the different purposes that give rise to interactions between adults and children. From this point of view, features which characterise classroom talk are found to be functionally effective in achieving the interactional purposes that teachers wish to achieve.

The final chapter considers the place of literacy in a child's linguistic development. Learning to read and write is a central part of schooling in almost all literate cultures and is associated with the development of cognitive skills of reasoning and abstract problem-solving that are highly valued in such cultures. It has been suggested by Olson (1977) and others that it is in mastering the written mode that the child acquires these higher order cognitive skills, since, in this mode, meaning is found in the text alone and is independent of the interpersonal and pragmatic pressures which contribute to the exchange of meanings in speech. However, evidence from a tribe in Liberia, who have developed an indigenous written script, casts doubt on such generalised claims. Scribner & Cole (1978), who studied this tribe, suggest that the ability to read and write only facilitates cognitive skills in tasks that are closely related to the activities for which reading and writing are used.

In the second part of the chapter these different evaluations of the effects of the acquisition of literacy are considered in relation to the different levels of educational attainment that are characteristic of middle and working class groups in Western societies. Since the majority of children, whatever their social background, attain a level of functional literacy before they leave school, and spend a large proportion of their later years at school engaged in tasks that involve reading and writing, a greater equality in level of cognitive functioning might be expected, if the claims made for the generalised effects of literacy are correct. On the other hand, if the facilitation is restricted to activities which are closely related to the functions for which reading and writing are normally used – particularly outside the setting of the classroom – we might expect class-related differences in level of cognitive functioning across a wide range of tasks, since there are class-related differences in the uses that are made of reading and writing in everyday life, particularly in the demands made by different types of employment.

Of course the factors that contribute to inequality of educational achievement are both wider and less purely intellectual than those associated with the role of literacy in the daily life of individuals or whole sections of society. Furthermore, the relationship between the political and economic factors and those that are more specifically educational is neither simple nor uni-directional. Nevertheless, in terms of directness of effect and amenability to some degree of intervention, the value attached to literacy is important, since such attitudes are learned very early and they strongly colour the child's first experience of formal learning in school. Here again, there are important implications for both parents and teachers, some of which are discussed in the concluding section of the chapter.

A note on style

One problem has plagued us throughout. The English language does not have pronouns that are neutral for gender: when referring to a child, a parent, or a teacher a choice has to be made between 'he' or 'she' or else some awkward device used such as '(s)he'. No one solution to the problem was acceptable to all the authors so, in the interests of stylistic consistency, the editor imposed the following convention. Where both a singular child and a singular adult are referred to in the same sentence or in closely related sentences, 'he' will be used to refer to the child and 'she' to the adult. Although, as it happens, the adults most frequently involved in conversation with young children are female, this editorial decision should not be taken as an implicit undervaluing of the important role of fathers and male teachers in the care and education of children; nor should it be taken as an indication of a covert desire to 'keep women in their place'. We apologise to any readers who find the convention offensive.

1

Language as interaction

GORDON WELLS

'Not to let a word get in the way of its sentence
Nor to let a sentence get in the way of its intention,
But to send your mind out to meet the intention as a guest;
THAT is understanding.'

Chinese proverb, fourth century B.C.

Most people, if asked what a language is, would almost certainly answer in terms of 'sounds', 'words' and 'sentences'. They would probably also refer to something less clearly defined which they might call 'meaning'. And they might just possibly add something about the purposes that language – both spoken and written – serves in the interpersonal transactions that constitute so large a part of everyday life. Such an ordering of priorities no doubt owes much to the way in which 'language' is encountered during the process of education: in dictionaries, in the form of comprehension exercises, and in lessons on grammar and spelling. It also corresponds quite closely to the relative emphasis that has been given to the various aspects of language in the long tradition of serious study that goes back as far as Aristotle and even earlier.

The same emphasis on sounds, words and sentences, treated as units within a formal system, has also characterised the greater part of the work carried out in the present century by linguists and others who have attempted to study language 'scientifically'. Two characteristics of language in particular have provided the main focus of attention: firstly, that within any language only certain combinations of sounds and words are permitted, and that these permitted combinations can be expressed in the form of a limited number of general principles of construction or structural rules; and secondly that, although the number of rules and the items to which they apply, is finite, the number of sentences that can be formed from them is potentially infinite. Much effort has been devoted, therefore, to the attempt to specify very precisely the rules of phonology and grammar that account for the structural organisation of sounds within syllables and words within phrases, clauses and sentences, and to do so in a way which will **generate** all and only the sentences recognised as grammatical within a particular language.

The result is that, although we now know a considerable amount about the organisation of the formal systems of language in isolation from the contexts in which they are used, we are still largely ignorant about the principles that underlie the orderliness of conversation and about the ways in which language in use is sensitive to subtle differences in the social context and in the purposes of the participants. That is to say we are still far from being able to give satisfactory answers to such questions as 'Why do people say what they do?' or 'How do we know what a speaker means by what he says?'

Fortunately, these latter questions have begun to be investigated more intensively in the last decade or so, and it is being increasingly recognised that the ancient Chinese proverb, quoted above, applies not only to successful communication but also to the *study* of the means by which that communication is achieved. Understanding language involves more than attending to the words and sentences that are spoken or written: unless we look beyond the forms to the intentions that they **realise** – the experiences that are referred to, the purposes that give rise to them and the situations in which they occur – we shall not achieve a full understanding, either of the sentences themselves or of language as a human phenomenon. Neither shall we be in a position to discover how it is that the human infant, initially uninformed as to what a language is or what it is for, rather rapidly masters sounds, words and sentences through interacting with his immediate family in the furtherance of various types of collaborative activity. The emphasis in this chapter, therefore, will be on language as a medium of interaction, and on the way in which meanings are communicated through talk.

Conversation: the negotiation of meaning
In order to focus on the situated and functional nature of language in

use and on the interactional context in which language learning takes
place, it may be helpful to consider an excerpt from a conversation
between a child and his mother that was recorded during the course
of an ordinary morning at home (see table 1.1). Mark, aged 28
months, is trying to persuade his mother to break off from her
household tasks in order to play with him. She, in her turn, tries to
get him to carry out a small task for her and a large part of the
conversation is given over to ensuring that Mark correctly interprets
her intention and successfully carries out the task. When this has
finally been achieved, Mark reissues his original request, to which his
mother finally accedes.

Table 1.1. *A conversation between a child and his mother*†

1 Mark: Play Mummy(v)		
2	Mother: All right	
3 Mark: [ʃɪʃ] wash up Mummy(v)? (=have you finished washing up?)		
4	Mother: Pardon?	
5 Mark: [ʃɪʃ] wash up?		
6	Mother: Yes	
7 Mark: Oh		
8	Mother: Let me just dry my hands	
9 Mark: Alright		
10 In there		[Mark looks for towel]
11	Mother: Here	
12 Mark: [ɪəɑ] (=here you are)		[Mark gives towel to Mother]
13	Mother: Just a minute	
14	Will you put the top back on the washing basket please	
15 Mark: Uh?		
16 Uh?		
17	Mother: Put the top back on the washing basket	
18 Mark: On there Mummy(v)?		
19 On there?		
20	Mother: Yes	
21	No not the towel in there	

22		The top of the basket on it
23 Mark: Alright		
24 Mark: On there		
25	Uh?	
26	Uh?	
27		Mother: Put the lid . . on top of the basket
28 Mark: On er—on there?		
29		Mother: Yes please
30 Mark: Alright		
31	You dry hands	
32		Mother: I've dried my hands now
33 Mark: Put towel in there		
34		Mother: No it's not dirty
35 Mark: Tis		
36		Mother: No it isn't
37 Mark: Tis		
38	Mummy(v) play	
39	Play Mummy(v)	
40		Mother: Well I will play if you put the top on the basket
41 Mark: Alright		
42	There	[Mark puts top on basket]
43	There	
44	Play Mummy(v)	
45	Mummy(v) come on	

† The conventions of transcription are given in the Appendix, where a version of this transcript to which a coding of intonation has been added will also be found.

In spite of the relative linguistic immaturity of one of the participants, this interchange clearly illustrates many of the features that characterise any successful conversational interaction. And it is, in fact, typical of a great deal of talk between parents and young children.

The first point to note is that the two participants in the conversation alternate in taking turns to speak, each listening while the other speaks and waiting for the other to finish before starting his or her turn. Secondly, we can see that, on the whole, what is said in each turn is coherently related to what was said by the previous speaker, and so it is reasonable to infer that both participants are understanding each other's messages and framing their subsequent messages in the light of that understanding. Thirdly, the talk seems to be systematically related to the physical situation in which it occurs and to the intentions of the speakers in relation to that situation. Indeed, in this particular case it appears that both participants implicitly recognise that a 'contract' has been negotiated: if Mark puts the lid on the basket for his mother, she will be under some obligation to meet his request for her to play with him.

We can see, therefore, that Mark and his mother, like any successful conversationalists, are engaging in a collaborative activity. Collaborative, firstly, in the orderly sequencing of speaking and listening **turns**; collaborative, secondly, in relating the meanings expressed in each turn to those in the turns that precede and follow; collaborative, finally, in agreeing on the objects and actions in the shared situation to which these meanings are intended to apply.

However, the fact that such successful collaboration is typical of conversation, even where young children are concerned, should not lead us to treat it as unworthy of attention, or to take it for granted. Indeed, we shall argue below that collaboration in the negotiation of conversational meaning is both a major part of what the child has to learn and also a necessary condition for that learning to take place. But first let us look more closely at how this collaboration is achieved.

The sequential structure of discourse

As we have seen, one of the most noticeable characteristics of conversation is the orderliness with which participants take turns in speaking, rarely overlapping or leaving long periods of silence. In almost all forms of conversation, in fact, there seems to be a generally observed convention that, at any time, one – but only one – participant should speak, and that he or she should have the right to decide when there should be a change of speaker and, in multi-participant talk, who the next speaker should be.

Ensuring a smooth transition from one speaking turn to the next is thus fundamental to the sequential structuring of conversation, and it depends upon several forms of behaviour. These include the speaker looking away from the listener for most of his turn and looking back again when he is ready to cede the floor; the use of pause-fillers to signal that a period of silence is not to be taken as the end of the turn; and, where a multi-clause turn is intended, planning it in such a way as to minimise the danger of interruption, by the use of appropriate intonation, by announcing in advance the proposed structure of the turn with such devices as 'on the one hand', 'for the following reasons' and so on. Such procedures do not invariably result in the speaker keeping the floor but, when interruptions do occur, they are nearly always at points at which the speaker might have decided to complete his turn.

It is, of course, important to realise that the listener, as well as the speaker, contributes to the successful management of turn-taking in discourse. The signals given by the speaker can only be effective if the listener is carefully monitoring the changes of gaze and facial and bodily gestures of the speaker and attending to the way in which his utterance is constructed and delivered in order to know when it is appropriate for him to 'take over the floor'. Indeed, as Sacks, Schegloff & Jefferson (1974) point out, the fact that the speaker plans his turn with the needs of the listener in mind provides a strong motivation for the listener to pay continuous attention to the way in which the message is expressed as well as to its content, so that he is able to judge when and how to continue the discourse. Even a brief lapse of attention by the listener can lead to a temporary breakdown of the conversation.

Although providing an essential basic framework, however, the management of the temporal sequencing of turns is only one aspect of the organisation of discourse. Conversations occur because the participants have interactional purposes of various kinds to fulfil, and it is the negotiation of these purposes which creates the structure of particular conversations within the turn-taking framework. In order to understand the principles that account for this more 'delicate' level of organisation, it will be helpful to think of discourse as having two interrelated dimensions: the sequential chaining in which one turn follows another (the **syntagmatic** dimension), and the choice as to what is done at each link in the chain (the **paradigmatic** dimension) (see figure 1.1). We shall be considering the paradigmatic dimension in greater detail below, but for the moment it will be sufficient to think of a choice being made in each turn from options such as asking and answering questions, offering and accepting or refusing services, greeting, and so on.

It will already be apparent from these examples, though, that the options on the paradigmatic dimension from which choice is made at each turn are not entirely independent and unrelated. A question expects, and usually receives, an answer; one greeting tends to be followed by another. And so the expectation that one option sets up for a particular sequel provides a structural link between the turns that contain these options, when these are considered on the syntagmatic dimension. In fact, conversations usually consist of groups of turns linked together by both syntagmatic and paradigmatic relations between adjacent turns, and a full understanding of the organisation of discourse requires both these dimensions to be considered together. For the sake of simplicity of exposition, however, we shall continue to concentrate on the syntagmatic dimension of sequential structure here, moving on to the paradigmatic dimension in the next section.

Consider first the simple case of patterns such as: A asks a question and B provides an answer; or A makes a request and B agrees to the request. In such reciprocally related pairs of single-utterance turns – called **adjacency pairs** by Sacks et al. (1974) – there is a strong expectation that, following the first of the pair, the next utterance will be the second part of the appropriate pair. In fact this expectation is so strong, they suggest, that the omission of the second part will be worthy of remark, and failure to supply it may be treated as a breach of convention for which the offender is held accountable. With this in mind, Mark's insistence to 'come on' (45) may perhaps be heard as just such an implicit reprimand to his mother for not responding to his immediately preceding request.

Figure 1.1. The relationship between the syntagmatic and paradigmatic dimensions of discourse

PARADIGMATIC DIMENSION

Options selected from:

Greeting	Request	Statement
Call	Offer	Question
Available	Accept	Answer
Thank	Comply	Challenge ... etc.

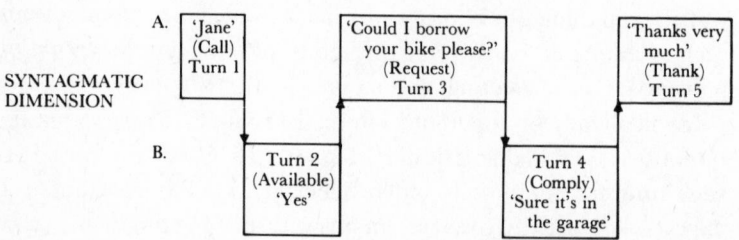

Useful though the idea of adjacency pairs is, it is of only limited explanatory value, because not all adjacent turns that are heard as related form pairs of this kind. However, the more basic idea that a turn may either *prospectively* set up expectations about the sort of turn that will follow or *retrospectively* meet expectations set up by a previous turn does provide us with a structural principle of very general application. Labelled **exchange**, such a two-part structure is considered by a number of researchers to be the basic unit of discourse (e.g. Halliday, 1977; Sinclair & Coulthard, 1975), and the two **moves** of which an exchange is constituted are labelled **initiate** and **respond**.

Several examples of this basic structural pattern can be seen in the extract involving Mark and his mother:

| 1 | Mark: | Play Mummy (v) | Initiate ⎤ |
| 2 | Mother: | Alright | Respond ⎦ |

| 8 | Mother: | Let me just dry my hands | Initiate ⎤ |
| 9 | Mark: | Alright | Respond ⎦ |

| 31 | Mark: | You dry hands | Initiate ⎤ |
| 32 | Mother: | I've dried my hands now | Respond ⎦ |

Whilst the first two of these examples may appropriately be described as adjacency pairs, this is less clearly the case with the third example. Yet all three have in common the basic exchange structure of initiate–respond.

However, conversations are not usually limited to single exchanges, as is clear from our illustrative extract. By what principles, then, are minimal exchanges extended to form longer stretches of discourse, whilst still retaining internal coherence?

Devices for sustaining discourse

One very obvious device for sustaining a sequence of discourse is maintaining continuity of topic, that is, talking in successive exchanges about the same, or a relevantly related, topic. However, this notion is not as simple as it might appear, and a distinction needs to be drawn between talking 'to a topic' and 'talking topically'. Talking to a topic typically occurs in rather formal settings, where there is an agenda or some other means of controlling the topic over successive turns. In casual conversation, on the other hand, the topic tends to shift and change as the discourse develops. Thus, as Sacks remarks, 'when one presents a topic, except under rather exceptional circumstances, one may be assured that others will try to *talk topically* with what you've talked about, but you can't be assured that the topic you intended is the topic they will talk to' (Sacks, 1968: 11). Compare, for example, the way in which a plan to demolish a block of flats in order to build a ring road would be discussed (a) at a Council meeting and (b) by two or three occupants of the flats who happened to meet by chance in the local pub. Nevertheless, in spite of the lack of straightforward topical continuity, most casual conversation is not incoherent, nor do conversational participants on the whole fail to follow the drift of each other's contributions.

The reason for this, it has been suggested, is that participants in general observe, and expect other to observe, a **cooperative principle** of something like the following form:

'Make your conversational contribution such as is required, at the stage at which it occurs, by the accepted purpose or direction of the talk exchange in which you are engaged.'
(Grice, 1975: 45)

If participants observe this tacitly agreed principle, even when 'talking topically', hearers can expect that a speaker's contribution will somehow be relevant, and can search for appropriate **implicatures** (see below, p. 53) that will enable them to discover that relevance by bridging the gap between the topic of one turn and that of the following turn. In the last resort, therefore, almost all pairs of adjacent turns can be interpreted as in some relevantly related, since there are indefinitely many implicatures, of varying degrees of indirectness, that can be found to provide possible links.

However, there are many cases in casual, as well as in more formal, conversation where the connections between exchanges are made explicit. In the following examples, the device used is the making of **cohesive** ties through repetition and pronominal reference (see below, p. 57).

Mother:	What are you going to *play* with now?	Initiate	Exch. 1
Mark:	I'm going to *play toys*	Respond	
Mother:	*They're* in the corner	Initiate	Exch. 2
Mark:	Oh	Respond	

Mark:	*Can* I have other *piece* of meat Mummy(v)?	Initiate	Exch. 1
Mother:	Yes . . .	Respond	
	May I have a *piece* for Helen please?	Initiate	Exch. 2
Mark:	Mm	Respond	

And in the following example, in addition to the cohesive tie of pronominal reference, the two exchanges are linked by the feature **contrast** – although the contrast here depends upon the implicit assumption that one doesn't put towels that are not dirty in the washing basket:

33	Mark:	Put *towel* in there	Initiate	Exch. 1
34	Mother:	No	Respond	
		it's not dirty	Initiate	Exch. 2
35	Mark:	'Tis.	Respond	

A third device for sustaining a sequence of conversation, and one which often accompanies topical continuity, is seen in the last example (and also in the immediately preceding one). Mother's turn (34) contains two moves, the first move providing a response in one exchange and the second move initiating the next.[1] A more condensed version of this **linking** device occurs when the second, responding, move of the first exchange is omitted altogether, but is implied by the initiating move of the next exchange, as in this sequence of linked exchanges from an earlier point in the same recording of Mark:

Mark:	Mark play in Mark's car	Initiate	Exch. 1
Mother:	Shall I bring it down?	(Respond)	
		Initiate	Exch. 2
Mark:	No	Respond	

---

[1] Of course, turns are not limited to two moves, but it may still be appropriate to think of the beginning and some subsequent part of a multi-clause turn realising these two moves, whilst the remainder is left unanalysed with respect to discourse move. Alternatively, it may be better to think of some turns including a **complex move** which itself can be analysed in terms of constituent **acts** (cf. Sinclair & Coulthard, 1975). Our own adult–child conversational data contain very few turns involving more than two moves, so we have not had to reach a decision on this issue.

	I ride it up there	Initiate	Exch. 3
Mother:	We'll have to close Vickie's door	(Respond) Initiate	
Mark:	No	Respond	Exch. 4

In order to understand the principles that underlie this and other structural devices for linking exchanges, we need to look again at the basic organisation. So far, it is the sequential dimension that has been emphasised, as the description of moves in terms of their initiating or responding position in the syntagmatic structure of the exchange makes clear. Now we need to consider the paradigmatic dimension: the options from which selections are made to fill the positions that have been syntagmatically defined.

Linking exchanges: the main move types

Considered from this point of view, the many different types of conversational contribution through which participants' inter-actional purposes are realised can be grouped together into three rather abstract types of move. These arise from the basic dynamics of any social interaction, whether it is expressed verbally or carried out by non-verbal means. That is, in initiating any social interchange, a participant either (a) **gives** something to the other participant or (b) **solicits** something from him. Then, in response, the second partici-pant completes the exchange by respectively (c) **acknowledging** what was given or giving what was solicited.[2] This gives rise to two basic types of exchange:

	Initiate		*Respond*
(1)	Solicit	–	Give
(2)	Give	–	Acknowledge

Understanding of how participants jointly construct quite long sequences of conversation by linking exchanges of these two types is still very limited, so the following paragraphs must be seen as extremely tentative. Nevertheless it does seem that several linking devices depend upon the different degrees of expectation for a fol-lowing response set up by the three types of move just described.

---

[2] Although couched in slightly different terms, these distinctions are found in Halliday (1977).

From this point of view, the three move types can be thought of as occupying different segments on a scale of **prospectiveness**.

At one end of the scale are solicits, which are strongly prospective in their expectation of a response; at the other end of the scale, acknowledges have little or no prospective force at all. Solicits always initiate a new exchange; acknowledges hardly ever do so. Give moves, on the other hand, occupy an intermediate position, having a prospective potential which may or may not be realised, depending upon the type of exchange in which they occur. In addition, any move type may be increased in prospectiveness by the addition of a tag or the selection of the intonational option of higher than usual pitch. Since the basic organising principle of the exchange is that the two sequentially defined moves should be arranged in terms of decreasing prospectiveness, the selection of a move type to fill the response position which has a greater degree of prospectiveness than that predicted by the move in first position provides a variety of ways of linking exchanges into longer sequences (Wells, MacLure & Montgomery, 1979).

One such possibility has already been illustrated (pp. 31–2), where the acknowledging response was made only implicitly, its place being taken by a move type with a greater degree of prospectiveness. This is just one of the devices that can be used to link two exchanges together. Rather similar is the addition of a tag to a give or acknowledge move, which has the effect of increasing the prospectiveness of that move (shown by the addition of '+' to the move type), as in the following example:

Mark:	Where's Pappa's pen draw on there? (= that I want to use to draw on there)	I	Solicit	Exch. 1
Mother:	You left it at Clifton didn't you?	$\{ {}^R_I \}$	Give +	
Mark:	No	R	Give	Exch. 2

The use of higher than usual pitch can also have the same effect:

Stella:	'Z̃at/ . . . Daddy(v)?	I	Solicit	Exch. 1
Father:	'P̃addling pool	$\{ {}^R_I \}$	Give+	
Stella:	'P̃addling pool	R	Give	Exch. 2

In this latter example, Father's use of high pitch seems to invite Stella to produce an imitation in response to his own utterance.

Another device for linking exchanges, which is also frequently used with a didactic purpose, is following up a responding give with an evaluative acknowledgment.

Teacher:	What did the first tiger take off Little Black Sambo?	I	Solicit	Exch. 1
Children:	His coat $\left\{ \begin{matrix} R \\ (I) \end{matrix} \right\}$ Give			
Teacher:	That's right	R	Ack.	Exch. 2

Here it is the double potential of the give move that is being exploited. Although the children's give is made solely in response to the teacher's solicit, the teacher goes on to treat this give as itself the initiation of a further exchange, to which an acknowledge is an appropriate response. The fact that the initiating function is imposed, after the event, by the teacher is shown by the ( ) round the symbol for initiate.

This particular pattern has been treated by some analysts (e.g. Mehan, 1978; Sinclair & Coulthard, 1975) as a three-part exchange, with the **follow-up** having equal status with the initiate and respond moves in the structure of the exchange. However, since this pattern is only one of several in which two or more exchanges are linked together to form a longer sequence, there seems no reason to give it a special status. Perhaps the original reason for treating this sequence as a basic exchange type was its frequency in classroom interaction, which was the type of data studied by both Sinclair & Coulthard and Mehan. However, we have found this particular pattern to occur quite frequently in the home as well, and not always with the adult as the initiator and evaluator, as the following example shows:

Thomas:	What's[ə] down there?	I	Solicit	Exch. 1
Adult:	That's the tape recorder $\left\{ \begin{matrix} R \\ (I) \end{matrix} \right\}$ Give			
Thomas:	'corder	R	Ack.	Exch. 2

It seems most satisfactory, therefore, to treat this pattern as a sequence of two linked exhanges, recognising that when it occurs in a didactic context, the acknowledging move will almost invariably be of an evaluative kind.

One further pattern of linked exchanges is worthy of mention, since it is so frequent in an adult–child interaction. The following is a typical example (the symbols are explained below):

3	Mark:	[ʃɪʃ] wash up Mummy (v)? (=have you finished washing up?)	I	Solicit ⎤	
					Exch. 1
4	Mother:	Pardon?	{Ret. / I}	Solicit ⎦	
					Exch. 2
5	Mark:	[ʃɪʃ] wash up?	{R / I₂}	Give/ Solicit ⎦	
					Exch. 3
6	Mother:	Yes	R	Give ⎦	

Such sequences have been described as involving 'contingent queries' (Garvey, 1977), since the second move solicits a reiteration or clarification of the previous utterance. Whilst this move is clearly a form of reply to the opening solicit, as well as initiating a new exchange, it does not meet in full the expectations set up by the previous move. Rather, it replies only to the fact that there was an initiation, and not at all to its function. For this reason, it can be seen as a **return**, rather than as a full response. The following move also plays a part in two exchanges: in repeating his original question, Mark both responds to his mother's initiation, giving the repetition that was solicited, but at the same time he also *re*-initiates his original exchange with a solicit, to which, in the subsequent response, his mother gives the information that was requested.

We can summarise the discussion so far by recalling the short dialogue presented in figure 1.1. The five turns of that sequence of discourse can now be seen to make up three exchanges. The first exchange opens up the channel and functions as what might be called a **pre-sequence** exchange. The next two turns constitute a second exchange organised around the request to borrow the bike. The third exchange is linked to the second by the follow-up device, and acknowledges the offer that was implied in the second part of the second exchange.

Before leaving the structural description of the exchange, one further point needs to be made, and that concerns the relation between verbal and nonverbal behaviour. As we have already noted, social exchanges may be performed either verbally or nonverbally. Since our concern is with language and its development, we have naturally concentrated on verbal exchanges and shall continue to do so. However, we should not forget that communication can take place through other channels than the verbal. Gesture, as we shall see in the following chapter, is one such channel, and it is particularly important as a precursor of verbal communication. Gesture can also play a part in predominantly verbal exchanges, either as an accompaniment to the verbal message or, on occasions, instead of it. This can take the form of conventional gestures, such as an affirmative nod of the head or a shrug of the shoulders or, in responding to a solicit that requests an action of some sort, the actual performance of the action. In conversation between adults, it is common for the performance of the action to be accompanied by some form of verbal response as well, but this is not obligatory; children, however, very frequently merely perform the requested action without any verbal response. We must be prepared, therefore, to recognise that some moves in discourse may be realised entirely nonverbally.

The repertoire of speech acts

So far we have been chiefly concerned with the sequential organisation of discourse. Nevertheless, as we have seen, this cannot be fully understood independently of a consideration of the way in which the positions in the sequential structure are filled by move types (defined in terms of the broad type of function that they perform in the dynamics of interpersonal interaction). In this section we shall be

Figure 1.2. An illustration of move and exchange structure

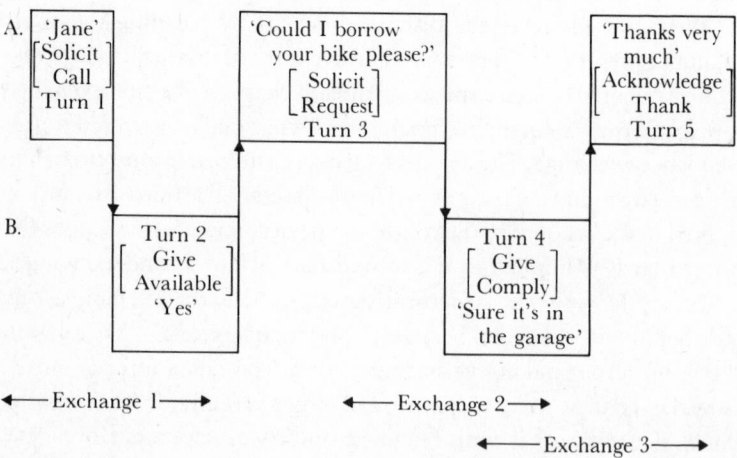

looking in more detail at the repertoire of functions from which a choice is made at each sequential position, and at the factors which influence which option is chosen. However this section, too, must be treated as exploratory, as there are still many problems to be resolved. In particular, in the investigation of the different functions, particular categories have tended to be considered in isolation from their conversational context, and little attention has so far been given to the ways in which different functions tend to be sequentially related. Nevertheless, the potential contribution of this line of investigation to an understanding of conversational organisation is sufficiently important to make it worth considering in some detail.

Viewed from a functional perspective, moves in discourse have been described as **speech acts,** and Austin (1962), who was one of the first writers to stress this action orientation of utterances, aptly entitled his book *How to Do Things with Words.* Austin started from the observation that certain utterances, such as 'I declare this fête open' or 'I bet you five pounds Blue Fizz wins the Derby', actually perform the actions of opening or betting by virtue of the successful making of the utterance. However, after further investigation, he came to the conclusion that a speech act of some kind is performed in the making of every utterance. In some cases, such as 'I command you to open this door', the type of act is overtly marked by the presence of an **illocutionary** verb in the utterance. However, even without 'I command you', 'Open this door' is still a command. Either form of utterance, therefore, performs the same speech act – in this case that of 'commanding'.

If every utterance performs one or more speech acts, an important question is: How many different types of speech act are there? Austin (1962) listed many more than a hundred, and indeed it seemed that the only limit to the number that might be proposed was the number of illocutionary verbs in the language. However, since this is a matter that is specific to the lexicon of a particular language, or even of a particular dialect (which could change overnight with the addition of a new lexical item), it does not seem that the existence of an illocutionary verb is, in itself, evidence of a corresponding distinct act. Secondly, there seem to be several clusters of verbs, such as 'command', 'direct', 'order', 'bid', 'request', etc., which are synonymous on one very important dimension and different from each other only with respect to less essential dimensions. If we could identify these dimensions and place them in order of importance, perhaps we should be able to define the major classes of speech act and construct an ordered taxonomy. Adopting just such an approach, Searle (1977), identified twelve dimensions, of which the most important are:

(i)   The purpose of the act: whether the act is, for example, an attempt to get the hearer to do something, or a representation (which may be true or false) of a state of affairs, or an undertaking by the speaker to do something, etc.

(ii) The direction of fit between words and world: for some acts, part of the purpose is to formulate the proposition to match a state of affairs in the world; for others, the purpose is to bring the world to a state that matches the proposition; in still others, successful performance guarantees the fit between world and words.

(iii) Expressed psychological state: this may be believing, wanting, intending, etc.

On the basis of these three dimensions, Searle proposed five major classes of speech act, which he defines as follows:

Representatives. This class has as its purpose to commit the speaker (in varying degrees) to something being the case. The direction of fit is that the proposition match the world, and the psychological state is that of belief.

Directives. The purpose of this class is to attempt (with varying degrees of force) to get the hearer to do something. The direction of fit is to bring the world to match the proposition, and the psychological state is that of want.

Commissives. The purpose is to commit the speaker to some future action. The direction of fit is, as for directives, bringing the world to match the proposition, and the psychological state is that of intention.

Expressives. The purpose of this class is to express the psychological state of the speaker with respect to the proposition, e.g. 'thank', 'apologise', 'deplore', etc. There

is no direction of fit and the psychological state is that
which is expressed.

Declarations. The defining characteristic of this class is that
in successfully performing one of these acts, the speaker
brings about a correspondence between proposition and
state of affairs in the world.

(Searle, 1977: 10–15)

This classification is summarised in table 1.2.

Other dimensions, which permit a sub-categorisation of types of
act within these classes, include the strength with which the purpose
is presented, the relative status of the participants, the way the
utterance relates to the interests of speaker and hearer, and so on.

However, although this is a useful attempt to provide explicit
criteria for constructing a finite taxonomy, it is open to a number of
criticisms. One of these concerns the allocation of information-
seeking questions to the class of directives. It is true, as Searle argues,
that a question has as part of its purpose the attempt to get the hearer
to do something, namely answer; but from another point of view,
one could equally argue that a question is concerned either to discover whether something is the case (yes/no question) or to obtain a
fuller representation of what is the case (wh- question). On these
grounds, questions could be argued to form a sub-class of representatives, and this position receives further support from the fact that
the attempt is to get the hearer to produce an utterance in which the

Table 1.2. *A classification of types of speech act (after Searle, 1977)*

	Direction of fit	Psychological state	Example
Representatives	Words match world	Belief	'I've dried my hands now'
Directives	World match words	Want	'Put the top back on the washing basket'
Commissives	World match words	Intention	'Well I will play if you you put the top on the basket'
Expressives	–	As expressed	'Thank goodness'
Declaratives	Words create state in world	–	'I declare the fête open'

proposition will match a state of affairs in the world. On the other hand, it is equally true that the psychological state underlying a question is that of wanting information. Since both these arguments have some force, perhaps the best solution would be to treat questions as a separate class of acts, related on one dimension to representatives and on another dimension to directives.

A second problem concerns the classes of act that have been omitted. The taxonomy, as it stands, seems to be chiefly concerned with acts that would typically initiate an exchange, and no mention is made specifically of responses. One solution would be to assign responses to the classes to which their respective initiating acts belonged but, as we have already seen in the case of questions and answers, this may also be problematic. A further group of acts that is not mentioned includes the various types of contingent query (e.g. 'Pardon?') and their appropriate responses. Arguments could no doubt be advanced for treating them, like questions, as directives but, for the same sorts of reasons, these are not entirely convincing.

The relationship between form and function

However, even if a modified taxonomy could be agreed upon that overcame these difficulties, another very difficult problem would remain: that of knowing which of the possible acts is being performed by a particular utterance. For, in general, there is no simple one-to-one correspondence between the form of an utterance and the speech act it is intended to perform. Here too Searle (1969) has attempted to provide a solution, by the precise specification of the conditions that have to be met for an utterance to count as a satisfactory performance of a particular kind of act. For example, he gives the following conditions for a **request**:

> For a speaker (S) appropriately to make a request the propositional content of his utterance must refer to an act (A) to be carried out in the future by the hearer (H), and it must also be the case that:
>
> (i)   H is able to do A and S believes H is able to do A.
> (ii) It is not obvious to both S and H that H will do A in the normal course of events of his own accord.
> (iii) S wants H to do A.
> (iv) The utterance counts as an attempt to get H to do A.

> Equally, for the utterance to be successful as a request, it is necessary that H should recognise that, in uttering it, S intends H to do A.

From the hearer's point of view, however, it still remains a problem in many cases to know, from the form of the utterance, which act the utterance is intended to perform. As we have seen, this is sometimes overtly marked, as in 'I promise to repay you next week', and in other cases one of a number of locutions which are conventionally associated with particular kinds of speech act may be used, such as, 'Would you mind Xing . . .' But in many cases the form of utterance does not mark the function overtly. Such utterances, therefore, when considered in isolation, are functionally ambiguous.

Of course there are advantages to be gained from fuzziness of this kind, since participants can exploit it in order to achieve a variety of interactional purposes. Consider, for example, a wife at a party who considers that her husband is drinking too much. If, as he seems about to accept the offer of another glass, she says, 'It's getting very late, dear', she may intend, and be heard as intending, to request him to take her home and therefore not to have the proffered drink. However, if he takes issue with this interpretation and accuses her of interfering, her retreat is secure, for she can justly argue that she had only remarked that it was getting late. However, what may be exploited to advantage by participants remains a serious problem for those who attempt to give a systematic and determinate account of how participants succeed in understanding which acts particular utterances are intended to perform.

There seem to be at least two major areas of difficulty. The first is illustrated by the preceding anecdote, in which the wife's utterances can be heard as realising several different acts simultaneously. Is there any way in which one of these can be identified as the 'essential' meaning, the rest being merely subsidiary? Or do we have to allow that all the possibly intended acts have equal status? One solution proposed by Davies (1979) is to make a distinction between **first-order significance** and the **higher-order** levels of significance that are implied by the communication of that first-order significance in the particular context that obtains at the time of utterance. On these grounds, we might argue that, in the above example, it is the representative act concerning the lateness of the hour which is primary.

Just how complex a set of higher-order levels of significance can be judged to be intended by a particular utterance in context can be illustrated from a psychiatric interview studied by Labov & Fanshel (1977). In the course of the interview, the patient Rhoda explained how she had telephoned her mother, who had been staying away from home with her married daughter for some time:

An-nd so – when – I called her t'day, I said 'Well when do you plan to come home?'

In analysing this utterance, Labov & Fanshel find that, on the basis of the first-level significance, five higher-order levels of significance are implied in this context:

R. continues the narrative and *gives information* (1) to support her assertion that she carried out the therapist's suggestion that she should ask relevant others for help. R. *requests information* (2) on the time that her mother intends to come home, and thereby *requests indirectly* (3) that her mother come home, thereby carrying out the therapist's suggestion and thereby *challenging* (4) her mother indirectly for not performing her role as head of the household properly, simultaneously *admitting* (5) her own limitations and simultaneously *asserting* (6) again that she carried out the therapist's suggestion.

(adapted from Labov & Fanshel, 1977: 160)

Not all problems can be resolved by appeal to higher-order levels of significance, however, since some utterances remain resolutely pluri-functional, or at least ambivalent in function. One particularly large area of interaction in which this is the case concerns the making of requests. The most direct form of request is expressed through the imperative mood, but whilst this may be appropriate for a superior addressing an inferior within a sharply defined social hierarchy, it is less frequently used between equals.

Instead, the indirectness of the relationship between form and function is systematically exploited in order to soften acts which, because they involve the speaker in attempting to control the listener, may cause offence. A considerable number of forms, more or less conventional, is available by means of which a request may be made more indirectly, for example:

(1)   Can you shut the door?
(2)   Are you going to shut the door?
(3)   Would you mind shutting the door?
(4)   The door is still open
(5)   Ooh! It's cold in here
        etc.

Some of these forms ((1)–(3)), as Searle (1975) has pointed out, make appeal to one or other of the conditions that have to be met in the making of a request and so the grounds for treating them as requests, although indirectly put, are clear. However, this is not the case for (4) and (5). Out of context, there is no way of telling from their form whether they are intended as requests, very indirectly expressed, or whether they are intended, respectively, as statement and exclamation. Similarly, when Mark is asked by his mother, who is holding two differently coloured Easter eggs, 'Which one do you like best?', it is impossible to tell from the form of the utterance alone whether she is asking for information about his preference or offering him whichever he prefers.

As participants, however, we are rarely at a loss, since in arriving at an interpretation of an utterance we can draw upon a wide variety of nonlinguistic cues in the situational context in order to resolve such ambiguities. In addition, there seems to be a general predisposition to treat any utterance as **action-oriented**, if such an interpretation can be heard as appropriate in context. Certainly, young children behave in this way: both Ervin-Trip (in press) and Shatz (1978a) report that children as young as 3 years of age are as likely to respond appropriately to indirectly expressed requests as they are to direct requests.

Such a predisposition could be expressed in the form of general principles for conversational interaction such as the following:

(i)   If the propositional content can be heard as having
        implications for action in the context in which it is uttered,
        it should be so heard.

and

(ii) If that action is one which the speaker might wish to have
        carried out and it is within the hearer's capability to carry

out, then the hearer should treat the utterance as a request
that he carry out the action.

or

(iii) If the action is one that the hearer might wish to have
carried out and it is within the speaker's capability to carry
it out, then the utterance should be treated as an offer by
the speaker to carry out that action.

There is, however, another dimension to the form–function relationship which applies particularly to requests. As already suggested
by Searle's analysis, a direct request, if uttered under the appropriate
conditions, leaves little or no discretion to the hearer as to whether to
carry out the requested action or not. An indirect request, on the
other hand, by raising one of these conditions or some relevant
aspect of the context as a matter of information, allows the hearer
the option of responding to that information rather than to the
implicit request, and thus of refusing the request without causing
serious loss of face on either side. Because direct requests assume
compliance, they are only socially appropriate where the speaker has
the right to make such an assumption, either because of higher status
in a power hierarchy, such as the armed forces, or because of the
reciprocal expectation of support that exists between friends. Indirectness, by contrast, is an expression of the speaker's unwilling-
ness to make such an assumption and is thus an appropriately polite
mode for a request made by an inferior to his superior or by one who
does not wish, or is not able, to claim familiarity.
    Dictates relating to relative power may not always be in agreement
with those relating to familiarity and politeness, however, and so, in
context, more than one message may be transmitted. For example,
when the managing director says to one of his employees 'I wonder
whether you could manage to start work on time' or a teacher asks
'Who's whistling?' they are choosing to express their purposes in
indirect forms which play down their power to control. At the same
time, however, there is usually little doubt that, because of their
status, they expect their requests to be complied with. Ervin-Tripp
(in press) cites an interesting example where misunderstanding
occurred: a foreign student who said to her landlady 'Can we move
the rubbish bins over here?' was surprised to receive the reply, 'I

didn't know you had a room-mate.' The landlady clearly did not expect to be requested to assist in carrying out the action and so interpreted the 'Can we . . .' as a request for permission by more than one person; the student either was not aware of her inferior status, and so of the inappropriateness of asking the landlady to help, or she mistakenly used 'we' in an attempt to be polite. But whichever explanation is correct, it points up the need to consider social features of the situation, as well as the form of the utterance, in arriving at an interpretation.

However, whilst principles for the interpretation of utterances, such as those that have been considered in relation to requests, may quite accurately reflect, in general terms, some of the procedures that participants make use of in relating form to speech act function, they still leave largely unexplained the particular criteria that are appealed to in specific instances. It must be concluded, therefore, that we are still far from an adequate understanding of this aspect of the organisation of discourse.

Articulating the two dimensions of discourse

Given the unresolved problems encountered in the attempt to provide defining criteria for the recognition of speech acts, it is obviously not yet possible to give a detailed account of the way in which the syntagmatic and paradigmatic dimensions of discourse are related. Yet there can be little doubt that they *are* systematically related. One possibility, tentatively advanced by Wells, MacLure & Montgomery (1979), is that the three move types, solicit, give and acknowledge, provide the link, mapping onto the various classes of speech act (however defined) on the one hand, and entering into the sequential structure of the exchange and longer stretches of discourse on the other. At the same time, certain formal features of utterances, such as the mood system and the intonational systems of tone and pitch height can also be shown to be systematically associated with choice of move type.

Whatever the merits of this particular proposal, however, it is clear that there are quite strong constraints on the options, both formal and functional, that can be appropriately selected by a speaker at different points in the syntagmatic structure of any exchange or sequence of linked exchanges. Likewise there are constraints on the possible interpretations that a hearer can put upon particular utterances, depending on their sequential position. Certain writers have likened these constraints to the syntactic rules which define the regularities in the structure of sentences, but that is surely too strong. A better analogy might be to the principles that influence the strokes that players successively make in a ball game such as tennis.

Even this analogy is less than satisfactory, however, as it implies a more strictly goal-oriented activity than is the case in the majority of conversations, where, as much as to win points, the object is to keep the ball in play. To this end, conversational participants are willing to ignore 'faults in service', to return balls that have gone 'out' and even, if necessary, to redefine the rules. The way in which a rally proceeds thus bears only a probabilistic relation to the predetermined, rule-governed sequences that might be prescribed by theory. However what the analogy does serve to highlight is the essentially collaborative way in which discourse is constructed, each participant in turn setting up opportunities and constraints for the move to follow as well as responding to the opportunities and constraints set up by the previous move.

Conversation: the triangle of communication

In the first part of this chapter we have looked at linguistic interaction almost exclusively in terms of the way in which utterances by different speakers sequentially contribute to the meaning that is jointly and collaboratively constructed. In so doing, we have concentrated on the moves that are made and the relationships between those moves, ignoring almost completely the psycholinguistic processes that individual participants engage in as they make and interpret those moves. In the remainder of this chapter we shall attempt to complete the picture by examining these processes in more detail, trying to establish the main components involved in the production and comprehension of a single utterance. For this purpose we shall concentrate on utterance 27 from the original extract given in table 1.1:

Mother: Put the lid . . . on top of the basket

As has already been argued with respect to the organisation of discourse, linguistic interaction is a collaborative activity, and this applies just as much to the production and interpretation of individual utterances as it does to longer stretches of discourse. Any act of linguistic communication involves the establishment of a triangular relationship between the sender, the receiver and the context of situation. The sender intends that, as a result of his communication, the receiver should come to attend to the same situation as himself and construe it in the same way.[3] For the communication to be successful, therefore, it is necessary (a) that the receiver should come to attend to the situation as intended by the sender; (b) that the sender should know that the receiver is so doing; and (c) that the receiver should know that the sender knows that this is the case. That is to say they need to establish **intersubjectivity** about the situation to which the communication refers.

Not all communications concern a shared, immediately perceptible situation, as in the example concerning the washing basket; nor do they always involve a speaker and a hearer. The paragraph that you are reading now involves a writer and a reader, and the situation that is the focus of our intersubjective attention is a generalised abstraction from our individual experience as communicators. In both cases, however, collaboration is required: the sender attempting to make his interpretation of the situation, and his intention within that situation, intelligible to the receiver; and the receiver using a variety of cues derived from the linguistic signal, his past experience and his own interpretation of the situation, in order to arrive at the meaning he judges to be intended by the sender.

In using the term 'situation' for the third point of the triangle, however, there is a certain ambiguity: at one and the same time it refers both to the context and to the content of the communication. This is not accidental. Although the physical setting of a communication – the context of market, classroom or club – may influence the way in which the participants relate to each other, and thus what they say, the more important situation is the one that is created by

---

[3] This formulation is based upon the more precise account of sufficient conditions for meaning proposed by Grice (1957). In an extended discussion of linguistic behaviour from a philosophical point of view, Bennett (1976) offers the following version:

'U (utterer) did x meaning that P if there is someone A (audience) such that U did x intending

(i) that A should come to believe P,
(ii) that A should be aware of intention (i), and
(iii) that the awareness mentioned in (ii) should be part of A's reason for believing P.' (p. 124)

means of their communication. It is precisely because words, and the sentences in which they occur, are symbols, separate from, but conventionally related to, the objects and events of our experience, that they enable us to create the intersubjectively agreed situations of our communication, whether the objects and events focused on are immediately present or not.

Constructing the message

The first stage in the production of an utterance is the construction of the message to be communicated. But this involves processes of interpretation and organisation that are not restricted to language. Almost all human behaviour is goal-directed, organised by **plans** which are nested one inside another, with higher-level plans requiring sequences of plans at lower levels for their implementation (Miller, Galanter & Pribram, 1960). In our example, the plan is to bring about a state of affairs in which the lid is on the washing basket – a plan which could clearly be carried out in a number of ways, one of which would involve the mother carrying out the action herself. An alternative – and one which is almost essential where the goal is some form of collaborative activity – is to make use of communication as a means of carrying out a higher-level plan. This is what Mark's mother does when she asks him to carry out the action for her.

Where the plan is complex, its communication may require a whole series of messages, as for example when instructing someone to carry out an intricate task such as assembling a kit or when telling a story. But whether part of a series or standing alone, each message can itself be, for convenience, theoretically separated into a number of components. The first of these concerns the **purpose** of the communication.

As we saw in the earlier discussion of speech acts, an important part of the speaker's intention in communicating is to bring about some effect – to carry out a verbal action. There, we were looking at speech acts from the point of view of the relationships between moves in the sequential structure of discourse, but the categories that were distinguished can equally be taken to describe the sorts of purposes that speakers may have in the implementation of higher-level plans: purposes such as directing (influencing the listener to act), representing (adding to or modifying the listener's knowledge), expressing feeling and so on. In most cases the effect that is intended involves the listener in some way, and Halliday (1970) refers to this component as the **interpersonal function**. In the case of our example the message clearly has a directive purpose: to get Mark to carry out an action.

Closely linked to purpose is the second component: the **topic** of the message. This concerns the events or states of affairs – the situation – to which the plan that has given rise to the message applies. Constructing the topic of the message involves selecting and organising the relevant present and past experience.

For experience to be available to be drawn upon in carrying out a plan, whether through communication or by some other means, it must be internally represented in some form. Psychologists are not entirely in agreement about the form in which experience is stored in memory, but clearly it must be systematically organised with numerous cross-references so that it can be readily accessed either for the interpretation of incoming sensory information or for the various types of mental process that can be gathered together under the general label 'thinking'. As well as integrating information received through different sensory modalities, this **internal representation of experience** also makes use of typical episode structures or 'scripts' (Schank & Abelson, 1977) in order to integrate experiences over time, and project future outcomes and possibilities.

Whilst the organisation of language – its grammar and vocabulary – must be closely matched to this internal representation and almost certainly comes to influence the way in which experience is represented, the internal representation of experience itself clearly does not consist of a set of sentences ready-made to fit the constantly changing detail of moment-by-moment experience. Even the recognition of individual objects does not involve a direct link between percept and lexical item; rather both are linked through some form of conceptual organisation which is brought into play when the object has to be referred to verbally (Miller & Johnson-Laird, 1976). Language and experience, therefore, are not in any simple one-to-one correspondence.

There are two further reasons for recognising a separation between language and the way in which experience is internally represented, which were pointed out by Vygotsky (1962) in his discussion of language and thought. Firstly, experience is personal and particular, whereas the categories of language, whether lexical or grammatical, are public and general; secondly, experience is multi-dimensional and simultaneous, whereas the act of speaking or writing requires this to be converted into an ordered arrangement of constituents that can ultimately be expressed through a temporarily organised sequence of sounds or marks on a page. If these arguments are correct, it follows that, in order to communicate through language, a speaker first has to identify and organise conceptually those elements of present or past experience that are relevant to his current plan, and then to reorganise, or 'translate', this personal and particular configuration into the categories of meaning that are publicly available in the semantic structure of his native language.

What is involved in this stage of topic construction has only recently begun to be investigated (e.g. Chafe, 1977; Schank & Abelson, 1977), as linguists and psychologists have started to explore the semantic interface between personal experience and the organisation of meaning in particular languages. Learning to manage this interface thus represents a major part of what is involved in language acquisition. This topic will be more fully discussed in chapters 2 and 3; for the moment, it is sufficient to emphasise the general point that speaking (and listening) require the manipulation of more than one form of representation, and a process of translation between them that involves substantial reorganisation (Fodor, Bever & Garrett, 1974).

If we attempt to apply these ideas to the construction of the topic in the utterance that we are focusing upon, we might arrive at a sketch such as the following: In order to formulate the topic relevant to her plan of getting Mark to replace the lid on the basket, his mother first has to interpret certain patterns of visual stimulation as evidence of the presence of two particular objects located in a certain relation to each other and to herself and Mark (also, of course, other patterns as evidence of the presence of Mark apparently disposed to listen to her request); she then has to conceptualise the desired end state and how it might be achieved; and finally she has to match this with a particular semantic structure, which might be stated in terms such as 'Agent Cause Object to Move to be in a specified ("on") Relation with respect to a Location', with the various roles in this event being taken by the particular entities: Mark, the lid and the basket, respectively.

Thirdly, messages frequently also have an **attitudinal** component, involving one or more of the following: the speaker's affective response to the situation and his or her involvement in the topic being discussed (realised, for example, as '*I really am very worried* that George will be unable to get a job'); his estimate, in the case of an informing message, of the probability of the information being correct (e.g. '*It is probable that/Perhaps* he is at home'); his attitude to the hearer on such dimensions as friendliness, familiarity, etc. (shown, for example, in the form chosen to realise a request, e.g. '*Would you mind* putting the book back on the shelf when you've finished with it'). There are no obvious realisations of attitude in the extract from which our example is taken, except perhaps the addition of the politeness term 'please' in the mother's utterance (14). This is not surprising, as the means for expressing attitudinal qualifications are relatively late to emerge and, probably for this reason, are relatively rare in speech to young children.

The attitudinal component is usually congruent with the purpose and topic components of the message, but it can happen that, without the speaker necessarily being conscious of it, his 'real' attitude is expressed in a way which conflicts with the rest of the message. When this happens, the realisation of the conflicting attitude is typically paralinguistic (for example, the tremor in the voice or the averted gaze which belies the claim to certainty in 'I know I gave it back to you', or the peremptory tone of voice which belies the indirectness of the request 'I wonder if it is possible for you to do this immediately'). Where this occurs, there are in effect two contradictory messages being transmitted simultaneously and, perhaps not surprisingly, it has been shown that it is the apparently unintentional one that is most likely to be attended to (Argyle, 1969).

Taking account of the context

The discussion so far has treated the construction of the message as if it occurred in an interactional vacuum. But, as we saw in the earlier discussion of the organisation of discourse, there are quite strong constraints on what moves a speaker can appropriately make at each successive point in the unfolding of a conversational sequence; and the selection and organisation of the purpose and topic of the message must take these constraints into account in a number of ways. Since there does not seem to be any agreed way of referring to this aspect of the message, let us introduce the term **orientation**. We can think of orientation, therefore, as the adjustment of purpose, topic and attitude to take account of the particular context in which the message is to be communicated.

One aspect of orientation that has already been considered in relation to discourse, is the selection of a speech act which will simultaneously realise the speaker's intended purpose and be capable of being mapped on to a move type that is appropriate to that point in a sequence. Even more fundamentally, the decision to produce an utterance at all, as well as its purpose and topic, may be almost entirely a matter of orientation to the expectations set up by the previous speaker's utterance. Our example utterance is a case in point; for it seems highly unlikely that the mother would have repeated her earlier instruction if Mark had not solicited the repetition.

With respect to topic, orientation influences both what information is included and how it is organised. One of the most important decisions a speaker has to make concerns the amount of information relevant to his topic that he can assume to be already shared with his intended hearer. To underestimate what his hearer already knows will lead him to appear to be 'talking down', which may cause his hearer to feel insulted; on the other hand, to overestimate is to risk failing to communicate effectively altogether, as the hearer searches his representation of past experience in vain to find relevant information to which he can relate what he hears.

There are at least three levels at which such judgments about what is shared knowledge have to be made. The most general concerns cultural assumptions – what is taken to be 'common knowledge' amongst members of a particular culture, by virtue of their membership of that culture. Secondly, there is knowledge known to be shared as a result of personal experience; and thirdly there is knowledge which has already been established as shared during the course of the present conversation. In some respects it is this last level which is the most important, since it is by successfully managing the introduction, foregrounding and linking of items of information from one utterance to the next that conversational participants create coherence in their joint production of discourse and reassure each other that mutual understanding is taking place.

One of the ways in which speakers organise their utterances to achieve this effect depends on a distinction between information which is **given** and information which is **new**. Each utterance can be expected to contain some information which is presented as already belonging to the intersubjective pool of shared knowledge, as a result of earlier mention in the conversation, or at least as being easily assimilable to that pool by inspection of the situational context or by appeal to past experience. This information can therefore be treated as given. The remainder of the utterance offers new information relevant to that which was given. One aspect of orientation, therefore, is the construction of the message so that the hearer is able to recognise which part of the information is to be taken as given and which is new.

As we saw earlier, however, what is presented as given information is not always directly recognisable as such by the hearer, and indeed conversation would be rather tedious if all connections between utterances were spelt out in full. Nevertheless, as Clark & Haviland (1977) point out, mutual understanding is only possible if participants behave as if they were parties to an agreement to the effect that the speaker will construct his message so that his hearer *is able* to discover the unique referent identified by each item of information that is introduced. This they call the **given–new contract**. The speaker has to make sure, therefore, that, if what he offers as given has not already been specifically mentioned, the hearer will be able easily to make the **implicature** that allows him to locate the intended referent in memory or in the situation.

In the case of the utterance concerning the washing basket, both the intended referents are clear, since there is only one lid and one basket, both visible to speaker and hearer and both having already been mentioned in the immediately preceding conversation. However, it is easy to imagine a slightly different conversation in which the link between utterances is not so obvious. For example,

> Child: This towel needs to go to the wash
> Mother: The basket is behind the door

Here, 'The basket' is treated as given information in the mother's utterance, although it had not been previously mentioned. However, if the child as hearer were aware that articles in his household needing to be washed were placed in a particular basket, he would be able to draw the implicature that the basket his mother was referring to was the basket for dirty washing and he would then understand the relevance of the new information that it was behind the door.

The orientation of the speaker's message is also responsive to other aspects of the context, particularly the social setting or event of which the communication is a part. In the particular example we are focusing upon there is little evidence of adjustment to the context as such, but the form of the mother's utterance certainly seems to be adjusted to the gap in skill between herself and Mark and, if we were to examine extracts from other contexts, we should find evidence of both child and mother adjusting their messages when speaking to Mark's baby sister, to Mark's father, or to unfamiliar visitors. We should also find examples of utterances by Mark which showed some ability to orient his meaning to take account of the perceived or anticipated attitude of his mother to his intended or current activities. Perhaps, indeed, this is what we are seeing in his solicitous offering of the towel to his mother.

These various kinds of orientation to the anticipated needs of the hearer are thus an important part of the selecting and organising of meaning which, it has been suggested, constitute the first stage in the production of an utterance. It is also in making these adjustments that the speaker most obviously engages in a collaborative activity and observes the Cooperative Principle in conversation that was discussed above (p. 30).

Before going further, let us recapitulate the discussion so far. Communication, it has been argued, brings into being within the context of situation a triangular relationship between sender, receiver and the field of intersubjective attention, where this field may concern some aspect of the situational context or may be created from the participants' representation of experience by means of the communication itself. In the construction of a particular message to further his current plan, the speaker selects the relevant aspects of his internally represented personal and particular experience and formulates them in terms of categories of meaning within the shared and public language that he speaks. For convenience, these meanings can be described in terms of a purpose the utterance is intended to achieve, a topic which provides its propositional content and an attitudinal component. At the same time, the organisation of the message is given an orientation to the requirements of the specific interactional context in which it is to be communicated.

The result of this process of construction we shall call a **meaning intention**, which is what the sender wants the receiver to understand as the result of his communication.

Encoding the meaning intention

The next stage in the production of the utterance is the encoding of this meaning intention. As we have already seen, linguistic communication involves a translation between the form of representation in which cognitive operations are carried out and the temporal sequence of linguistic items which constitute the speech event. As Fodor et al. (1974) remark in discussing comprehension, utterances can transmit thoughts only because hearers know how to translate them into the language in which thinking is done. Clearly, the reverse of this procedure is equally necessary in the production of utterances, although the detail of how 'thoughts' are converted into the form that the utterance will take is still, as we have seen, a matter of considerable theoretical discussion. One part of this procedure is carried out, we have suggested, in the formulation of a meaning intention in terms of categories of purpose, topic and attitude. However, there must also be a second stage at which the meaning intention is encoded in terms of the formal resources of the language: lexical items, syntactic structures, intonation patterns and gestures. Finally, in a third stage, the resulting pattern of items in structure is given physical expression through patterns of sound or some form of visual representation.

For many linguists, the resources involved in these latter two stages and their systematic organisation are what constitute the essence of language; how people use the sentences that are constructed from these resources being considered outside the province of linguistic investigation. This is particularly true of Chomsky and other **transformational-generative** grammarians, who also make a sharp distinction between **competence** (the knowledge that a native speaker/hearer has about the formal organisation of his language, which can be expressed in the form of rules of various kinds) and **performance** (the processes of speaking, listening, making linguistic judgments, etc., which draw upon competence, but which also involve memory, heuristic processing strategies and so on) (Chomsky, 1965). Other linguists and sociolinguists, on the other hand, have argued that what a native speaker knows also includes how to use language appropriately to make reference to objects and events in the world, how to engage effectively in linguistic interaction and so on. The term **communicative competence** has been coined, in opposition to the 'grammatical competence' of transformational grammar, in order to emphasise this broader conception of what constitutes linguistic knowledge (Campbell & Wales, 1970; Hymes, 1972).

Like Halliday (1970, 1977), however, we find it more helpful to think in terms of what a speaker/hearer is *able to do* rather than in terms of what he knows. This view is also shared by certain psycholinguists. Miller & Johnson-Laird (1976), for example, have suggested that the rules of syntax, such as those proposed in transformational grammar, are not so much components of the language user's competence, playing an important role in performance, as generalisations that the language user may eventually come to derive from the procedures that he uses. We see the formal organisation of language, therefore, as a resource: systems of options of lexis, syntax and intonation, through which meaning intentions are encoded, or realised.

Rather like translation from one language to another, however, realisation is not a straightforward matter of one-to-one correspondence between units of meaning and units of form. On the one hand, a particular meaning may be realised simultaneously by options from more than one of the formal systems (e.g. 'politeness' may be realised in making a request by the selection of interrogative rather than imperative mood, with associated past as opposed to nonpast tense, and the addition of the lexical items 'mind' and 'please', as in 'Would you mind shutting the door please?'). On the other hand, one formal item may simultaneously realise more than one aspect of meaning (e.g. in 'Did he go out?', 'did' both encodes the reference to past time, and functions, in inversion with the subject 'he', to mark the sentence as interrogative, thus realising in this context the purpose 'request information').

Nevertheless, although many-to-one relationships in both directions are the rule rather than the exception, it is fairly accurate to say that the different aspects of meaning tend to be more closely linked to some rather than others of the formal systems of realisation. Thus topic tends to be most strongly associated with the selection of the lexical verb and the lexical content of the noun phrases associated with it in the case roles of **agent, patient, location**, etc., and with the syntactic organisation of these noun phrases as **subject, object,**

adjunct, etc., of the clause. Topic is also associated with the syntactic systems of **tense** and **aspect**. Purpose, as we have seen, is strongly associated with the syntactic system of **mood**, and thus with the relationship between subject and the first element of the verb. Attitude is clearly associated with the selection of lexical items according to their affective associations, as opposed to their referential meaning; it is also associated with a number of lexical items or phrases such as 'think', 'in my opinion', 'possibly', etc. and with the system of modal verbs (e.g. 'might', 'could', etc.) as the realisation of tentativeness and uncertainty.

The realisations of orientation are less easy to characterise, however. Just as each of the other aspects of meaning is adjusted to fit the message to the conversational and situational context in which it is to be communicated, so the formal realisations of these adjustments are to be found in lexical selection, syntactic organisation and intonational patterning.

One particularly important aspect of the realisation of orientation is the organisation of the structure of the utterance to signal the given–new distinction discussed above. Information which is presented as given, it will be recalled, is assumed to be already available to the hearer from the preceding conversation, either directly or by means of 'implicature' (cf. p. 53). Given information typically occurs in the early part of the sentence, whilst new information tends to follow in the latter part;[4] and whilst new information is presented in full, given information is typically presented in a more allusive fashion with links back to the earlier mention being made through some form of **cohesion**.

This can be illustrated by means of a version of the washing basket extract which might have, but did not actually, occur:

1   Child: Look here's the lid
2   Mother: Put *it* on the basket
3   Child: I have   [Child has put the lid *into* the basket]
4   Mother: I don't think *so*
5   No put *it* on *it*

---

[4] This is not always the case as, for reasons of emphasis, new information can be put at the beginning of the sentence by means of various types of **thematisation** (cf. Halliday, 1967b), for example, 'A page of the thesis was what William was chewing.'

In this short extract, information is carried forward from one utterance to the next using several of the different types of cohesion (cf.
Halliday & Hasan, 1976). In 2, 'the lid' is the given information, and
here it is realised by means of **anaphoric reference**: 'it' refers the
hearer back to a previous occurrence of 'the lid' in 1. In 3 there is an
example of **ellipsis**: in the context, 'put it on the basket' can be
supplied from the previous utterance to complete the meaning of the
elliptical 'I have'. 4 involves the **substitution** of 'so' for the whole
clause 'you have put it on the basket' elliptically contained in 3.
Finally, the two anaphoric pronouns in 5 refer back, respectively to
'the lid' in 1 and 'the basket' in 2.

Another way of looking at the realisation of the information
structure here is in terms of relative emphasis. Werth (forthcoming)
suggests that items of information are assigned one of three possible
levels of emphasis. New information, as might be expected, is
brought into **focus**; given information, on the other hand, is given a
reduced status. The third possibility, illustrated in 5 above, is that of
contrast. An item of given information, '*in* the basket' in this case,
which is directly available from the situation, is used as the point of
comparison for a contrasting item, '*on* the basket'. As we have
already seen, reduced emphasis tends to be associated with cohesive
options such as pronominal reference, substitution and ellipsis.
Focus, on the other hand, is associated with full lexical specification.

Also associated with all the categories of emphasis, and with the
orientation of the message more generally, are the systems of **intonation**. In discussing intonation, however, we first have to consider the
division of the utterance into **tone units**, for it is to tone units, rather
than to clauses or utterances, that the systems of intonational contrast apply. Not all utterances are divided into more than one tone
unit, but where such a segmentation is made, it has the effect of
presenting the 'matter' contained in the utterance in a number of
chunks, each one involving choices with respect to the various systems of intonational contrast.

In order to illustrate what is meant by tone unit, consider the
following invented examples, where / marks a boundary between
tone units:

(1) John gave the 'apple and the 'pear to his 'sister / but the
     ba'nanas he kept for him'self

(2) John gave the 'apple / and the 'pear / to his 'sister / but the
      ba'nanas / he 'kept for him'self

In the first case the message is presented as just two tone units,
corresponding to the two opposed sets of fruit. In the second, by
contrast, each entity mentioned, except John, is presented in a separate tone unit. The larger the number of tone units, the greater the
number of opportunities for choices of emphasis, and the smaller the
amount of information to be processed in each chunk. Not surprisingly, therefore, a high ratio of tone units per utterance tends to be
found in contexts where dramatic effect is intended and also in
speech addressed to young children. As we shall see below, the
repeated request addressed to Mark is divided into two tone-units.

Each tone unit contains at least one syllable which is acoustically
prominent (marked ' in the examples above) and this syllable, or the
last such syllable where there is more than one, is the **tonic** syllable,
on which choices are made with respect to two systems involving
pitch: **tone** (direction of pitch movement), which has three basic
options: **rising, falling** and **level**; and **pitch height**, which may be
high, mid or **low**.

Two meaning contrasts seem to be associated with choice of tone;
in the first, rising tone (shown as ⟋) indicates that the 'matter' of
the tone unit is being presented by the speaker as knowledge assumed
to be shared, whilst falling tone (⟍) indicates that the matter is not
assumed to be shared (Brazil, 1975). The other contrast associated
with tone is whether the matter which is presented is complete or
incomplete, with rising tone indicating that, at this point, the sequence is incomplete and that there is at least one tone unit to follow.
This contrast is particularly frequent in lectures and in reading
aloud, where tone units not occurring at the end of a sentence tend to
be uttered with rising tone. In conversation, utterances ending on
rising tone are likely to be heard as expecting a response. (However,
it does not follow that those ending on a falling tone are heard as not
expecting a response, since the expectation of a response is also
related to mood choice and, more generally, to move type and
exchange structure (cf. pp. 32–4).) Level tone, which is relatively rare
in Standard English, is neutral with respect to both these oppositions.

The opposition between complete and incomplete is also associated with the choice of pitch height on the tonic syllable, with high

pitch being heard as expecting a continuation and low pitch as offering an opportunity to close the sequence. In addition, high pitch on a prominent syllable may also indicate that a contrast is intended (e.g. 'Mother: No put it 'on it', p. 57 above), whilst low pitch indicates that the matter of the tone unit can be taken as essentially equivalent to that contributed in a previous tone unit (Brazil, 1978). As will be clear from the brief sketch, however, the role of intonation in the realisation of the different aspects of orientation is complex, and, as yet, not very well understood.

Nevertheless, if we return to Mark and the washing basket, we can now see that its form realises a number of options of orientation:

'Put the 'lid / . . on 'top of the 'basket

Firstly, by breaking the utterance into two tone units, separated by a brief pause, his mother organises the message as two chunks, corresponding to the two objects that Mark is to act upon. Secondly, by selecting rising tone in the first tone unit, she indicates that she is assuming that the fact that it is the lid that is to be moved is already a matter on which they are agreed; what is new (or being treated as new) is where he has to put it. Thirdly, the use of the definite article in referring to both lid and basket indicates that she assumes that Mark already knows which particular objects are being referred to. Finally, in contrast to her initial request (14), which was indirect, the present request is direct, though this is probably more in the interests of formal simplification to ensure understanding than as an expression of any change in the actual or desired status or authority relationship between them.

Following this brief account of some of the formal systems taken one by one, we can look again at his mother's utterance to Mark and note how the different aspects of meaning are simultaneously realised in the various options that are selected in the formal organisation of the utterance.

The purpose of the message, to request action of the hearer, is realised by the selection of imperative mood, that is to say by the omission of the grammatical subject and the selection of the nonfinite form of the verb. The topic of the message, that an agent (the hearer) cause a change of location (put on) of the patient (the lid) with respect to the goal location (the basket) at the time (now), is realised through the selection of the lexical items in brackets and their allocation to the grammatical constituents subject, main verb, object and adjunct in the unmarked order VOA. (Note that, as a result of the imperative mood, the subject is omitted and the verb is unmarked for tense.) As no option is selected in the attitudinal component, there is no realisation of attitude in this utterance.

In the realisation of orientation, there are two tone units: the first, which takes rising tone and high pitch, contains the given information, and the second, which takes falling tone and high pitch, contains the new information. Because the objects referred to in this utterance both are perceptually present and have already been referred to, they are treated as definite.

In what is a relatively simple utterance, all the main formal characteristics can be accounted for in terms of the systems described above. This is represented diagrammatically in figure 1.3.

The final stages in the production process take this plan for an utterance, recode it in terms of phonological structure (i.e. as a temporally organised sequence of segments of sound) and execute the resulting programme by activating the muscles that control the lungs, vocal cords, throat, tongue, jaws and lips to produce an integrated sequence of movements that modify the outgoing breath to produce the characteristic sound that we recognise as speech.

Of necessity, this account of the production of an utterance has been highly schematic; parts of it too, are in need of much more empirical validation before they can be accepted as proven fact. One qualification, in particular, needs to be made, and that concerns the uni-directionality of the processes implied by the above account. Although there is evidence in rather general terms for the temporal succession of the stages that have been outlined, it is clear that the message does not have to be constructed in full before a start can be made on putting it into execution. Evidence from the study of errors and the location and duration of pauses in speech (Fromkin, 1973), for example, indicates that pauses tend to occur just before items with high informational value, suggesting that although the general organisation of his meaning intention is sufficiently well developed for the first part of his utterance to be executed, a choice with respect to some subordinate part is causing the speaker a momentary difficulty. There is also a feedback effect in the opposite direction, as the speaker monitors the encoding and transmission of his utterance, leading on some occasions to self-corrections of various kinds. A

62

Figure 1.3. Relationship between context, meaning and form for one utterance

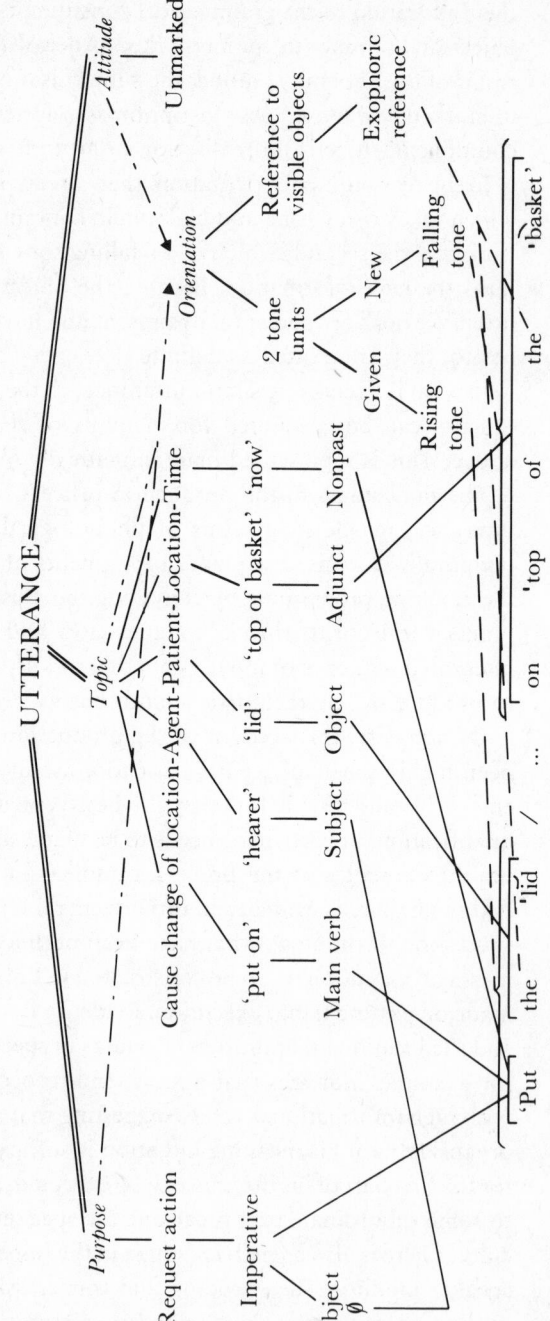

more important consequence of feedback is that by comparing the verbal formulation actually transmitted with the initial meaning intention, a speaker has the opportunity to become more aware of his own thoughts and to modify and develop them. This is even more true of writing, where there is greater opportunity for correction and revision (cf. chapter 7).

Comprehension: understanding what is intended

Now let us turn to the other side of the communication process – the reception and interpretation of the signal transmitted by the sender, whether it be spoken or written. In the previous sections we considered the major components involved in the production of an utterance and sketched the relationships between them. When we come to consider the receiver, we can see that he too requires the same components but, as will become clear, the relationship between the components in the comprehension of an utterance is rather different. In particular, comprehension differs from production in the way in which the non-linguistic representation of experience is related to the linguistic encoding of the message.

As we have already seen, the task of the speaker is to translate the representation of particular and personal experience into a linguistically oriented meaning intention, which can be encoded by selecting and organising appropriate options from his repertoire of vocabulary, grammar and intonation to create a plan for an utterance, which is finally articulated as speech. At each stage in this task the speaker is guided by the plan that his communication is to serve and, throughout the process, as a template against which to check the result, he has available a representation of the situation to which his message applies, either derived through direct perception or in the form of an already activated area of internally represented experience.

The hearer, on the other hand, does not have such a representation available; indeed his task is precisely to create such a representation on the basis of the information that is made available to him in the incoming speech signal. It might seem, therefore, as if the processes involved in comprehension could be represented as a simple inversion of the sequence of production: auditory discrimination and segmentation of the speech signal yielding a sequence of words in

syntactic structure from which the meaning could be decoded, leading to an amplification or modification of the listener's representation of experience and current plan.

In broad outline, of course, processes of this sort must take place,
if the speech signal is to lead to the listener understanding the
meaning intended by the speaker. However, on the basis of research
carried out to date, it seems unlikely that such a simple, uni-
directional model accurately describes what typically occurs.

In the first place, just as nonverbal perception involves an interaction between information received by the senses and expectations
derived from past experience, so the perception of linguistic information involves a similar interaction between the actual speech signal
and expectations derived from various sources, including redundancy within the formal structure of the message itself, accompanying paralinguistic signals and information from the conversational
and cultural contexts within which the message occurs (Clark, 1978;
Marslen-Wilson, Tyler & Seidenberg, 1978).

Secondly, even when the speech signal has been decoded as a
semantic structure, the linguistic units of which it is constructed only
label abstract classes and entities and the relations between them.
They do not, in themselves, fully specify how they are to be integrated into the particular framework of meanings that have been
established as shared knowledge in the preceding interaction, nor
how they are to be related to the particular objects and events that
they refer to in the field of intersubjective attention. The interpretation of the message can only be achieved, therefore, by the listener
drawing upon information from sources other than the signal itself,
and in particular from his interpretation of the total context (Bransford & McCarrell, 1974).

Much of this information is already available to him, however.
For, like the speaker, the hearer is actively engaged in construing the
situational context in the light of his own past experience and current
plan, and this information includes the actions of the speaker, his
gestures, facial expression and direction of gaze. So, even before the
speaker begins to produce his utterance, the listener will have formed
certain general expectations about the speaker's intentions, which
will dispose him to treat certain messages as more probable than
others. The greater the amount of 'common ground' that has already
been established, either in the preceding conversation or as the result

of shared experience, the more detailed and accurate these expectations are likely to be.

Expectations about complete messages can rarely be very precise, however, given the wide range of things a person may say, even in well-defined situations. But once the speaker has begun to produce, and the listener to process, the utterance, progressively stronger expectations are aroused as the utterance proceeds in an almost inverse relation to the difficulty of choice experienced by the speaker. These expectations are of three general kinds, corresponding to the types of redundancy mentioned above: relationships between lexical items, corresponding to the relationships that hold with varying degrees of likelihood between objects and events in the world of experience; relationships between items within semantic/syntactic structures; and relationships between units of speech sound. In the following invented example, involving two parents discussing how they spent the weekend, all three types of redundancy converge in predicting the completion of the second utterance:

A: John and I went to Weston at the weekend and the children rode the ponies on the sands.

B: That must have been fun. We went to Bristol and ours saw the white tigers at the z—.

In arriving at this completion, experience narrows down the locations in Britain where one can see white tigers to a small set; such locations are referred to by nouns and, following a spatial preposition and the definite article, a noun is the most probable sequel; nouns with initial consonant 'z', which refer to such locations, can be reduced to the single possibility: 'zoo'.

This is no doubt an extreme case, for not every word in an utterance can be predicted with such certainty. Nevertheless, evidence from a variety of sources all leads to an account in terms of bringing information to the task of understanding as well as extracting it from the speech signal.

From this point of view, consider the **cloze** procedure, in which written texts have words removed at regular intervals. Subjects in experiments involving this procedure have little difficulty in suggesting words that make sense in the gaps and, if they are given additional information about the length of the word or its initial letters, can frequently provide correct solutions, particularly if the subject matter is familiar (Heatlie & Ramsey, 1971). A second, and rather compelling, source of evidence of the role of expectations is found in the misreadings we can be led into by our familiarity with the most frequent structural patterns in the language. The following text caused the present writer to puzzle for some considerable time before the intended meaning became clear:

> 'The wild Ginseng men sought and found
> with considerable difficulty
> could not begin to meet
> the great demand for the magic root.'[5]

Perhaps the most convincing evidence, however, is to be found in the skill with which parents seem to arrive, more often than not, at satisfactory interpretations of their children's utterances even when these are, to varying degrees, inadequate in specificity of reference, completeness of expression, pronunciation, or a combination of these. However, by drawing upon their interpretation of the situation and their experience of the child's characteristic interests and desires, parents are able to arrive at the child's probable meaning intentions, making use of whatever linguistic cues are available and supplying the remaining information from other sources. In just this way, it appears, Mark's mother succeeds in understanding his question '[ʃɪʃ] wash up Mummy?'

However, the problems faced by parents, or by subjects in 'cloze' experiments, and the strategies they use to resolve them, differ only in degree from those in which any conversational participant is involved. For the achievement of comprehension always involves a complex interaction of informational cues from a variety of sources. It must be stressed, however, that the relative weight that is given to the different types of cue is not constant across all situations, but depends upon a variety of factors, such as the purpose for which the participants are communicating, the relationship between them, the familiarity of the topic, the availability of nonlinguistic behavioural and situational cues, and the form and quality of the actual signal.

Awareness of the constructive, multi-cued nature of the comprehension process helps us to understand how listeners can overcome inadequacies in the message or noise in the communication

---

[5] Commas after 'Ginseng' and 'difficulty' make the task considerably easier. They were not present in the advertisement in which this sentence was found.

channel. It also helps us to see how strategies that give particular emphasis to one sort of cue may be successful in some situations yet lead to error in others. This seems to be the explanation of many of the miscues produced by beginning readers, and of the systematic but erroneous responses that young children produce on tests of comprehension (cf. chapter 5). At the same time, it can help us to see the appropriateness of the utterance whose production we have examined in such detail, and indeed of the whole sequence of conversation in which it occurred.

From Mark's point of view, the purpose of this conversation is to get his mother to play, and so his motivation to understand and perform the action requested by his mother is high, once he has understood that her compliance is conditional upon his performance of the task. The objects on which the action is to be performed are also present in the situation, and it is a task which is well within Mark's capabilities. However, since the performance of the task is dependent upon his correctly understanding the linguistic instruction, it is important that it should be made as easy as possible for him to relate the formal organisation of the utterance to other cues available in the situation, and to use the resulting meaning intention to create and direct a plan of action. And this is what his mother's total communication seems intuitively designed to achieve:

'Put the 'lid / . . on 'top of the 'basket

By separating the utterance into two tone units, she helps to define the sequence in which the action is to be performed; at the same time, by pointing to the lid by gesture and gaze and by giving prominent stress and rising tone to the corresponding word in her utterance, she maximises the chances of his correctly identifying her intended referent. Then, having assured herself that he has understood that much, she moves her gaze to the basket as she produces the second tone unit, once again giving prominent stress to the words in her utterance that specify the location where the lid is to be put. In this way she organises the verbal and nonverbal cues in her communication to match the cues available from the disposition of the referent objects in the shared situation. That Mark finally carries out the request is evidence that he has comprehended the message and, although less directly, this in turn provides an indication of the success of his mother's strategy.

Having charted at great length the progress of a single utterance
through the reciprocal processes of production and comprehension
(as summarised diagrammatically in figure 1.4), we can now see why
Grice stresses the importance of conversational cooperativeness and
why other writers have used terms such as 'intersubjectivity' and
'negotiation of meaning'. For conversation is only possible through
collaboration: the speaker constructing and encoding his message in
a form that he judges will make his meaning intention readily available to the listener, and the listener making use of all the relevant cues
to construct and interpret the meaning that he judges to match that
intended by the speaker.

Conclusion

In this chapter we have attempted to provide a brief sketch of what is
involved in communicating through language by examining one
particular sequence of parent–child interaction, and then by considering how a single utterance is constructed and interpreted in its
context of socially situated interaction.

It has been assumed throughout that linguistic communication is
only possible because individual participants share a tacit agreement
as to the way in which utterances are related to the situations in
which they are used. It has also been assumed that such relationships
are systematic and amenable to description in generalised terms. At
the same time, it has to be admitted that, in some areas, linguists and
other students of linguistic communication have not as yet been able
to offer such a generalised account in terms that accord with participants' intuitions. What, then, is the relationship between the
descriptions of language use that are offered by analysts and the
actual production and interpretation of utterances by participants in
particular situated contexts of communication?

Most analysts take it as axiomatic that this relationship should be
as close as possible, as is suggested by the following quotation:

'Contextualisation can be looked at from two points of view.
We can think of it as the process whereby the native speaker
of a language produces contextually appropriate and internally
coherent utterances – a process which . . . involves a lot more
than knowledge of the language system. We can also think of
it as a process which the linguist carries out in his description

Figure 1.4. A model of the communication situation

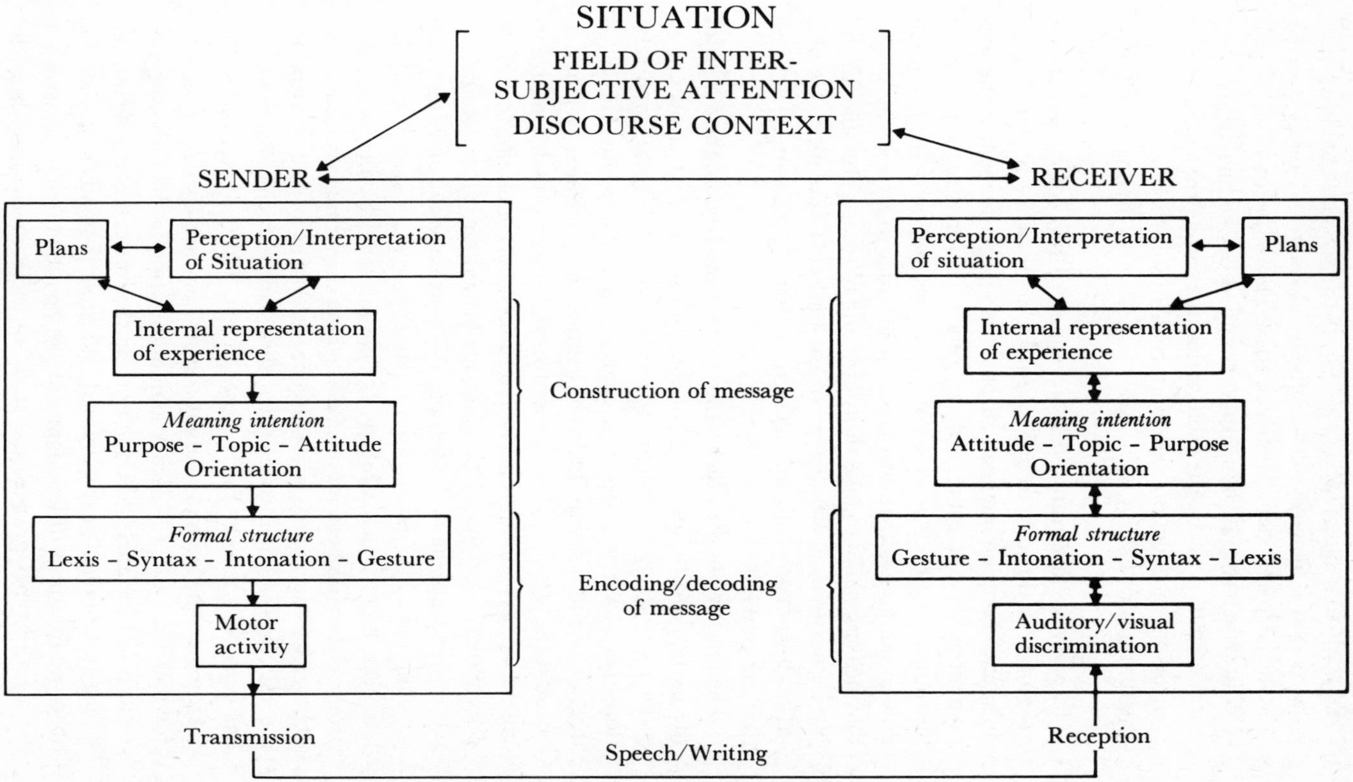

SITUATION
FIELD OF INTER-
SUBJECTIVE ATTENTION
DISCOURSE CONTEXT

RECEIVER

| Plans |
| Perception/Interpretation of situation |
| Internal representation of experience |
| *Meaning intention* Attitude – Topic – Purpose Orientation |
| *Formal structure* Gesture – Intonation – Syntax – Lexis |
| Auditory/visual discrimination |

Reception

Construction of message

Encoding/decoding of message

Speech/Writing

SENDER

| Perception/Interpretation of Situation |
| Internal representation of experience |
| *Meaning intention* Purpose – Topic – Attitude Orientation |
| *Formal structure* Lexis – Syntax – Intonation – Gesture |
| Motor activity |
| Plans |

Transmission

of particular languages. In so far as the semantic analysis of a
particular language is descriptively adequate . . . there must be
some correspondence between these two kinds of
contextualisation: the factors identified by the linguist as
contextual must be the factors that determine the native
speaker's production and interpretation of utterances in actual
situations of use.'
                                                    (Lyons, 1977: 610)

In practice, however, the achievement of this correspondence is
proving very difficult to attain. At the heart of the problem is the
difference between the goals of analysts and participants. The participant is always concerned to convey or interpret a particular
meaning intention that arises out of an interaction in the here-and-
now of a unique situational context. In order to achieve this objective, he is prepared to take short-cuts and to trade upon shared, and
often unexpressed, knowledge of the particular situation. He also
makes use of communicative resources that include more than those
that are purely linguistic.

The analyst, on the other hand, seeks to go beyond the details of
the particular utterance, and of the context in which it occurs, in
order to arrive at statements and rules about categories, and relationships between categories, that are true for whole classes of
utterances and contexts. In order to attain this goal, he is prepared to
'standardise' the data that he has observed and recorded, concentrating on what is common in the data and ignoring all but the major
systematic variations in the language behaviour of the community
whose language he is describing. As a strategy for arriving at an
account of the internal organisation of the language system itself this
has been highly successful, as is demonstrated by the very great
progress that has been made in describing the grammar of hundreds
of languages during the last half-century. At this level of description,
too, the correspondence between analyst's and participant's categories
has been shown to be fairly close (Levelt, 1978; Massaro, 1975).

However, the attempt to apply this strategy to the study of the way
in which the system is used in communication is much more problematic. For the analyst, it is important that the categories he utilises
should be discrete, clearly defined and finite in number, so that the
observed instances of language use can be unambiguously assigned
to category types prior to the study of their interrelationships. In

addition, if his description is to correspond with the factors that determine the native speaker's production and interpretation of utterances in actual situations of use, warrant for the categories he proposes must be sought in participants' behaviour. From both these points of view, the description of utterance meaning is proving extremely difficult. As we have seen, there is as yet no agreement on the number of speech act categories that should be recognised and, although the generalised conditions that have to be met for an utterance to count as a successful performance of a type of act have been specified for a limited number of acts, the decision as to which act or acts a particular utterance is performing in context is frequently problematic.

So fundamental do these difficulties appear to analysts working in the Ethnomethodological tradition, that they have abandoned the attempt to arrive at generalisable categories altogether, arguing that, since no exhaustive account can be given, in terms of the features of the analytic categories themselves, as to how the meaning of an utterance is recognised as an instance of a particular category, it is simply not possible to specify the meaning of an utterance independently of its actual occasion of use. As a result, Conversational Analysts, as this group is called, have shifted their focus of attention to the study of the methods and procedures that participants employ in order to decide what is meant and to 'remedy the essential indexicality and opaqueness of speech' (Wootton, 1975: 61–2).

Given the fact that one of the essential features of language is that it allows the uniqueness of individual experience to be encoded in terms of a finite system of publicly available, generalised resources, it is inevitable that some aspects of the intended and received meaning of particular utterances will escape a description of language use which is made from the point of view of the system. It may also be the case that, although the formal categories of phonology, lexis and grammar have been found to be discrete and mutually exclusive, this will prove to be much less true of the categories of meaning, and particularly of functional meaning. Nevertheless, as Wootton himself argues, it is also true that 'people do operate with a sense that what they see and hear is of a specific, definite kind' (in press: 100–1), and this is further attested by the existence, already noted, of a rich array of lexical verbs for talking about the functions that utterances perform.

The position adopted here, therefore, is that it is certainly worth continuing with the attempt to arrive at a systematic account of the categories that operate in linguistic interaction, whilst recognising that such an approach cannot provide an exhaustive account of the way in which meaning is negotiated in particular conversations. As has been repeatedly stressed throughout this chapter, the exchange of conversational meaning is essentially a cooperative enterprise: participants collaborating in adapting the shared code of symbolic representation to the particular requirements of their interactional intentions. Not surprisingly, therefore, other strategies of investigation will be required, including those that focus on the procedures that participants use to determine the intended meaning in context of particular utterances and sequences of utterances. As Vygotsky observed half a century ago, in order to understand a person's utterance,

> 'it is not sufficient to understand his words – we must also understand his thought. But even that is not enough – we must also know its motivation. No analysis of an utterance is complete until that plane is reached.' (1962: 151)

There are still many gaps in our understanding of the total process, and these will only be filled by further cross-disciplinal investigation. Nevertheless, the outline is clear enough for us to approach the study of children's acquisition and development of linguistic communication with a general idea of what it is that they have to learn and of the context of interaction within which that learning takes place. It is to these questions that we shall turn in the remaining chapters of this book.

2

Becoming a communicator

GORDON WELLS

What the child can do today in co-operation, tomorrow he will be able to do on his own.

(Vygotsky, 1962)

In the first chapter we considered in broad outline what is involved in linguistic interaction. As we saw, successful communication is a collaborative enterprise, in which each participant in his turn as speaker constructs and encodes his message so that it both adequately conveys his intention and also orients to the informational needs and expectations of the hearer at that point in the conversation. At the same time, the hearer plays his part by drawing upon a variety of sources of information in the situation and his past experience in order to interpret and fill out the message that he decodes from the actual speech signal. In performing these tasks, both speaker and hearer engage in a number of interrelated processes: translating between personal experience and the semantic structure of their common language; encoding and decoding meaning intentions through lexical items in grammatical structures; and integrating the phonological, prosodic and gestural patterns by means of which the message is given physical realisation. These are the processes that the language learner has to master, and in this chapter we shall consider how the young child sets about this task.

Attempts to explain the development of language, however, are closely tied to the beliefs that are held about the nature of language itself and about the way in which it should be studied. As was suggested at the beginning of the previous chapter, these beliefs have changed quite considerably in the last two decades, with important consequences for research on language development.

There have, in fact, been four major emphases, corresponding to the different facets of language that have been brought into focus: syntax, semantics, pragmatics and discourse. Each focus has led to different issues being given prominence in the attempt to explain how language is acquired; and one aim of this chapter is to review these different types of explanation. Proponents of the different theories tend to present them as if they were in competition, but it is probably better to see them as each contributing cumulatively to an increasingly rounded account. Certainly it is our view that, with each new emphasis, the account that can be given of development has been progressively enriched. For this reason, the exposition of the different theoretical emphases follows their chronological emergence. Then, having concentrated on broad and universal characteristics of development, the chapter will conclude with a brief consideration of variation – differences between children in rate and style of development, and possible causes of those differences.

Syntactic development: innate and environmental influences
The major impetus to recent work on the development of language came from two works published by Chomsky at the end of the 1950s: *Syntactic Structures* (Chomsky, 1957) was the first exposition of the theory of transformational-generative grammar; a review of Skinner's (1957) *Verbal Behaviour* (Chomsky, 1959) was a thorough-going refutation of behaviourist explanations of language behaviour and language learning. The impact of these two works was far-reaching, for it set the direction that most research was to take during the whole of the next decade.

Chomsky's theory of language gives the central role to linguistic form – syntax and morphophonology. Language, on this account, is essentially a set of rules for combining and permuting syntactically defined categories to account for the relationship between meaning and sound at the level of the sentence. The rules are generative because, with the addition of a lexicon, they account for the infinitely large number of sentences that can potentially occur in any language. Some of the rules are held to be universal – applicable to all human languages; these are the rules that generate the underlying, or **deep**, structure of a sentence – the form of the sentence which is most closely related to its semantic interpretation, its meaning. Other rules transform this underlying structure into the **surface** form, which is given physical realisation in speech. These rules are, of course, specific to particular languages, but their form is governed by principles that are universal (Chomsky, 1965, 1968).

As an overall theory of language this account has limitations – as was suggested in chapter 1. However there is no doubt that the precise formulation that it provides of the formal organisation of language in terms of a set of explicit rules has been of enormous benefit to researchers in providing a descriptive tool for the study of language behaviour. As a matter of historical accident, the publication of *Syntactic Structures* also coincided quite closely with the advent of the portable tape recorder as a tool for research. The result was that, in the early 1960s for the first time, a methodology became available for the recording of naturally occurring conversation and its subsequent systematic description in terms of the syntactic structure of its constituent utterances.

Students of language development were quick to see the advantages of this new methodology, and a considerable number of studies were carried out in which the aim was to describe the child's progressive mastery of the grammar of his language by specifying the rules required to generate the sentences produced and comprehended at successive points in his development. The most comprehensive of these was Brown's pioneering study of Adam, Eve and Sarah (Brown, Cazden & Bellugi, 1969) involving American English. Languages other than English that have been investigated somewhat similarly include: Samoan (Kernan, 1969), Finnish (Bowerman, 1973), Dutch (Schaerlaekens, 1973), Serbo-Croatian (Savić, 1975). These studies represent a major advance in the field of child language, in that they provide systematic and theoretically grounded documentation of the basic facts of syntactic development across a variety of different languages. (The findings of the earlier studies by Kernan and Bowerman and those of two other studies of English, by Miller & Ervin (1964) and Bloom (1970), are fully reviewed by Brown in *A First Language* (1973).)

Transformational-generative grammar, however, is more than a descriptive framework. Indeed it claims to be essentially a theory of knowledge about language (competence), with strong implications for how that knowledge is acquired. At a conference in 1963 Chomsky criticised those investigating child language by means of syntactic descriptions of samples of recorded speech, charging them with failing to make the (in his view) crucial distinction between **competence** and **performance**, and with underestimating the abstractness of the rules that young language learners acquire (Chomsky, 1964). Indeed, in all his writings on the subject, Chomsky has stressed the abstractness of the rule system that the child comes to know, and the absence of evidence in the speech that he hears from which this rule system can be induced by principles of learning such as those that Skinner (1957) proposed (cf. Chomsky, 1968: ch. 3, for a full exposition of the argument). Taking into account, in addition, the early age and the speed at which this impressive feat of learning occurs, the most satisfactory explanation, in Chomsky's view, is that the child is innately equipped with a **language acquisition device** (LAD), which includes knowledge of the universal principles of human language, together with procedures for discovering how those principles apply to the particular language to which he is exposed.

In the intellectual climate of the time, Chomsky's proposals aroused fierce argument. There were, and still are, outspoken critics (e.g. Derwing, 1973; Morton, 1971), but there were also some who accepted the basic argument and endeavoured to apply it in an explanation of the facts of syntactic development as they were then known. Perhaps the most thorough-going such attempt is to be found in the early work of McNeill (1966, 1970).

If language were no more than the syntactically organised formal system that it is presented as in Chomsky's writings, the argument for LAD would be extremely compelling. But language as experienced by the language learner is clearly a great deal more than a formal system for generating sentences. Its words and structures are used to refer to objects and events in the environment and the relationship between language and experience is systematic, even if not transparent. Utterances are also social acts, related to the ongoing context of activity in ways that, although more complex, are similar to the purposeful nonlinguistic actions and gestures from which they develop. But most importantly, language as experienced by the developing child occurs in a context of interaction, where the child's communication partner both modifies the input to the child in response to the understanding that he manifests, and provides feedback on the way in which his own attempts to communicate are interpreted. From the beginning, therefore, language is experienced as a means of communication with significant others who, although they do not deliberately 'teach', actively mediate between the child, their shared situation, and the formal language system.

These various influential aspects of the total context within which language development takes place will be considered in more detail below. For the moment, though, enough has been said to demonstrate the substantial assistance that is available from his environment to aid the language-learning child, and so to cast doubt on the strong claims made for the innate LAD as the major determinant of development.

Chomsky too has not been unaffected by the evidence for the importance of cognitive and social factors in language development. But, characteristically, his response has been to postulate additional innate faculties:

> 'Alongside of the language faculty [i.e. LAD] and interacting with it in the most intimate way is the faculty of mind that constructs what might be called "common-sense understanding", a system of beliefs, expectations and knowledge concerning the nature and behaviour of objects, their place in the system of "natural kinds", the organization of these categories, and the properties that determine the categorization of objects and the analysis of events. A general "innateness hypothesis" will also include principles that bear on the place and role of people in a social world, the nature and conditions of work, the structure of human action, will and choice, and so on.' (Chomsky, 1976: 35)

What conclusion should be drawn, then, on the issue of the language acquisition device? That humans are innately predisposed to learn a language is certainly true. But to say that, in our present state of knowledge, is to say little more than that humans, and only humans, are biologically constructed in such a way that they naturally and spontaneously learn a language of a recognisably human form if they grow up normally in an environment where such a language is being used. The fact that cases have been reported of individuals who have succeeded in developing some degree of linguistic mastery in spite of severe environmental deprivation attests to the strength of this predisposition, but does not provide evidence as to the specific form or forms this predisposition takes.

Indeed the evidence is still extremely sparse, and certainly not sufficient to support an hypothesis as specific as that embodied in LAD.

What evidence we have is largely based on inference from inter-
species comparisons and from the study of language pathology. For
example, the gradual emergence over the course of evolution of
human language as we know it is clearly dependent on the speech
sound producing capabilities of the vocal tract and on the acuity of
our hearing over the frequency range of the sounds so produced. And
the possession of well-functioning organs with these capabilities is a
necessary condition for normal language development. Equally, the
neuro-physiological structure of the brain must have evolved to a
form which is capable of supporting the processes involved in
linguistic behaviour, and there is ample evidence that damage to
certain areas of the brain impairs normal language functioning in
adult life. However, the brain has remarkable plasticity in the early
years of life, and functions associated with certain areas of the brain
in adults have been successfully mastered by individuals who are
known to have undergone injury to those areas in early childhood
(Lenneberg, 1967). So, whilst it seems that a human brain is a
necessary precondition for learning a human language, no positive
evidence has so far been found for a claim that any particular area of
the brain is necessarily involved in the initial stages of acquisition.
(For a good review of these issues, see Marshall, 1979.)

As already suggested, the innate predisposition for language also
involves the cognitive abilities that are necessary for the individual to
interact with, and interpret, his social and physical environment –
abilities which, in rudimentary form, are almost certainly innate.
Indeed some theorists have gone so far as to reject the claims for a
specifically linguistic component of the innate predisposition for
language altogether, arguing instead that language development can
be adequately explained as one particular specialised outcome of the
interaction between general cognitive and social abilities and a normal social environment which includes linguistic communication.
But such a conclusion is certainly premature.

Although there is a large area of overlap between linguistic and
other cognitive structures and processes, we should not underestimate what is specific to language. As we saw in chapter 1 (p. 55), the
linguistic representation of experience in speech and writing (and
probably also in signing) involves two levels of abstract categories

which are not the same abstract categories as are involved in the nonlinguistic internal representation of the same experience. Talking and thinking, although related, are not the same activity. Nevertheless, it might be argued that, despite their autonomy, the two abstract systems are related in such a way that it is a relatively straightforward task for the children to discover the relationship and to use his nonlinguistic representation as a basis for his mastery of the system of linguistic representation.

This is the argument that is to be developed in the next section, and it is one which has considerable plausibility. At the same time, however, it must be pointed out that, even though there may be a systematic relationship between the categories of thought and the categories of linguistic meaning, there are still organisational principles specific to linguistic form – the rules of syntax and morphophonology of particular languages – that have to be learned, and it is still uncertain how far the process of mastering these principles may require some innate structure or 'knowledge' of a language-specific kind.

What is certain, however, is that neither innate endowment – whatever form that may be found to take – nor linguistic environment, however richly structured, is alone sufficient to account for the development of language. Both are necessary, and the process of development involves a continuing interaction between them. For, at each point, what features of the environment are influential in affecting further growth is dependent upon the current state of development achieved by the initial structure and this in turn depends upon the sort of environment with which it has already interacted.

The cognitive basis of language development

If a focus on syntax tends to emphasise what is specific to language, by concentrating on the internal organisation of the formal system, a focus on semantics tends to lead outwards to a consideration of the relationships between language and other activities such as thinking about, and referring to, objects and events in the world around us. In the study of child language, such a movement began to take place in the late 1960s, when psychologists concerned with early cognitive development began to take an interest in the new wave of studies of children's language, and attention began to be systematically focused on the semantic dimension of language development. The result of the ensuing interaction between linguists and psychologists has been a new impetus to the study of children's meanings and the emergence of an alternative theory of language development.

Of course this is not to say that the meanings expressed and understood by young children had not been systematically studied in earlier times. In fact there is a long tradition of diary studies of individual children going back to the last century, in which considerable attention was devoted to the meanings of early words (cf. Blumenthal, 1970, for a review). What was new about the studies of the development of word meanings embarked upon in the late 1960s was the systematic investigation of groups of children, using experimental as well as observational techniques, and the application of current semantic theories to the description and explanation of the data obtained (Clark, 1973a; Huttenlocher, 1974; Nelson, 1973).

Since the subject of the development of word meanings is considered in detail in chapter 3, it will be sufficient here to mention only the most salient of the results of these studies. As might be expected, early words tend to refer to the familiar objects in the 'here-and-now' of the child's experience, particularly people, animals, and things that move or cause other things to move, the objects that the child most frequently acts upon, and the actions and states that result from his actions.

Learning the meaning of any new word involves learning how it is used to talk about relevant objects, actions or relations in the world of experience. However, since all words except proper names, such as 'Mary' or 'Fido', apply to classes of objects, actions and relations, and not to particular instances, the child's task eventually involves learning two sorts of relationship. Firstly, he has to learn how the word relates to the appropriate conceptual category, and secondly he has to learn how it relates to other words in the same semantic domain.

With respect to this second sort of learning, semantic theory has provided a useful framework for considering relationships between words in the form of 'semantic features', as is explained in chapter 3. For example, the similarity and dissimilarity in the meanings of the words 'child' and 'puppy' can be described in terms of the semantic features 'animate', 'mammal', and 'immature', which they share, and the features 'human' or 'canine' on which they contrast. However, although such features are useful in allowing a description to be made, from outside, of what the child seems to know about relationships between words, it seems unlikely that they enter directly into the early learning of word meaning although such a theory was put forward at one stage (Clark, 1973a).

In fact, starting to learn about the relationships between words within particular semantic domains is likely to be delayed until at least some words in that domain have become firmly established in terms of the first type of meaning relationship, that is to say the relationship between word and conceptual category. The basis for the young child's learning of this relationship, it has frequently been suggested, is to be found in his pre-linguistic knowledge. As Clark has more recently put it: 'It is the child's cognitive, non-linguistic, knowledge that provides him with his first hypotheses about what words might mean – what the mapping is between what he knows and the words that others use' (1977: 147).

But the task is not quite as simple as this account might suggest, for the child's concepts are not necessarily organised in ways that map very directly onto meanings as these are encoded in the adult speech that he hears and, in addition, his own conceptual organisation is constantly changing as a result of new experience. It seems likely, therefore, that the mapping is a two-way process: existing concepts providing a clue to the meanings of words heard, and words heard leading to a modification of existing concepts, with the situational context in both cases providing additional support in establishing the relationship on particular occasions. Such a two-way process seems to be implied by Katherine Nelson when she remarks that 'the young child's efforts to make sense of the world through forming concepts and learning words are a first manifestation of a continuing process of stabilizing an inherently unstable experience in order to operate on it and make predictions about it' (1977: 119).

Given the instability of the child's concepts and also of his grasp of the relationship between concept and word meaning, it is not surprising that his words are not always used in exactly the same way as adults use them. There are many accounts of early words being **overextended**, for example 'doggy' being used to name all four-legged animals (Lewis, 1963). Although less easily observable, **underextensions** also occur, as when a child restricts the use of a word to a particular sub-set of the class in question: in reply to the command 'Get off the furniture', one girl of just over 2 years of age was heard to reply 'That's not the furniture, it's a chair.'

However, as will be clear from the foregoing discussion, although we may describe such 'errors' as over- or underextensions, it is not always easy to tell whether the discrepancy between child and adult usage results from conceptual or linguistic confusion, or simply from paucity of available words. In fact the latter explanation is rarely considered, although it seems very likely that whilst the child's vocabulary is small, the words that are available will sometimes be used 'incorrectly' to communicate wants and interests in particular situations for which the appropriate word has not yet been learnt. Instead of being treated as evidence of the child's limitations, however, such analogic extensions could equally well be seen as evidence that the child is already aware, at least in a rudimentary way, of two important features of language: that it is an open creative system, and that meaning in spoken communication is a matter of negotiation.

In this section so far we have considered semantic development in terms of the learning of the meaning of individual words and the concepts that underlie them. This is the form of learning that is most apparent during the period of one-word utterances. However, the fact that the child is limited to the production of utterances one word long does not mean that there are not important developments towards the communication of the kinds of relational meaning that are expressed sententially in adult speech, as Bloom (1973) and Greenfield & Smith (1976) have shown. And by the time that the child begins to produce utterances in which two or more words are combined, it is fully apparent that he controls relational meanings as well as meanings encoded by particular words.

The first cited evidence of a child expressing meanings of this sort at the beginning of the period of multi-word utterances is the now famous example given by Bloom (1970). In the course of one observation, when her **mean length of utterance** (MLU) was 1.32 morphemes, Kathryn twice produced the utterance 'Mommy sock' in two different contexts: (a) Kathryn picking up her mother's sock; (b) Mommy putting Kathryn's sock on Kathryn. Clearly it is not the meaning of the two words 'Mommy' and 'sock' that is different in the two contexts, but rather the relational meaning which connects them. In the first case Kathryn was understood to be expressing a relationship of possession between 'Mommy' and 'sock' and in the second a relationship between agent and object acted upon.

Bloom's was one of the first studies that attempted explicitly to make judgments about the semantic intentions of early structured utterances, based upon clues from the context and behaviour in the situation in which the utterances occurred. Previous researchers had also made use of similar clues, of course, as it would be impossible to produce an intelligible transcription of any speech without attributing semantic intentions. But in this study, for the first time, the semantic intentions attributed to the child's utterances were made the focus of the research.

The attribution of meaning intentions to early utterances is often difficult in a language such as English, in which many of the important distinctions between relational meanings (for example, which of two mentioned animate beings is agent and which is object) is signalled only by word order. In the example quoted above it was the difference in context that allowed the distinction in meaning to be picked up, and this is frequently the most important clue to the meaning intended by the child. However studies of other languages, in which there is a greater use of affixes (e.g. case inflexions in languages such as Serbo-Croatian) to mark the semantic relations between nominals, confirm that the same universal set of semantic relations finds expression in children's early utterances in every language so far investigated.

Analysing data from studies of English, Swedish, Mexican-Spanish, Finnish and Samoan from this point of view, Brown (1973) lists the two-term semantic relations given in table 2.1 as the most prevalent in what he calles Stage I (MLU = approx. 1.75).[1] Other researchers have labelled the relations somewhat differently, and in some cases have made further distinctions within the categories proposed by Brown (e.g. Slobin, Antinucci, Wells et al. 1972; Wells, 1973); but there is general agreement that, with the addition of the 'three operations of reference' – nomination (e.g. 'there ball'),

[1] Rather than use age as the basis of comparison between children, Brown proposed mean length of utterance (MLU), measured in morphemes. This index of development was calculated for each recorded observation according to a set of rules. The period of development during which MLU increased from 1.00 to more than 4.00 morphemes was then divided into five stages, and each observation assigned to one of these stages, on the basis of MLU and 'upper bound', that is to say length of longest utterance. The mid-points of each stage are: Stage I, 1.75; Stage II, 2.25; Stage III, 2.75; Stage IV, 3.50; Stage V, 4.00 (Brown, 1973: 53–7).

recurrence ('more ball') and nonexistence ('all-gone ball') (Brown, 1973), these meanings account for the majority of utterances produced at this stage.

Like the meanings of the first words, these relational meanings are grounded in the here-and-now and seem to reflect a similar interest in things that can move and cause other things to move (agents), in the objects that can be moved or acted upon, in the locations and attributes of these objects, and in the actions that cause them to change their location or state. It is not surprising, therefore, that the basis for the learning of these relational meanings has been sought in the conceptual organisation of experience that has already been established by the time the child starts to produce structured speech.

First proposed in the early 1970s (Macnamara, 1972; Slobin, 1973), the hypothesis that cognitive development provides a prerequisite basis for the development of language – the **cognition hypothesis** (Cromer, 1974) – has been the subject of a number of empirical investigations which have drawn upon the theories of both linguists and psychologists. From linguistics has come the descriptive framework provided by **case grammar** (Chafe, 1970; Fillmore, 1968), in which the underlying propositional structure of sentences is analysed in terms of a limited set of participant roles (e.g. agent, experiencer, patient, possessor, etc.) and the types of state, relation or event in which these participants are involved.

From psychology, it is Piaget's account of the development of sensorimotor intelligence that has been most frequently taken as the basis of comparison, since this is not only the most comprehensive

Table 2.1. *Prevalent semantic relations in early speech (from Brown, 1973: 173)*

Two-term relations	Example
Agent and action	Adam go
Action and object	Kick ball
Agent and object	Mummy sock
Action and locative (or location)	Sit chair
Entity and locative (or location)	Lady home
Possessor and possession	Daddy chair
Entity and attributive	Yellow block
Demonstrative and entity	That dog

account of early cognitive development, but it also has the advantage of being expressed in terms which match the descriptive categories of case grammar quite closely. In *The Psychology of the Child*, for example, this development is described as follows:

'In the course of the first eighteen months there occurs a kind of Copernican revolution ... whereby the child eventually comes to regard himself as an object among others in a universe that is made up of permanent objects (that is, structured in a spatio-temporal manner, and in which there is at work a causality that is both localised in space and objectified in things.' (Piaget & Inhelder, 1969: 13)

If the cognition hypothesis is correct, it should be possible to predict, on the basis of Piaget's description of cognitive development, which meanings will be the first to be expressed and the approximate order in which new meanings will be added to the child's repertoire. This has been tested in two studies (Edwards, 1978; Wells, 1974a), in which longitudinal speech data were collected over a considerable period after the onset of structured utterances and analysed in case-grammatical terms. In both cases, when the order of emergence of meaning relations in the speech samples was compared with the order predicted from cognitive development, a reasonable match was found, although there were a number of discrepancies, which will be discussed below. However, the general conclusion to be drawn from these and other studies that have attempted to investigate the cognitive basis for language development is well summed up by Brown (1973) at the end of his very detailed analysis of his own and other researchers' data:

'In sum, I think, that the first sentences express the construction of reality which is the terminal achievement of sensori-motor intelligence. What has been acquired on the plane of motor intelligence (the permanence of form and substance of immediate objects) and the structure of immediate space and time does not need to be formed all over again on the plane of representation. Representation starts with just those meanings that are most available to it, propositions about action schemas involving agents and objects, assertions of non-existence, recurrence, location and so on ... In suggesting that the meanings of the constructions of Stage I derive from sensori-motor intelligence, in Piaget's sense, I mean also to suggest that these meanings probably are universal in human kind but not that they are innate.' (pp. 200–1)

There seems to be general agreement, therefore, that the conceptually organised representation of experience that is built up in the pre-linguistic period is a prerequisite basis for the acquisition of semantic structures and of their lexico-grammatical expression. In this sense, language development has a cognitive basis.

Some writers, however, have described the relationship between cognition and language as if the whole of language development could be explained as an extension of pre-linguistic cognitive development. But this is unwarranted. The fact that prior cognitive development is a necessary condition for the development of language does not mean that it is sufficient. And there are several reasons for thinking that it is *not* sufficient. The first concerns the difference between cognitive and linguistic representations, which has already been discussed in relation to the learning of first words. However, the problem of making the match between the two is even greater when what has to be related is the cognitive representation of a complete event, and the linguistic representation of that same event.

Although we do not know the precise form that cognitive representation takes, we do know that it is different from the objects and events that are represented. We also know that the actual form of utterances – syntactically structured sequences of words (or, more precisely, morphemes) realised through temporally organised sequences of units of sound – is different from the semantic representations – the meanings – that they encode. And, as has been taken for granted by all researchers, cognitive representation is different from semantic representation. The relationship between cognitive representation and linguistic expression – between thinking and speaking – is therefore an abstract one, requiring several stages of translation to get from one to the other (Macnamara, 1977).

Learning a language thus certainly requires the cognitive basis of previously acquired conceptual categories or schemata in order to make sense of the categories of meaning that are linguistically expressed. It also involves the child in discovering the principles that

govern the form in which each meaning is expressed in the language
to which he is exposed. Writing about the learning of locative forms,
Johnston & Slobin (1979) describe the process of matching conceptual categories to linguistic forms in terms of traversing a 'waiting
room':

> 'Each linguistic form has its own waiting room: the entry door
> is opened with the underlying notion as key; the key to the
> exit door is the appropriate linguistic form. The child receives
> the entry key when he discerns, primarily on nonlinguistic
> grounds the existence of a given locative notion. The entry is
> thus determined by conceptual acquisition of the sort generally
> referred to as COGNITIVE development. The problems to be
> solved in the waiting room are both SEMANTIC and
> MORPHOLOGICO-SYNTACTIC. The child must figure out
> just what aspects of the particular notion are encoded in the
> language, and what means are used for the encoding. The
> solutions take varying amounts of time, depending on
> linguistic factors, but finally, the child leaves that particular
> waiting room with the appropriate "semantic" key in hand.'
> (p. 544)

If the entry key is provided by cognition, the exit key is specifically
linguistic and, as already suggested, its manufacture may well
involve capabilities of a specifically linguistic kind.

A second reason for insisting that language development is not just
an extension of sensorimotor intelligence is implied in the sentence
that was deliberately omitted from the quotation of Brown's conclusion on page 85. Referring to linguistic representation, he adds:
'But representation carries intelligence beyond the sensorimotor.
Representation is a new level of operation which quickly moves to
meanings that go beyond immediate space and practical action'
(Brown 1973: 200). The point that he is making is that the relationship between thought and language is not one-way, but interactive.
Sensorimotor intelligence may provide the basis for breaking into
language but, once acquired, language becomes a means of extending the range and complexity of thought. Linguistic messages can
lead us to reorganise our internal representations just as much as
nonlinguistic, practical, understanding of a particular situation
facilitates understanding of linguistic messages about that situation.

But it is in their combination in linguistically organised symbolic representation – language used as a tool for thinking, as Bruner (Bruner, Olver & Greenfield, 1966) describes it – that the interaction between thought and language is most fully developed. This topic will be returned to in the final chapter.

The social and pragmatic basis of language

There is a further reason for not accepting the cognition hypothesis as a full account of the basis of language development, at least in the form in which it has been outlined so far, and that is the narrowness of the definitions of 'cognition' and 'meaning' that have been invoked. In terms of the model of linguistic communication that was outlined in chapter 1, it is only the **topic**, or ideational content, of messages that has been included in this account of meaning; whilst cognition has been almost entirely restricted to the sensorimotor schemas involved in the development of understanding of the physical world of objects. To put it somewhat differently, the emphasis in this account of conceptual and semantic development is strongly influenced by a more general concern with logico-mathematical reasoning and with the structure of the propositions in which such reasoning is formulated.

Of course these are important aspects of a child's development, particularly valued in literate cultures such as ours. On their own, however, they give a rather unbalanced picture of early cognitive development, and equally of the early development of linguistic communication. For what is missing from this account is any adequate recognition of the social, interpersonal, dimension of the child's early experience and of the pragmatic functions that are served by his own earliest utterances and those that are addressed to him.

Evidence for the importance of the pragmatic, or social, dimension of meaning has been accumulating rapidly during the last decade, and it has come from a number of sources. Let us consider first the evidence from the child's own utterances in the studies of the emergence of early meanings referred to in the previous section. Both Edwards (1978) and Wells (1974a) found that, along with the meaning relations predicted by Piagetian theory, the earliest structured utterances included evaluative meanings, such as 'nice', 'naughty' and 'dirty', as well as references to possession – both categories of meaning that depend on cultural values, which cannot be discovered on the basis of interaction with the physical world alone. Wells also noted that the very earliest two-word utterances were predominantly of the form **operator** + **nominal**, where the operator was a 'word' (often idiosyncratic) signalling a pragmatic intention, such as / ɔ̃ / for wanting or / ʊk / for indicating, whilst the nominal identified the object wanted or indicated. A similar observation has also been made by Dore (1975).

However, it is not necessary to wait until the two-word utterance stage to find evidence of pragmatic meanings in children's utterances, as a number of recent studies have shown. One of the first researchers to adopt a functional approach to the study of language development was Halliday (1975), who carried out an intensive, 'diary'-based study of his own child, Nigel.

For Halliday, the beginnings of language are marked by the emergence of recognisable, stable, vocalisation-meaning pairs, and this, in the case of Nigel occurred at about the age of 9 months. What is particularly interesting, in the present context, is that the meanings attributed to these utterances by his parents were entirely pragmatic, that is to say they were to do with the interpersonal purposes that they judged Nigel wished to achieve. The **functional** terms that Halliday used, together with his glosses on the generalised meaning of each function, are given in table 2.2. The emphasis in Halliday's account is on language as 'meaning potential' – a cultural resource for social interaction – which has its beginnings in the, often idiosyncratic, interchanges between the child and his immediate caregivers.

Table 2.2. *The interpersonal functions of early utterances (from Halliday, 1975: 19–21)*

Functional terms	Meaning glosses
Instrumental	'I want'
Regulatory	'Do as I tell you'
Interactional	'Me and you'
Personal	'Here I come'
Heuristic	'Tell me why'
Imaginative	'Let's pretend'
Informative	'I've got something to tell you'

Nigel's earliest utterances, like those of many children, owed little to the form of adult words and were only intelligible to his parents. For this reason, Halliday refers to this first stage as **proto-language**.

As the form of Nigel's utterances progressed from proto-language to that of adult speech, there was also a development in the functions expressed. Not all of the functions listed in table 2.2 were present from the beginning, and Halliday hypothesised that they would appear 'in the order listed, and in any case with the "informative" significantly last' (1975: 37). In the event, the hypothesis received only rather general support, for the first four functions appeared together as a group, with the next two both beginning to appear by 15 months. However, the informative function was clearly last, appearing only at the age of about 21 months. Taken as a whole, though, this sequence confirms Halliday's suggestion that the earliest proto-language utterances are primarily interpersonal in meaning, concerned chiefly with the initiation and maintenance of social interaction.

Using a somewhat different descriptive framework – that of **speech acts** (described in chapter 1) – Dore (1975) reached the similar conclusion that the single-word utterances of 1-year-old children are primarily the realisation of 'primitive speech acts', such as 'request', 'protest', 'calling', 'greeting'. Carter, too, in her longitudinal study of the development of one child's prelinguistic vocalisation into recognisable words (Carter, 1974) notes that, although the phonetic form of these vocalisations changed over the period studied, the gestures which nearly always accompanied them were constant in their meaning and clearly goal-directed. She concludes, therefore, that the significance of the child's vocalisation–gesture pairs was fundamentally pragmatic, and most frequently aimed at obtaining the assistance of others in altering his environment in various ways (Carter, 1979).

A similar pragmatic orientation was noted in the first clearly intentional communications of the Italian children studied by Bates, Camaioni & Volterro (1975). At about 10 months two types of communicative act emerged: the first they called 'proto-imperative', which was defined as the intentional use of an adult to obtain a wanted object; the second they called 'proto-declarative', defined as the intentional use of an object to obtain adult attention, by pointing, showing, etc. Both these pragmatically oriented communications were realised initially by gestures, then subsequently by one-word utterances. Only in a later stage, beginning somewhere between 12 and 16 months, they report, were words first used with referential value.

Although there is wide variation in the age at which the first 'proposition-oriented' utterances are reported to occur in these studies, there is complete agreement that they occur considerably later than those with a purely pragmatic, interpersonal function. As Griffiths (1979) puts it, in his review of this early stage of development: to begin with, one-word utterances have only illocutionary force and no propositional content. Using gesture to indicate a desired or interesting object is the first step in the direction of introducing content. This is soon followed by the use of object names with a similar referential function, and by the first two-word operator + nominal constructions already referred to. But the first utterances which can truly be said to have propositional content do not appear until the child is able to communicate information to someone who does not already possess that information (the informative function), and that requires the development of grammar and also a more sophisticated understanding of communication than is present at the one-word stage (Halliday, 1975).

If we now turn to the few studies that have been made of early comprehension, at first sight there seems to be some contradiction. Not only is the number of different words reliably understood in the period 10–20 months greater than the number produced, but the most frequently occurring are words for objects and actions. That is to say, it is the referential, or even the propositional, aspect of language that children seem to *comprehend* first. Huttenlocher (1974), who noted this asymmetry between production and comprehension in her own longitudinal study of four children, offers two complementary explanations. The first is that many of the words that a young child understands may contain relatively unfamiliar or difficult sound patterns, which effectively deters the child from trying to utter them, thus reducing the number of words observed in production. The second concerns the different processes involved in production and comprehension: in order to comprehend a word, a child has to recognise the sound patterns and then recall the associated concept and match that to the particular object or action in the situation. In production, on the other hand, the route is from recognition of the particular object or action as an instance of a conceptual category to recall and articulation of the associated word (cf. chapter 3, p. 140), for further discussion of the processes involved).

Assuming that recall of concepts is simpler than recall of words, and that identifying a referent object or action is simpler than articulating a pattern of sound, these explanations could account for the difference between the two vocabularies in terms of size. However, they do not account for the difference of composition. To explain this we need to consider a number of other factors.

One such factor is the possibly distorting effect of the way in which the results were obtained. Studies of production are dependent on the child actually choosing to speak at a time when the researcher, or one of the parents, is in a position to make a note of the utterance and its apparent meaning. Some words that the child produces may only occur in situations where they go unnoted. In studying comprehension, on the other hand, researchers typically rely on systematically 'testing' children in the course of their spontaneous activities, as Huttenlocher did, and inevitably restrict the words tested to those for which there is a corresponding, clearly perceptible object or action. Not surprisingly, therefore, it is these words that are found to be the most reliably understood.

However, there is a further point to be made about Huttenlocher's classification of the words that children were able to comprehend. The two main classes of words are referred to as the *names* of objects and actions, thus emphasising their referential function. But for many of the words, particularly the action words, the way in which the child showed his comprehension was in response to a request to carry out the action; for these words, therefore, it would be just as appropriate to describe them pragmatically as instructions to do 'peekaboo' or 'bye-bye' as to call them names for the actions concerned.

Even when these biases in the methods of data collection and description have been taken into account, however, the fact still remains that, between the ages of approximately 1 and 1½ years, the vast majority of children appear to comprehend proportionally more words for objects and actions than they produce. Suggesting, as Huttenlocher does, that the explanation for the particular words that children learn to understand is the importance in their lives of the associated objects and actions, although in all probability true, does not advance us any further. Presumably the same arguments should also apply to the words they learn to produce, but, as we have seen, these tend to include rather few names of objects and actions until well on into the period when structured utterances are the norm.

An alternative explanation suggested by Wells (1975) is that the asymmetry results from the slightly different communicative aims that parent and child may have during the period when the child is learning his first words. In addition to the fact that the adult may be quite deliberately trying to teach the names of familiar objects, her emphasis in addressing the child is likely to be on the object or event being referred to, since it can be assumed that the purpose of the communication will be more-or-less self-evident from previous shared experiences of similar situations and routines, and from accompanying nonlinguistic behaviour. For the child, on the other hand, it is the pragmatic function of his communication that has priority, for this is what provides the motivation for utterance. Precise specification of the persons or objects that are required to complete his purpose is less important since he can use gestures or other nonlinguistic means to indicate these, or rely on them being understood in context without the need for specific reference, once his purpose has been understood. If this is correct, the asymmetry is a result of the different focus of attention that the child is required to make in the two roles of hearer and speaker in order to participate successfully in linguistic interaction.

This explanation is not opposed to those put forward by Huttenlocher, but it goes beyond them in suggesting that the distinction between comprehension and production may also result from the different communicative strategies involved (cf. chapter 3, pp. 147ff, for further discussion of strategies for comprehension). Nevertheless, these different strategies arise from a common pragmatic goal – that of succeeding in communicating with another person about some purpose with respect to a particular aspect of the familiar, shared environment.

Two main points have emerged, then, from this consideration of the stage leading to the first structured utterances. The first is that there is no sharp discontinuity in the developmental progress from gesture to proto-linguistic expressions and on to structured utterances that are firmly based in the adult linguistic system. The second is that the earliest linguistic communication is strongly interpersonal in orientation, being concerned chiefly with the exchange of pragmatic meaning. A further point that is stressed in all the studies of production is that these pragmatic meanings remain recognisable throughout this period of development, despite changes in the form of realisation. Thus, the pragmatic function is not only the child's means of entry into linguistic communication, it also provides the essential continuity in the development of the means of realisation from gesture to lexico-grammar.

Interaction and the development of intersubjectivity

The previous section stressed the pragmatic orientation of children's earliest use of language – interpersonal communication aimed at regulating joint activities. A decade ago, the idea that a child so young could be capable of successfully participating in social interaction would have seemed highly implausible. According to the Piagetian account of development, the child at this age is still almost entirely egocentric in perspective, and his cognitive schemas are restricted to those arising from his sensorimotor interaction with the physical world. To take part in, and learn from, social interaction, on the other hand, requires the child to have developed quite sophisticated communication skills and this, in turn, implies the development of cognitive schemas about himself and others and about the ways in which people and objects can be related in an intersubjective field of attention (Shields, 1978). He must, for example, have some understanding that the world he experiences is similarly experienced by other people, and that his communications, like theirs, will be interpreted as expressing intentions with respect to this shared world. Sophisticated though such skills may appear to be for the child just beginning to use single 'words', that this is indeed the case is suggested by a number of lines of research which have focused on the infant's earliest learning and the context in which it takes place.

In his account of cognitive development, Piaget has stressed the importance of feedback which is contingent upon the child's behaviour, and he has shown this can arise from the child's sensorimotor exploration of his physical environment. However, as Snow (1978) points out, in the early months before he has developed the ability to sit up and reach out and take hold of objects, it is only in interaction with those who care for him that the infant is able to experience feedback concerning the effect of his behaviour. Here, however, there is ample opportunity. Since the newborn infant is completely dependent on his caretakers for survival, the adults who fulfil this function have to be able to discern his needs, and in the attempt to do this they tend to treat any change in his behaviour as potentially significant. Thus the infant's crying, or sounds of contentment, although involuntary components of physiological states in the first instance, are imbued with meaning by caretaking adults, who respond with contingent behaviour which, repeated regularly many times a day, provides the infant with his first opportunity to learn the cause–effect relationship.

But the infant's behaviour is not for long restricted to undifferentiated crying or gurgling, as a number of recent studies have demonstrated. As early as a few weeks, he manifests certain other behaviours, which have the effect of eliciting adult behaviour of a more social, communicative kind. These include a preference for faces (Schaffer, 1971), attention to and discrimination of adult speech sounds (Eimas et al. 1971) and an increasing range of vocal sounds. By about 6 weeks the infant produces facial gestures and changes of gaze which adults perceive as communicative in intention (Stern, 1974), and by 4–6 months he is able to follow an adult's line of regard when the adult looks away from the infant to another place (Scaife & Bruner, 1975). The result is that, during the routines of feeding, bathing and dressing and at times when he is awake and comfortable with other people around, the infant will have many opportunities for learning of an essentially social kind, as adults respond to these various behaviours by vocalising, smiling, touching and looking where the infant is looking.

Given this adult responsiveness, it is not surprising that infants initially show more interest in people than in inanimate objects (Stern, 1977), and direct some of their earliest and most elaborate spontaneous behaviours towards interaction with people (Trevarthen, Hubley & Sheeran, 1975). It seems reasonable to conclude therefore, as Schaffer (1977) does, that a great deal of the infant's earliest learning is social in nature, and that he is biologically pre-adapted to behave in ways which will elicit opportunities for such learning.

If the infant's earliest and most active interactions with his environment involve other persons, the first objects he encounters are also shaped by human activity to serve humanly conceived ends. The spoons and bottles, clothes and furniture, cuddly toys and wooden bricks are all functional with respect to the infant's needs as these are perceived in the culture into which he is born, and they are frequently met with in the context of some form of interpersonal activity. Even the physical environment, therefore, is organised and experienced within a cultural frame of reference, so the child's earliest learning from interaction with the objects around him cannot also but be socially based. It is for these reasons that Trevarthen claims that 'human intelligence develops from the start as an interpersonal process and that the maturation of consciousness and the ability to act with voluntary control in the physical world is a product rather than an ingredient of this process' (1974: 230).

That adults are generally responsive to infants is a matter of common observation, but it is only recently that the significance of this for subsequent development had been fully recognised, as the result of a wide variety of studies of mother–child interaction (cf. Schaffer, 1977). We have already briefly considered some of the implications for cognitive development, so in the remainder of this section we shall concentrate on communicative development.

In the discussion of communication in chapter 1, it was argued that all communication involves a triangular relationship between sender, receiver and situational context. However, in the very earliest communication between mother and child, there is little substantive content. As Newson puts it, 'the infant begins by becoming actively engaged in the "process" of communicative interaction as a step towards acquiring "content" in the form of mental constructs or understandings, which he begins to share with persons only as he regularly engages in communication' (1977: 48).

Establishing the 'process' of communication is largely the task of the mother or other caretaker and requires that she be attentive to the potentially communicative gestures and vocalisations the infant produces, synchronising her own activity so that a temporal pattern is built up of alternating reciprocal acts of communicating and attentional responses. Since the infant spontaneously initiates interaction by look or gesture, the mother's role is essentially one of following his lead, pointing up the reciprocal structure of turn-taking and orchestrating the dynamics of each interactive episode so that the infant discovers the predictable structure of such communicative exchanges. As early as a few weeks the resulting patterns of interaction can appropriately be described as 'proto-conversation' (Trevarthen, 1974).

'Content' is introduced into the interaction in various ways, but all are related to what has been called 'intersubjective attention'. When the mother looks at her infant and then follows his line of regard, perhaps pointing to, touching, or picking up the object concerned, she gives the infant evidence that they are attending to the same aspect of their environment. Or when, in the course of a repeated ritualised play routine like tickling, she matches the infant's anticipatory gesture with a significant pause, she emphasises their shared awareness of the sequence of activity and of the individual segments of which it is constituted. At this stage, objects and actions are not yet being referred to directly but, as the content of the oft-repeated games and caring routines, they provide a scaffolding for the synchronisation of attention and later of reciprocally related activity, by means of which is established the intersubjective awareness of each other's attention that allows the child to transcend his initial egocentricity (Bruner, 1977).

The development from person–person communication to communication about the shared world of intersubjective attention has been studied in detail by Trevarthen and his colleagues. On the basis of video recorded observational studies throughout the first year, they have identified three major phases in the development of the infant's interaction with people and objects. In the first phase, which they call 'primary intersubjectivity', the infant is capable of voluntarily engaging in interactive communication with his mother and also of rudimentary adaptive behaviour to objects, but he cannot engage in both sorts of activity simultaneously. In the second, intermediate, phase, the infant is able to participate actively in routinised games, either person–person games involving, for example, tickling and hiding, or object–person games such as, in the presence of another person, moving or dropping an object whilst watching the other person's response and laughing. By this stage the infant is also capable of quite elaborate play with objects alone, as he explores the various actions he can perform upon them. But it is only in the third phase, towards the end of the first year, that these two forms of activity are combined in what Trevarthen and his colleagues call 'secondary intersubjectivity'. Now the infant's interaction with another person can encompass their shared attention to an object as, for example, when the mother shows the infant how to do a task, he attempts to carry it out, then looks at her and both are pleased (Trevarthen & Hubley, 1978).

Although communication between infant and caretaker is initially achieved nonverbally, through gesture, vocalisation and looking, language enters into the infant's earliest experience of social interaction in a number of ways. From the beginning, the infant's environment is one in which speech is associated with many of those routine transactions, such as feeding and dressing, that provide the basis for some of his earliest meaning structures, as has already been suggested. In such contexts, caretakers typically comment upon the object or activity of shared attention and expand and elaborate on the meaning attributed to the infant's own communicative behaviour. In so doing they not only draw the infant into an intersubjective involvement in the activity of the moment, but, by the frequent repetition of matching words and phrases to the recurrent patterns of such activities, they provide the infant with information about which aspects of experience are culturally salient and, at the same time, a model of the way in which culturally significant meanings are given linguistic realisation.

On the basis of observations of her own interaction with her daughter, Ferrier (1978) emphasises the repetitious, ritualised and context-dependent nature of much parental communication:

'Observing my own behaviour when my daughter was about fifteen months old, I discovered that whenever I took my daughter out of her cot I said "Hello my love. Where's my nice girl?" Whenever I sat her in her high chair I said "Upsadaisy. There's a good girl. Bib on. There we are." Whenever she fell down (at this point at least half a dozen times a day) I said "Upsadaisy." Whenever she sneezed, I said "Atchoo" . . . (My daughter's first word was "Pretty", which had its roots in a bed-time ritual of admiring the geraniums on a window-sill halfway up the stairs.)' (p. 302)

However, if it is the regularity and invariance of these routines which allows the infant to make the connection between the situational context and the utterances that are spoken within it, it can also be the source of errors, since the relationship between context and utterance is not transparent. Ferrier recounts the history of one such error arising from a context that must be familiar to every parent:

'[ɸʰ] (Phew!) – an item which I systematically used for a while when I entered my daughter's bedroom each morning to be greeted by a rather offensive smell. My utterance was an exclamation and its "application" (Lyons, 1968: 434) was the smell. My daughter after a couple of days produced it in the same setting i.e. her cot in the morning but when in fact the smell was absent. For her it was a form of greeting and tied initially to that particular routine. Shortly afterwards I extended its use to nappy-changing situations in which for me the utterance had the same function and application – for her the function appeared to be simply "ostension" and its application was her nappy. She subsequently used the term outside the nappy-changing situation to refer to nappies both clean and dirty and finally to the nappy bucket which normally contained nappies but which was, on this particular occasion, empty.

'The initial use of the term as a greeting suggests that
(a) the recurring social situation of greeting her mother in the morning was for her the dominant feature of its use, and
(b) that her own noxious odour did not have the perceptual salience for her it did for me!
The fact that the term acquired an ostensive or perhaps naming function in the nappy-changing situation indicates
(a) that which particular features of physical context an utterance is referring to is not always obvious to the language learner, and
(b) that while for me the application of my utterance was my reaction to a smell, the referent of her utterance was the object which was sometimes the cause of the smell, i.e. the nappy.' (1978: 304–5)

Errors do occur, therefore, and these involve adult misinterpretations of their children's intentions as well as the sort of error cited above. Not surprisingly, therefore, a considerable proportion of adult utterances are devoted to expanding and checking their children's utterances, and to repeating and paraphrasing their own, and this adds another dimension of repetitiousness which may be helpful to the child.

However, such errors do not seem as a rule to impede successful communication and, in any case, in the early stages it is the response of making an interpretation of the child's communicative behaviour that is important, rather than its absolute correctness. For it is in this way that the child initially discovers that gestures and vocalisations have meaning and then, gradually, over many such routine inter-actions, what precise meaning they have.

As well as providing an opportunity for learning the relationships between particular utterances and aspects of the situations in which they occur, repetitive and ritualistic interactions also provide an opportunity to learn about the structure of conversation, with its pattern of reciprocally related turns. Such a pattern can already be seen in the communicative exchanges observed by Trevarthen in the stage of primary intersubjectivity, but at that point it is the adult who is chiefly responsible for creating this pattern, by the careful timing of her contributions. However, when the stage of secondary inter-subjectivity is reached, and the infant is able to attend simul-taneously to an object as well as to another person, ritualised games provide a particularly effective context for the development of basic conversational skills.

A number of such situations, including bath-time, playing with a mechanical toy and looking at a picture-book, have been observed by Bruner and his colleagues (Bruner, 1975a, 1978; Ratner & Bruner, 1978), and they suggest that the highly routinised trans-actions to which they give rise provide opportunities to set up 'standard action frames', in which vocal, and then verbal, signals are used to mark transition points in a joint activity. Here is one example:

'Ann had learned between 8 and 10 months to play a well modulated exchange game involving the handing back and forth of objects. When, at 13 months, the game was well organized, Ann picked up her mother's receiving "thank you". She used it both when giving and when receiving an object. After two weeks the expression dropped out of the giving position, nothing at first taking its place, but remained in the

receiving position. Meanwhile, the demand demonstrative
"look" was appearing in Ann's lexicon, used in referential
situations, as when looking at pictures in a book. At the end
of the thirteenth month, "look" was transposed as well into
the position at which Ann handed her mother an object.
"Look" was later replaced by "there" in the giving–taking
format.' (Bruner, 1975b: 90)

In this one case history is a condensed account of how, in the
context of playful collaborative routines, the child gradually learns
the reversibility of the roles of actor and recipient-of-action and
maps these on to the somewhat parallel roles of sender and receiver
of verbal communication. In this way the concept of dialogue is
established, first in the form of reciprocal action and then, gradually,
with the introduction of action-related utterances, in the use of
utterance as an alternative means of interpersonal action.

With the recognition of the importance of interaction, we have
reached the end of the historical review of changing emphases in the
study of language development. Although there will no doubt be
further changes, it is unlikely that any of the strands that have been
gradually woven into the complex picture of development will be
completely ignored in the future. At the same time, in following the
twists and turns in the search for the beginnings of language, we have
been led further and further back in the child's life to the earliest
interactions between mother and baby, which we have seen to be
essential for social and cognitive development as well as for the
emergence of specifically linguistic communication. It is for this
reason that the emphasis in this book is placed on interaction:
interaction between the various systems of representation and action
in the developing organism and interaction between the organism
and his human and physical environment.

Learning through conversation
In the previous sections of this chapter we have seen how the beginnings of language are to be found in the infant's pre-linguistic
interactions with his parents or other caregivers and the socially
structured world that they share. However, once he has discovered
the basic principles of linguistic communication, it is that characteristically linguistic form of interaction, conversation, which will

provide the context for his gradual mastery of the forms and structures of his mother tongue. It will also, of course, provide the opportunity for him to become more adept as a conversationalist and to extend the repertoire of social actions that he can perform through language. The question we now have to ask, therefore, is how the child learns from participating in conversation.

Let us at this point have a look at another conversation between Mark (whom we met in chapter 1) and his mother, when he had just begun to produce structured utterances. In the extract given in table 2.3, Mark, aged 23 months, is in the kitchen by the sink looking into

Table 2.3. *Conversations between Mark and Mother I*

1 Mark: Mummy(v)		[Mark is look-
2 Mummy		ing in a
3	Mother: What?	mirror and
4 Mark: There . there Mark		sees reflec-
5	Mother: Is that Mark?	tions of him-
6 Mark: Mummy		self and his
7	Mother: Mm	mother]
8 Mark: Mummy		
9	Mother: Yes that's Mummy	
10 Mark: *		
11 Mummy		
12 Mummy(v)		
13	Mother: Mm	
14 Mark: There Mummy		
15 Mummy(v)		
16 There . Mark there		
17	Mother: Look at Helen	
18	She's going to sleep	
	(long pause)	
19 Mark: [ɛəæ] (= look at that)		[Mark can see
20 Birds Mummy(v)		birds in the
21	Mother: Mm	garden]
22 Mark: Jubs (= birds)		
23	Mother: What are they doing ?	
24 Mark: Jubs bread		
25	Mother: Oh look	
26	They're eating the berries aren't they?	
27 Mark: Yeh		
28	Mother: That's their food	
29	They have berries for dinner	
30 Mark: Oh		

a mirror. His mother is engaged in domestic tasks, and his sister Helen (9 months) is in her high chair. As will be apparent from his contributions, Mark's linguistic resources are still extremely limited and his speech appears to be highly repetitive. Nevertheless, on listening to this extract one is struck by how much like ordinary conversation it sounds: turn-taking is well established, continuity of topic is maintained over several turns and there is every appearance that both participants are understanding each other's contributions. However, closer inspection shows that the relatively smooth flow of the conversation owes a great deal to the mother's skill in interpreting Mark's utterances and in responding in such a way that their joint contributions mesh together to produce a coherent conversational sequence.

As is to be expected in the light of the previous discussion of early utterances, Mark's contributions are predominantly pragmatic in orientation. In this extract, three different types of communicative act can be distinguished: attempting to initiate interaction (1,12,19); drawing his mother's attention to what currently interests him (4,6,20,24); and acknowledging his mother's communication (27,30). Words are beginning to be used referentially (6,14,20), and there are some utterances containing rudimentary propositions expressing the semantic relations of entity and location (4,14,16) and agent and object (24). In addition, intonation is being used with some degree of consistency,[2] particularly to distinguish initiating interaction (falling–rising tone) (1,12) from indicating a referent (falling tone) (2, 6, 8). In terms of Halliday's (1975) account of development (cf. p. 89 above), Mark has clearly moved beyond the proto-language stage, in which sounds are paired directly with meaning, to the stage where there is a rudimentary level of formal organisation between sound and meaning, a grammar which allows him 'to mean two things at once' (Halliday, 1975: 30). In 24, for example, the agent–object 'propositional' meaning relating birds and bread is combined with the pragmatic meaning of indicating.

If Mark's repertoire is limited, his mother's, we can reasonably assume, is similar to that of any normal adult. In this extract, however, her utterances are simple in form, and restricted in their semantic content to topics arising from the immediate situation, and

[2] A version of this and the extract in table 2.3 which includes a coding of intonation is contained in the Appendix.

in particular to those proposed by Mark. In this, as in her exaggerated intonation and frequent use of high pitch, her style is typical of a high proportion of the speech that is addressed by adults to children at this developmental stage (Snow, 1977). A further characteristic of much conversation involving children at this stage is the need for the adult to 'lead from behind', letting the child take the initiative and then using various devices to support and extend the topic that he has proposed (Wells, Montgomery & MacLure, 1979). It is probably significant, therefore, that in this extract it is only when Mark has initiated the topic that his mother's attempts to introduce new material meet with any response.

Several devices for sustaining conversation are apparent in this extract. The first is the mother's use of 'continuing' moves (5,23,26), which not only acknowledge Mark's indicating/informing initiations, but also simultaneously call for a further response. A similar function is performed by the high pitch and rising tone on several of her responses (5,7,9,13), which can be glossed as 'Yes, I'm interested and do go on.' A second significant feature of the mother's style is the liberal use of cohesion to maintain the linguistic coherence of the topic from one utterance to the next. For example, she uses simple lexical repetition (5,9), anaphoric reference ('she' in 18 and 'they', 'their' and 'that' in 23–9) and lexical collocation ('eat' – 'berries' – 'food' – 'berries' – 'dinner' in 26–9). In these latter utterances, in particular, spoken as both mother and child watch the birds through the kitchen window, Mark is being given the opportunity to learn both the referential links between words and structures and the objects and events to which they refer, and also the intralinguistic meaning relations that hold between these words which all belong to the same semantic field. Finally we might note that in both 25–6 and 28–9 the mother uses the upper part of her pitch range, and begins each turn with a high rise-fall (tone 5), which is an exaggerated version of the information-giving tone. In both turns, then, she seems to be drawing on a variety of conversational resources to extend the topic that Mark has proposed, and in doing so to draw his attention to the observable event and to the form in which that event is linguistically encoded.

Noting the formal simplicity that is characteristic of adult speech in conversations such as this, some researchers have suggested that adults deliberately simplify their speech in order to teach their children to talk. But such a self-consciously didactic aim does not seem to describe this extract nor, indeed, the majority of conversations that we have recorded. There are occasions, of course, where an adult enunciates a word particularly clearly – often with rising tone – with the intention of getting the child to repeat it; but this is almost entirely restricted to the teaching of new words. A group of mothers observed and later questioned by Garnica (1977) were all aware of modifying their speech when talking to their 2-year-olds in the sorts of ways already described. However, when asked why they spoke in this way, their answers were expressed in terms of making their communication with their children more effective, rather than in terms of trying to teach them to talk.

If this account is correct, it also serves to explain the high proportion of adult utterances that can be described as 'checking' or 'expanding' what the child has just said. The aim seems to be to achieve agreement about the child's intention before going on to respond to it in an appropriate way. This is not always easy, as many one- or two-word utterances, even in context, are indistinct in pronunciation or indeterminate in meaning, and it may take a number of turns before a mutually agreed interpretation is arrived at. The example in table 2.4 comes from a recording of Mark made a few weeks after the one given in table 2.3.

It seems, therefore, that it is a concern 'to understand and be understood, to keep two minds focussed on the same topic' (Brown, 1977: 12) that is the motivation for many of the characteristic

Table 2.4. *Conversations between Mark and Mother II*

Mark: Oh popped on		[The central
	Mother: Pardon?	heating boiler
Mark: It popped on		had just re-
	Mother: It popped on?	ignited]
Mark: Yeh		
	Mother: What did?	
Mark: Er – fire on		
	Mother: The fire?	
Mark: Yeh . . .		
Pop the . fire popped it fire		
	Mother: Oh yes	
	The fire popped on didn't it?	
Mark: Yeh		

features of parental speech, rather than a deliberate intention to teach. However, although attention may be focused on the negotiation of meaning, it seems likely that the simplification of form that results also has the effect of making it easier for the child to learn the relationship between form and meaning (Wells & Robinson, in press). Certainly, the mother's description of the birds eating berries in the extract above seems to provide Mark with an ideal opportunity to make such a connection.

As the child increases his mastery of the language system, the range of topics that are potentially available for inclusion expands dramatically, and this calls for further modification in the adult strategies for sustaining and extending the conversation, as can be seen in the extract from a recording made of Mark and his mother about two months later (table 2.5). Once again, Mark is looking out of the window, but this time he is asking a question about the whereabouts of a neighbour he had some minutes earlier seen working in the garden opposite.

There are many signs of the progress that Mark has made since the previous extract: the length and complexity of his utterances (e.g. 11,26,36), his ability to respond appropriately to information-seeking questions (17,22), the fact that his initial question and the answer that he himself provides concern persons and events recalled or imagined but not present in the here-and-now. Together, these enable him to participate in the conversation much more fully than two months earlier, and to build up what is, in effect, the first example of a 'story' in the recorded data.

At the same time, however, the fact that he is able to draw upon these newly acquired skills to such good effect owes a great deal to his mother's willingness to follow his lead, in spite of the fact that he rejects her original, and probably accurate, response to his opening question. She might easily have cut the conversation short by rejecting his suggestion with 'Don't be silly, darling, I've already told you he's gone into his house', or words to that effect. Instead, judging perhaps that encouragement of the creative power of language is more important, on this occasion, than insistence on factual accuracy, she first checks that she has correctly understood Mark's version of where the man has gone (12–14) and then helps him to develop a fantasised account of a shopping expedition, in which he himself takes over the role of principal actor.

Table 2.5. *Conversations between Mark and Mother III*

1	Mark:	Where man gone?	[Mark has seen
2		Where man gone?	a man work-
3		Mother:	I don't know	ing in his
4			I expect he's gone inside because it's snowing	garden]
5	Mark:	Where man gone?	
6		Mother:	In the house	
7	Mark:	Uh?	
8		Mother:	Into his house	
9	Mark:	No	
10		No	
11		Gone to shop Mummy(v)	[The local shop
12		Mother:	Gone where?	is close to
13	Mark:	Gone shop	Mark's house]
14		Mother:	To the shop?	
15	Mark:	Yeh	
16		Mother:	What's he going to buy?	
17	Mark:	Er – biscuits	
18		Mother:	Biscuits mm	
19	Mark:	Uh?	
20		Mother:	Mm	
21			What else?	
22	Mark:	Er – meat	
23		Mother:	Mm	
24	Mark:	Meat	
25		Er – sweeties	
26		Buy a big bag sweets	
27		Mother:	Buy sweets?	
28	Mark:	Yeh	
29		M – er – man – buy the man buy sweets	
30		Mother:	Will he?	
31	Mark:	Yeh	
32		Daddy buy sweets	
33		Daddy buy sweets	
34		Mother:	Why?	
35	Mark:	Oh er – [ə] shop	
36	Mark:	Mark do buy some– sweet –sweeties	
37		Mark buy some – um –	
38		Mark buy some – um –	
39		I did	

Because Mark is able to contribute new information to the topic himself, the devices she uses to sustain the conversation are somewhat different from those in the first extract, being mainly confined to 'feeding' him questions to elicit further information. But the overall strategy is similar: to accept his initiation and to help him to sustain and develop it. The story that is built up, therefore, owes as much to the implicit structure that she provides as it does to the material that Mark contributes. In this sense, the meaning is 'negotiated', and the resulting story is a collaborative achievement.

Three brief examples such as these cannot begin to represent the many different types of conversation which provide children with the opportunity to master the system of linguistic communication, but more examples will be considered in chapter 4. In the meantime, however, it should be clear that conversations such as those we have just examined, although clearly different from pre-speech conversations in important ways, nevertheless share many features with their antecedents. Firstly, there is the need for the adult to interpret the child's contribution in the light of the immediate context and the focus of joint attention; secondly, to maximise uptake, the adult's own contributions need to be closely related to the child's preceding communication and current interest; thirdly, whilst being modified in timing, form and content to the child's receptive capacities, these adult contributions must also provide the means whereby the child can enlarge his linguistic resources and, through them, his understanding of the content of the communication.

For his part, in attempting to achieve his communicative intentions, the child will need to make use of nonlinguistic strategies in order to supplement his limited linguistic resources: strategies for interpreting the context of situation and his interlocutor's actions and gestures in the case of reception, and strategies for combining action and gesture with speech in the case of production. From frequently repeated experiences of combining linguistic and nonlinguistic strategies in communicating about objects and events that come within the field of intersubjective attention, the child gradually masters the linguistic system and its relation to the interpersonal and ideational meanings it serves to encode.

The precise way in which this gradual increase in mastery is derived by the child from his moment-by-moment experiences of actual conversation is still largely unknown, although it continues to be a major focus of research (Macnamara, 1977; Snow & Ferguson, 1977). The general principle involved seems to be one of constructing a linguistic representation on the basis of the speech signal that he hears, and comparing that with the conceptual representation of the situation to which he believes the spoken message applies, using any other available cues to help him with the task – although it is clear that such a bald statement does not begin to do justice to the complex processes that are obviously involved (K. E. Nelson, 1977). Such a characterisation puts heavy emphasis on learning through listening – through making sense of what is heard – and this is probably correct. But there is also learning through speaking – through using the linguistic resources available to encode an intended meaning and, in the process, becoming clearer both about the meaning itself and the lexico-grammatical system through which it is realised.

Both listening and speaking, however, require that the child should have a conversational partner who is oriented to his needs as a language learner, if he is to derive the maximum benefit from his comparative matching of form and functional meaning. And it is in providing opportunities for the child to make and check such comparisons that the strategies of interaction discussed above seem likely to be particularly beneficial. For, where they occur, they provide help for the child in a variety of forms: firstly through feedback to his own communicative acts, which allows him to discover their interactive effect – the meanings, both interpersonal and ideational, that are attributed to them; and secondly, through confirmation and development of those meanings, in the form of actions and utterances which complete or extend them or encourage the child to do so himself. In addition, in the utterances of his conversational partner he also encounters 'model' linguistic encodings, in a variety of forms, which correspond to, and help to define, the meanings that he can derive nonlinguistically from his interpretation of the situational context.

Differences in development

Throughout this chapter so far we have talked about 'the child' as if all children were the same and their development followed an identical course. This was partly a matter of convenience for the purposes of exposition, but partly also a reflection of the bias in the way in which the subject has been studied during the last two decades. In keeping with Chomsky's emphasis on linguistic universals, the greater part of the research on the acquisition and development of language has looked for, or assumed, a universal pattern of development. And there does indeed seem to be a considerable amount of evidence to support such a view, both at the gross level of, for example, proto-linguistic idiosyncratic expressions appearing before recognisably adult-based words, and at the finer level of the order in which semantic relations and syntactic realisations are added to the child's repertoire (Brown, 1973; Wells & Woll, 1979). But it must also be stressed that only a handful of languages have been studied in detail so far, and the number of children involved in most cases has been so small as to preclude serious attention to individual or group differences.

Even within the studies that have been carried out, however, there have been observations that suggest that there may be quite large differences between individuals; and there is every reason to suppose that when different cultural groups are compared, they will also be found to differ in quite systematic ways (cf. Wells, 1979a, for a fuller review).

One very obvious source of variation is to be found in the structure of the language being learned. As was suggested in the discussion of the cognition hypothesis (pp. 86–7 above), the translation from conceptual to linguistic representation must take account of the particular set of meanings that is encoded in the language in question and the formal categories through which these are realised, and these are not identical from one language to another. In other words, different cultures give rise to different 'meaning potentials', and even where these are fairly similar, the patterns of formal organisation can be strikingly different.

Slobin and his colleagues have already carried out a number of cross-cultural studies designed to explore the effects of some of these differences (Slobin, 1973; Johnston & Slobin, 1979). They found that ease of learning of particular distinctions depends upon the transparency of the relationship between meanings and formal expression in the language in question. In the case of 'proto-typical events', the mapping from meanings to grammatical forms tends to be clear and direct in all the languages studied. But beyond these, the relationships may be less straightforward, as is illustrated in the following comparison:

> 'The Russian child must eventually extend his accusative inflection to mark the direct objects of verbs which are not part of the prototypical event of physical object manipulation. The English-speaking child must learn that causal agency in passives is not marked with a source preposition, *from*, but with a preposition of location *by*.' (Slobin, 1979: 23)

As might be expected, therefore, differences of this sort between languages affect both the rate of learning and the order in which particular distinctions are acquired.

As well as variation associated with differences between languages, there is also some evidence of differing styles of development within particular languages. Bloom and colleagues (Bloom, Lightbown & Hood, 1975), for example, have identified a difference, in the early stages of structured utterances, in the extent to which pronouns are used in preference to nouns, and Brown et al. (1969) noted that when the two girls in their study were equated for stage of development as measured by MLU, Eve's utterances tended to contain a greater number of content words in comparison with Sarah's, whilst in the marking of grammatical distinctions, such as number, Sarah made far fewer errors than Eve. There is also evidence of differences between children in the sort of words they learn when their vocabulary is just beginning to expand. Comparing the first fifty words of eighteen children, Nelson (1973) found that some children learned far more 'general names', whilst others learned 'personal–social words' and stereotyped phrases and expressions.

Nelson proposed that, in the acquisition of vocabulary, children could be divided into those with a preference for **referential** words and those with an **expressive** preference. More recently, she has suggested that such a distinction may be of rather wider significance, since along with the preference for personal–social words, expressive children also tend to be those who use pronouns rather than nouns, produce unanalysed phrases rather than constructed two-word combinations, and have clear intonation but poor segmental articulation (Nelson, 1979).

Whether such a difference in general style of development will be found to be a widespread phenomenon still remains to be seen, but from those studies that support a distinction between referential and expressive children, it is clear that what is involved is a continuum rather than a dichotomy. Many children do not exhibit a strong preference for either style, and even where a preference can be discerned in an individual child this may change from one context to another.

In her earlier monograph (Nelson, 1973), the referential–expressive distinction in style of vocabulary learning was attributed to a difference between children in their initial hypothesis about the essential function of language, which we might see as a relative emphasis on the ideational as opposed to the interpersonal function. Such an emphasis, it must be assumed, derives from children's early experience of conversational interaction with their parents and other members of the immediate family circle. More recently, Nelson (1979) has suggested that the relative emphasis on interpersonal–pragmatic meanings as opposed to ideational–referential meanings in parental speech results from the presence of an older sibling, but it seems probable that other factors are involved as well, such as the functions for which the parents themselves habitually use language (cf. chapter 7).

It was suggested earlier that the pragmatic and interpersonal functions of linguistic communication provide the way in to language for all children, since it is as an accompaniment to joint activity that language most frequently occurs in the child's early experience. If there is a difference between children in the relative emphasis that is given to ideational as opposed to interpersonal meanings in their conversation with their caregivers, it seems likely, therefore, that this only begins to produce a bias in the child's behaviour after the pragmatic function of language is well established.

That there should be differences between children, and between their parents, in their relative emphasis in different contexts on the ideational and the interpersonal functions of linguistic communication seems entirely plausible, just as there are differences between adults in other aspects of their speech to young children (see below). How important such differences are, however, for the course that development takes, for the rate at which it proceeds or for the level and type of mastery achieved, still remains to be investigated.

The type of variation that has received most attention so far is the rate at which language is acquired, and indeed differences on this dimension are very striking. Wells (in press a), for example, reports that, when compared in terms of MLU at $3\frac{1}{4}$ years, the most advanced children in the sample of 128 had an MLU of more than 6 morphemes – a value not attained by the average child until after the age of 5 years – whilst the least advanced children had an MLU of less than 2.5 morphemes, which is the value attained by the average child at $2\frac{1}{4}$ years: a range of about three years between most and least advanced. Some of this variation can almost certainly be attributed to differences between children in their initial endowment – their language learning ability, whatever that may prove to be – but, equally certainly, differences in social and physical environment play an important part. Clearly, an interaction between these two types of factor is involved but, as yet, there are no indications of their relative importance.

With respect to the first factor, it used to be believed that girls were in general more advanced than boys in learning their native language (McCarthy, 1954) but, in recent research, sex-related differences, if they have occurred at all, have been small and often not statistically significant (Woll, 1979). Where differences do occur, they seem to owe more to culturally based differences in the ways in which boys and girls are treated and talked to, rather than to any inherent difference between the sexes in their biologically based abilities as language learners.

Another potential cause of variation that has frequently been investigated is social background. Many of the earlier studies, such as those summarised in McCarthy (1954), reported a significant trend for children in families of lower socio-economic status to be delayed in their language development. This was attributed to a general impoverishment, both material and cultural, which restricted the range of language-related experiences of such children. However, it is not at all clear how far the observed retardation was the result of a failure, on the part of the researchers, to recognise a distinction between immature and nonstandard, dialectal forms; and this is an issue which has bedevilled educationally oriented discussions of language development (Labov, 1970). More recently, class-related differences which have been observed in children's linguistic behaviour have been attributed to differences in their characteristic orientation to meaning, resulting from the codes 'elaborated' and 'restricted', or 'restricted' only, underlying the uses of language that they experience in the contexts of primary socialisation (Bernstein, 1971). However, the evidence for a sharp distinction between codes and for the hypothesised relation between social class, codes and task-related language behaviour has been questioned in several recent publications (Edwards, 1976a, b; Robinson, 1978), while the results from the Bristol study suggest that social background is no longer – even if it once was – a strong determinant of either rate or style of development (Wells, in press a).

This is not to argue that none of the differences between children in their rate of development is attributable to their social environment. Indeed, it is precisely to differences in style of social and linguistic interaction that we are led by the theory of development outlined in this chapter. But there is no *a priori* reason to believe that such differences are based on either class or code.

One of the first attempts to investigate the effect of differing styles of interaction was the study of early vocabulary development by Nelson (1973), which has already been referred to above. In addition to the differences between the children, she also found two dimensions of the mothers' behaviour that were important for the children's development: the extent to which the mother was strongly directive of the interaction, and whether she was more likely to accept or to reject the child's contributions. As is suggested by the earlier discussion of strategies of interaction, an accepting and non-directive style was found to be most beneficial, with the acceptance–rejection dimension being the more important as far as long-term effect was concerned.

Evidence of a rather different kind has come from those investigating the linguistic characteristics of adult speech to children, which has been found, in all cultures, to be systematically modified in the direction of formal simplicity and semantic redundancy. However, there are still differences between adults using this register in the extent to which their speech is finely adjusted to their children's linguistic level, and such differences could be important for the children's development. This question has been addressed in a number of studies which have yielded some suggestive results (cf. Wells & Robinson, in press, for a review). Simplification or fine adjustment of linguistic form alone has not been found to be related to rate of progress (Newport, Gleitman & Gleitman, 1977), but in a study of a sample of rapidly developing children, Cross (1977) found that the speech they received was 'graded quite continuously in tune with their linguistic and communicative abilities' (p. 163). However, what was of greater importance was the semantic and interactional relevance of the mothers' speech, as was brought out in a subsequent study comparing fast and slow developers (Cross, 1978). What distinguished the speech of the mothers of the fast developers was the greater proportion of their utterances that were related to the preceding child utterances in the form of expansions and extensions of the child's contributions. Similar results have emerged from the Bristol study, with the additional finding that amount of speech is also important. Faster developing children tend simply to receive more speech, as well as a greater number of utterances which incorporate and extend matter previously contributed by the child or which are designed to focus and direct ongoing activity (Ellis & Wells, 1980; Wells, in press b; Wells, Barnes & Satterly, in preparation).

However, we should not be misled by these results into thinking that differences in parental speech style are a uni-directional cause of differences in the rate of the children's development. As in any interaction, there are two parties involved and both contribute to the eventual outcome. So, in looking at the differences between children in their experience of conversation, we find that what is important is the actual topics proposed and the way in which they are jointly negotiated and developed, and to this both child and adult contribute in varying proportions on different occasions.

As has been stressed throughout this chapter, learning to communicate is a collaborative affair. Right up to the early years of schooling and beyond, the adult is the more skilled participant, with a responsibility for helping the child to develop and extend his communicative skills, at first pre-verbally, then verbally, and later in written language. But at each stage, the child also has a contribution to make, stemming from his own interests and directed by his own purposes. The sort of interaction that will be most beneficial for his development, therefore, is that which gives due weight to the contribution of *both* parties, and emphasises mutuality and reciprocity in the meanings that are constructed and negotiated through talk. For in learning to communicate the child is also building his working model of reality: the values that he adopts and the abilities that he develops to understand and control the world in which he lives will owe much to those aspects of experience and interpersonal collaboration that are given salience in his day-by-day conversational interactions.

3

The development of comprehension

ALLAYNE BRIDGES, CHRIS SINHA and
VALERIE WALKERDINE

As we have seen in the previous chapters, the patterns of linguistic interaction which typify family life involve the child from the start as a conversational partner. And a crucial aspect of being an effective party to a conversation is the ability to understand the utterances of the other person. However, comprehension is much more than just the ability to understand isolated linguistic messages; indeed, that ability is a relatively late acquisition in the development of language. Comprehension means understanding, and we shall therefore emphasise all the many factors which contribute to the child's understanding, not just of language, but also of the interactive contexts which give rise to the use of language. Language forms and functions reflect and mould the coordination of seemingly disparate activities in diverse contexts into a unified and coherent setting for rule-governed interactions. Ways of speaking, then, depend upon context; but they are also the means whereby situational contexts are crystallised into interactional settings.

In this chapter, we shall consider the communication process from the standpoint of comprehension rather than production. We shall try to present an account which gives full weight to the cognitive complexity of language comprehension, and to the equally complex strategies which children draw upon to make sense of language. Our account begins at the earliest stages of language development, with a description of how children interpret simple utterances referring to aspects of the immediate context. We shall see that these young children actively seek to reconstruct for themselves the intentions of their mothers in communicating with them.

Next, we look at how children acquire an understanding of word meanings, and we see how their developing knowledge interacts with context in the construction of strategies of comprehension. Finally, we examine the strategies children employ when they try to come to grips with syntactic structure, and we see how here, too, the context of the utterance can provide both supportive and misleading information for the child's comprehension processes.

Language comprehension as a process

As we shall see, comprehension of language is a process of great psychological complexity. But both in carrying out this process, and in learning to carry it out, the child is aided by the way in which the adult speaker orients towards his needs in constructing a linguistic message and puts into practice Grice's **Cooperative Principle**, which was introduced in chapter 1. This principle can be stated as follows: 'speakers try to be informative, truthful, relevant and clear, and listeners interpret what they say on the assumption that they are trying to live up to these ideals' (Clark & Clark, 1977: 122). But we must also not forget that 'successful' communication does not always depend on such sincerity. People do not only talk to inform: they talk to impress, to deceive, to mystify, to evade, to defend and to attack. Habermas (1970) has noted that many forms of communication, in a society in which wealth and power are unequally distributed, are 'pathological'. They are instances of what Pateman (1975) calls 'repressive discourse', a discourse which depends upon and sustains inequalities of power. 'These repressive communications disguise their own nature, disguise social relationships and inhibit the possibility of becoming aware of that nature and those relations' (p. 60).

Relations of domination and subordination are presupposed in linguistic interaction at every level of the social context, from the mass media to the family. The rules of pathological communication also involve a sort of cooperation, though it is better described as complicity, in which the dominated person is required to cooperate in his or her domination. In the following example (Poussaint, 1967), a white policeman addresses a black professional in the USA:

'What's your name, boy?'
'Doctor Poussaint. I'm a physician . . .'

'What's your first name, boy?'
'Alvin.'

The black doctor is here complying with a rule of conversational inequality, which states that blacks may be addressed by whites as 'boy', but not vice versa, and that specialised status terms are applicable to whites, but not to blacks. Sometimes, however, the person who is subject to a bid for domination may resist. In the film *In the Heat of the Night*, Sidney Poitier plays a black policeman following up a case in the Deep South of the USA. A white policeman (Rod Steiger) addresses him: 'What do they call you in Chicago, boy?' Poitier answers: 'They call me *Mr* Tibbs.'

We can assume that, in the prehistory of humanity, the use of language to control those over whom one has power emerged at the same time as the use of language to cooperate with one's fellows in the labour process. In our society, class, sex, race and age are the main dimensions along which one's communicative potency is hierarchically graded. In any conversation between people, their similarities and differences in terms of these dimensions are of great importance in determining the content and form of both linguistic and nonlinguistic messages.

Children, in particular, must learn to attend to the covert as well as the overt messages conveyed in adult utterances, if they are to be socially successful comprehenders. When a parent says to a child 'You've left some dinner on your plate', this may well be an implicit command to finish his dinner. Children are faced daily with a world in which adults command more power than they, both at home and at school. They have to learn to cooperate with this situation if they are appropriately to understand the utterances which are addressed to them (cf. chapter 4). Therefore, we should widen the notion of the Cooperative Principle to cover cases in which speakers are, at least in part, evasive, deceitful, irrelevant and opaque; as well as those in which they are informative, truthful, relevant and clear.

This expanded version of the Cooperative Principle provides us with a useful framework for understanding the complex relationships between social relations and cognitive processes which are basic to language comprehension. For it will be readily apparent that the context of communication is of critical importance in determining the interpretation that a listener places upon a speaker's utterance.

Language comprehension is also an interactive process. To understand an utterance, the listener must be able to represent the context to which it refers. But in order fully to represent the meaning intention of the speaker, the listener must also understand in which particular way the speaker intends the listener to *modify* his representation of the context: in order to act upon it, assert something about it, answer a question about it, or whatever. Comprehension, then, consists in the construction and modification of relationships between what is already known, or represented, and what new information must be added to the existing representation.

In a sense, we can speak of language comprehension as a process which involves both *construction* and *deconstruction*. The listener must identify first what aspect of represented reality is being referred to, and construct an adequate representation of it. He must then identify the speaker's purpose, and relate this purpose, utilising the new information in the speaker's utterance, to his existing representation. As Smith (1975) says, 'comprehension means relating new experiences to what is already known' (p. 10).

In order to comply with the purpose of the speaker, the listener must also deconstruct his existing representation and integrate the new information into the old. Wells (1976), discussing comprehension and context, argues that 'comprehension is the result of an interactional process between the cues provided by the sender's utterance and the knowledge the receiver can bring to bear in interpreting those cues'. Wells goes on to quote Bransford & McCarrell (1974): 'The semantic content of a particular linguistic message is created only as the comprehender, guided by linguistic cues, specifies conditions under which the abstract relations can be realised given his knowledge of the world' (Wells, 1976: 28).

We should not, therefore, see the process of comprehension as being one in which the meaning is decoded *first*, and then acted upon *second* – for to really understand is to understand what is entailed by the relationship between message, intention and context. 'Context' is never just a given reality, but an intersubjectively constructed frame of reference, whose relationship to the utterance is specified, ultimately, by the intentions of the conversational participants. As Wells (1974b) says, 'communication takes place in a situation, but a situation which is actually brought into being by the act of communication and defined by the meanings that are exchanged within it'.

A recent experiment by Glucksberg, Hay & Danks (1976) neatly illustrates this point. Adult subjects were seated at a table on which stood various pieces of 'experimental apparatus' – tape recorders, microphone, lights and keys, etc. To the subject's right was a second table, on which lay various tools. After the subject was seated, the experimenter excused himself, saying 'I have to fix something – I'll be right back.' The experimenter went out carrying a screwdriver, and reappeared a few seconds later, holding up the screwdriver, saying 'Could you give me one that's different from this one?' The subjects, without exception, gave the experimenter another screwdriver. They treated the request for a different object in terms of their perceptions of the speaker's intention, gauged from their knowledge (or assumption based upon experience) about his ongoing activity. That is, in looking for something 'different', they looked for something that *preserved* the speaker's intention within the context, rather than searching for 'something completely different'. Clearly, such findings have implications for the way in which adults often try to test children's language comprehension in settings which deviate from the normal expectations of conversational interaction, and we shall take this point up in more detail in chapter 5.

A further question about the relationship between context and comprehension is the extent to which the development of communication and comprehension skills in children can be seen as a gradual freeing of the child from dependence upon immediate context. A number of educational theorists (Barnes, 1976; Britton, 1970) see this as being of great importance in enabling the child to represent, for himself and for others, hypothetical as well as actual states of affairs, and for developing structures of adult communication and reasoning (cf. also chapter 7). Although this view is plausible in a very general way, it should be clear from the foregoing that the process of comprehension depends upon context at every level of development. What is perhaps important is the way that the relationship between context and comprehension becomes embedded within increasingly complex structures of represented knowledge. These structures, while still contextually located, allow the individual to act in complex ways upon the representations themselves.

We have argued, so far, that comprehension should be seen as interactive and constructive: successful comprehension is dependent both upon the cooperative orientation of conversational partners to shared meanings, and upon their negotiation of a shared framework of relations between utterance and context. For this reason, comprehension should be seen as a unitary process. This process has many components: phonological and syntactic processing, the representation of deep semantic relations, the drawing of inferences from unstated presuppositions and implications, the programming of motor responses and so forth. But all these sub-processes are indissolubly interwoven in the active reconstruction by the listener of the meaning intention of the speaker.

Nevertheless, an adequate theory of comprehension must include a specification of its components, and of their relations to the whole process. Clark & Clark (1977) suggest that the study of comprehension

'divides naturally into two somewhat different areas of study. The first will be called the construction process. It is concerned with the way listeners construct an interpretation of a sentence from the speaker's words. They seem to begin by identifying surface structure, and end up with an interpretation that resembles an underlying representation. The second area of study will be called the utilization process. It is concerned with how listeners utilize this interpretation for further purposes – for registering new information, answering questions, following orders, registering promises and the like.' (p. 45)

They make it clear that the two processes are not truly separate. Thus, in constructing an interpretation, listeners are motivated from the beginning by the goal of identifying how they are intended to utilise the information conveyed in the speaker's utterance; and in utilising the information, they must continually refer back to their initial construction in order to produce a plausible utilisation programme. Further, the relationship in real time between processes being carried out at different levels (phonological, syntactic, semantic, pragmatic) is not a simple sequential one. Listeners can anticipate what is coming next on the basis of what has come before, and they tend to process information only to the extent – or 'depth' – that is really necessary for the task in hand. From their knowledge of context, they can, to use Bruner's (1974) phrase, go 'beyond the information given' in the utterance.

In the sections that follow, we shall see that the relations between construction and utilisation processes in comprehension undergo, separately, a series of developmental changes which reflect the increasing ability of the child to process information in more sophisticated ways. We shall see too, that these processes, while always complementary, become more distinguishable from each other during the course of development. Thus, for the youngest children, the comprehension process is best seen basically in terms of strategies to identify the activity that the speaker wishes the listener to carry out; whereas for older children, the process of constructing an interpretation of an utterance becomes partially differentiated from the process of utilisation. The dissociation is, of course, only partial. What matters is how these processes are organised in more complex modes of understanding. Ultimately, understanding what another person means is always a matter of understanding both what is said and what to do with what is said.

Fostering understanding: the characteristics of adult–child speech
An important point that is sometimes overlooked in experimental studies of language comprehension is that in everyday conversations, successful communication between two people is a two-sided problem; that is to say, the problem of making sure that a message is ultimately interpreted in the way it is intended is rarely the sole responsibility of the listener: the speaker is accountable too, for he is expected to make the task as easy as possible for the listener, by presenting what he wants to say in such a way that it is unambiguous, informative, relevant and appropriate to the listener's cognitive and linguistic capabilities. The likelihood of a satisfactory outcome in an everyday, verbal exchange, therefore, does not rest with either participant alone but is dependent on the combined efforts of both speaker and listener.

A collaborative model of communication such as this contrasts sharply with the more static model which has been the basis of the many investigations of children's language comprehension in the past. These test-like investigations have tended to view language comprehension as an asocial, almost automatic, mental activity, governed entirely by the availability (or otherwise) of certain links between cognitive and linguistic domains in memory, and consequently the circumstances of data collection have generally had an artificial and distinctly nonconversational ring to them. Few conversations in real life are as inflexible as these tests. For example, failure to recognise the name of an object is rarely sufficient to prevent the continuation of a verbal exchange or to preclude a mutually satisfactory conclusion to a conversation. Young children will draw on extralinguistic information, such as their knowledge of the most plausible event, to interpret what has been said to them. And parents, unlike test administrators, are prepared, if necessary and for as long as their children will cooperate, to modify, simplify, supplement or rephrase what they have to convey, until the children understand (or at least respond in a broadly appropriate way). So, instead of concentrating on the failures in communication that occur in laboratory tests (interesting though these errors are), let us turn to examine the amount of conversational support children receive and focus on the way in which parents manage to get their intended messages across, despite the obstacles and communication difficulties they inevitably encounter when talking to very young children.

Considerable evidence already exists regarding the nature and frequency of modifications parents routinely make when they are addressing their children. Two major benefits would follow if we could use such evidence as a source of indirect information about the children's maturity as listeners: firstly, it invites a more naturalistic approach to the study of children's development of receptive skills; and secondly, it offers researchers the opportunity to find out how children are brought to understand new words and phrases during the course of conversations.

Interest in various aspects of child-directed speech has grown rapidly during the past decade (see Ervin-Tripp & Mitchell-Kernan, 1977; Lewis & Rosenblum, 1977; Snow & Ferguson, 1977). The formal characteristics of mothers' speech to young children and the way in which it differs from adult–adult speech are by now well documented (Broen, 1972; Cross, 1977; Ferguson, 1964; Kobashigawa, 1969; Phillips, 1973; Snow, 1972). Baby talk or **motherese** is marked, for example, by slower rates of delivery, by greater redundancy and repetition, by fewer false starts, hesitations or incomplete sentences and by short, syntactically simple sentences (see Sachs, Brown & Salerno, 1976; Snow, 1977). The exact significance of some of these modifications (e.g. repetition) is not entirely clear, however, and is currently undergoing more thorough investigation (Benedict, 1978; Keenan, 1977; Newport & Gleitman, 1977;

Wells, Barnes & Satterley, in preparation). Of course, motherese is not restricted to mothers; fathers and other adults, including non-parents, make the same types of modification when talking to toddlers (Berko-Gleason, 1977); even 3- and 4-year-olds have been observed to adjust their speech in an appropriate direction when addressing 2-year-olds (Sachs & Devin, 1976; Shatz & Gelman, 1973). Evidently modifications of this sort are very pervasive. But what motivates their occurrence? What possible purpose can motherese serve?

Several investigators (e.g. Snow, 1972; Vorster, 1974) have argued that motherese is a way of teaching language, and that the function of the special characteristics of adults' speech is to enhance certain features and distinctions for children and thereby facilitate the learning of syntactic structure. Utterances spoken to 2-year-olds certainly do tend to be short and syntactically simple, but this is not always so, as Gelman & Shatz (1977) have pointed out. The occurrence of syntactically complex utterances, such as 'Well, let's see if we can find something to put inside' (spoken by a mother to her 2-year-old and reported by Gelman & Shatz), and the nonoccurrence of other simpler types of sentence poses great problems for any theoretical model which only recognises syntactic considerations.

Syntax, it would seem, is not the only or necessarily the most important level at which adults modify their message presentation when addressing children. Indeed some syntactic adjustments may yet prove to be merely the indirect result of higher-order modifications. Newport (1976), for example, has questioned whether adults are able to maintain fine-grained control over syntactic complexity independent of other (e.g. cognitive) considerations. Instead she proposes that 'speech modification may result from any number of nonsyntactic constraints on mother–child interaction, such as the adoption of a particular conversational role or a restriction of message content' (p. 180). Ervin-Tripp (1977b) and Brown (1977) have also drawn attention to the otherwise paradoxical use of complex polite forms of request utterances to young children, such as 'Why don't you put that away now?' when shorter, more explicit, forms exist.

Findings such as these have led Cross (1977), Newport, Gleitman & Gleitman (1977), Snow (1977) and others to argue that motherese is not so much a device designed specifically to teach language, but more a response to a particular social and communicative setting, and that the adjustments mothers make are motivated primarily by their aim to 'keep the conversation going' for as long as possible, at a level which is nontrivial yet rewarding to both partners. As such, modifications in speech to children are likely to occur not only along the dimension of syntactic simplification but also (and perhaps more obviously to the mothers) in terms of the constraints imposed by the children's relatively limited behavioural repertoire and attention span, which in turn have the effect of limiting the topics that may be discussed and restricting the range of activities that the mother and child can engage in together (Wells, in press b).

Obviously, the children's own immaturity constitutes the 'weak link' in the communication chain, but this only serves to increase the pressure on more sophisticated language users to convey in the clearest, least confusing way what they are talking about and what they mean the children to do thereby: to 'tailor' a particular message presentation to a child's current linguistic and cognitive skills (Berko-Gleason & Weintraub, 1978; Bloom, Rocissano & Hood, 1976). By studying the frequency, type and range of adults' accommodations to young listeners, therefore, we should be able to learn much about children's limitations as conversational partners.

To this end, a study of the adjustments in message content that mothers typically make was carried out in Bristol by Bridges (1979). Thirty-two mother–child pairs were engaged in an object-retrieval task in which the mother had to direct her child to fetch a variety of specific objects placed around the room. An object-retrieval task was chosen because it provided the opportunity to study a fairly common interaction situation between mother and child, in which there was an obvious goal (i.e. the retrieval of the object), but which nevertheless retained a considerable degree of flexibility regarding the means by which the mothers might achieve the goal. Sixteen 24-month-olds and sixteen 30-month-olds took part. The search sequences were recorded on video tape and the speech and nonverbal behaviour of both mother and child were later transcribed.

The structure of directive sequences

'Keeping the child on course' is a problem of which adults seem acutely aware when they are directing children's actions; and in this respect, the object-retrieval task was no exception. The ways in which the mothers went about asking for the object, directing their children's attention towards where the object lay, prompting and helping them when they seemed to be floundering, and discouraging interest in nonrelevant objects, all contributed to the overall structure of the mother–child interchanges. Examination of the transcripts of the search sequences revealed that there were several distinct conversational moves within the body of the search. One major group of such conversational moves, or 'speech acts', was that of **requests for action**. The retrieval game, by its very nature, invited repeated use of requests for action with the mothers asking their children to fetch up to eleven objects within a matter of a few minutes.

In its barest form, a request sequence consists of a **request** and an adequate and appropriate (verbal or nonverbal) **response**. Here is an example of a simple request–response sequence which was recorded during one of the retrieval games:

Child's behaviour	M's verbal behaviour	M's nonverbal behaviour
	Get me that scarf, love	Points to where scarf is
Follows point		
Steps towards scarf and picks up		

Pre-sequences

In more elaborate conversational exchanges, the request may be prefaced by a **pre-sequence** which serves to establish the topic of the conversation before the actual request is made. In other words, a mother may refer to the target-object before she makes clear what it is her child is being asked to do with that object. The actual request for action follows later. Here is an example of a pre-sequence–request–response sequence:

Child's behaviour	M's verbal behaviour	M's nonverbal behaviour
	On the tray there's a 'thing' – that thing on the tray	Looks and points towards tray
Looks at dog in M's pointing hand.		

Child's behaviour	M's *verbal* behaviour	M's *nonverbal* behaviour
Follows point		Lets pointing arm drop,
	Could you go and get	then points again to
	it for me?	tray and withdraws
		point
Fixates object, runs		
to tray and picks up		

Occasionally, a mother may introduce the topic of the target-object to her child by talking about its function or the circumstances in which the child has encountered a similar object in his past:

Child's behaviour	M's *verbal* behaviour	M's *nonverbal* behaviour
	Granny's got a scarf	Looks at C's face
	D'you remember?	
Nods	In her shopping bag	
Gaze falls to ball of		
wool	You see if you can find	
	one like Granny's	
	scarf	Sits up, monitors
Goes towards wool,		
picks up wool, offers		
to M	No	Shakes head

Sometimes, a mother may even direct her child's attention towards the target object in a pre-sequence-like move in which she does not actually refer to the object by name until after the child has already focused on it:

Child's behaviour	M's *verbal* behaviour	M's *nonverbal* behaviour
	Look	Points to puppet
Follows point to		
puppet		
Steps towards puppet		
	A puppet	
Goes closer to puppet		[*cont.*]

Child's behaviour	M's verbal behaviour	M's nonverbal behaviour
	Would you like to pick that up for Mummy?	Withdraws point
Crouches, picks up puppet, says 'up'		

Garvey (1975) has characterised pre-sequences as the preparation of propositional content. She reported that with the 3- to 6-year-old children she studied, a speaker only went on to make the formal request once the child being addressed had responded (either verbally, e.g. by saying 'yes', or nonverbally, by turning to look at the object mentioned). The children in the retrieval task, however, were very much younger and rarely responded verbally. Moreover, the mothers in the object-retrieval task seemed prepared to treat continued attention to the speaker as an acceptable response from their child listeners, so that making a request did not always depend on the child first making an overt response:

Child's behaviour	M's verbal behaviour	M's nonverbal behaviour
Looking steadfastly at M's face		Looking at C's face
	On the table, by the tissues, there is a stamp	
Continues to look at M's face		
	Could you find it?	
Looks towards table, walks to table and visually searches top		Watches C

Requests

Requests can be made in one of a number of ways. Indeed the many-to-one relationship between the form of an utterance and the function it serves within a conversational exchange is another area which has attracted considerable attention recently (see chapter 1). Linguistic philosophers such as Grice (1975) and Searle (1969,

1975) have suggested that the frequent mismatches between form and function may pose a special problem for children learning language. A sentence that has the form of a question, for example, can be used to request information, to request permission, to demand action or to persuade (Keenan, 1974). Conversely, the same speech act (e.g. a request for action) can be realised by several different formal constructions (see chapter 1, pp. 42–3). How does a child learn about all the different ways of requesting an action? From transcripts of office and hospital conversations between adults, Ervin-Tripp (1976, 1977a) has identified six categories of utterance types by which adult speakers effectively request actions or solicit goods and services from other people. These are:

(1) **imperatives** 'Give me that pen'
(2) **embedded imperatives** 'Would you lend me your pen?'
(3) **permission directives** 'May I have that pen now?'
(4) **question directives** 'Have you got a pen?'
(5) **statements of need or personal desire** 'I want the green pen'
(6) **hints** 'I'd write that down if I had a pen'

The rules for choosing amongst these options, Ervin-Tripp argues, depend on features of the social context, in particular the relative social status of speaker and listener, the degree to which compliance can be assumed and the participants' familiarity with each other and with the task. Discussing the comprehension of directives by children, she argues that question directives (in which the desired act and often the agent of the act are omitted) and hints should be less easily understood by young children because of their lack of explicitness (i.e. the degree to which they rely on inference to be understood appropriately). This is a prediction which can be tested using the data from the retrieval task.

If Ervin-Tripp's classification scheme is applied to the initial requests for action from the search sequences in the object-retrieval task, we find that about half the total search sequences were initiated by embedded imperatives (e.g. 'Can you fetch the X for mummy?'). The next most frequent approach was to use a question directive ('Where's the X?') in the case of the 24-month-old group or an imperative (e.g. 'Fetch me the X') for the 30-month-olds. One explanation for the high incidence of question directives to the younger group (33 per cent of all sequences) and the fact that they were relatively rare (only 8 per cent of all sequences) in the transcripts of 30-month-olds might be that mothers of the younger children attempt to segment the task into two temporally distinct parts: making sure first that the child is visually attending to the target-object and only then prompting action towards that object. That is to say, the use of a question directive might be equivalent to the use of a pre-sequence. Re-examination of the transcripts however did not reveal much support for such an hypothesis: only 5 of the 14 search sequences that were initiated by a question directive had clear-cut 'locate' and 'pick-up' subsequences. 'Where's the X?' would seem to operate as a fully functional request for action when addressed to 2-year-old children. But, as Shatz (1978b) has pointed out, we should not make the mistake of confusing the children's tendency to respond by fetching an object each time with an adult-like apprecia-tion of a sophisticated indirect request. Very young children are likely to respond to most utterances by performing an action, so the fact that a child responds nonverbally when asked 'Where's the X?' should not be surprising. The question as to why mothers of 24-month-olds should prefer this particular way of requesting an object rather than other equally short imperatives (such as 'Get the X') remains unanswered however, although it is interesting to note that Ervin-Tripp herself has commented elsewhere (Ervin-Tripp & Mil-ler, 1977) on the high frequency of ostensive and locative utterances in speech to children who are just beginning to talk, so it may be that the question directive 'Where's the X?' is a particular case of this general tendency.

Clarifications

After the request has been given, a mother will frequently provide additional relevant information to help her child identify the object that is wanted. Occasionally children may elicit this additional information (e.g. by turning back to look at their mothers), but such explicit solicitation is not always necessary: mothers will prompt their children in this way spontaneously. They seem to treat a child's continued failure to identify the object as sufficient reason for supplying additional 'clues' about the target-object in question.

Here are three examples of these clarification sequences:

C's behaviour	M's verbal behaviour	M's nonverbal behaviour
1	Where's the scarf, C?	
Moves into centre of room, scans floor, moves towards table, looks at M		
	It's the orange, the orange material	Points to scarf (twice), looks at scarf briefly
Steps towards scarf		
2	Would you go and get me the scarf please?	
Looks at M 'Mm?'		
	The scarf	
Goes towards table		
	Like Daddy's	
3	Can you find a stamp	Looks towards table
Looks towards table		
	Like we put on letters	
Goes to table and picks up stamp		

The nature of clues used in directive sequences

The characteristic feature of clarification sequences is the presence of 'clues' (i.e. items of additional relevant information). Clues are not restricted to post-request clarification sequences, however. Potentially useful information about the use, appearance or location of target-objects can be offered at almost any point in the search sequence: as part of the presequence, as part of the initial request, as part of subsequent repeat requests or in clarification sequences. Analysis of the transcripts of the retrieval game revealed nine categories of clues:

(i)   pointing

(ii)   directed gaze or head jerk
(iii) nonspecific verbal indicator (e.g. 'over there')
(iv)   use of locative term (e.g. 'in the box')
(v)   use of alternative or childish name (e.g. 'dolly' for puppet)
(vi)   labelling/single-word naming
(vii) naming within sentence frames
(viii) reference to physical attributes (e.g. 'little blue one')
(ix)   reference to nonobservable attributes either verbally or
       through mime (e.g. 'Granny's', 'like we put on letters')

Amongst the objects that mothers were asking their children to fetch during the object-retrieval task were three which the mothers did not necessarily expect their children to know by name. These were a (head)scarf, a (postage) stamp and a (glove) puppet. The most frequently employed hints during the search sequences for these 'unfamiliar' objects were naming and location clues. This was true for both the 24-month-old group and the 30-month-old group. There were, however, age-related differences in the frequency with which other types of clues were offered. For example, mothers of 30-month-olds, unlike mothers of 24-month-olds, refrained from pointing directly at the target-object; and whereas almost all of the clues which the younger children were offered concerned the current whereabouts of the object, the 30-month-olds were, in contrast, frequently prompted by clues relating to the target-object's functions, or the people, events and places associated with a similar object in the children's own previous experience (i.e. background information).

The inclusion of these background clues brings about a qualitative change in the aim of the conversation. Instead of the identity of the target-object being subsidiary to the main task of fetching, it becomes an explicit (and talked about) aspect of the game for the older children. That is, the mother's task changes from trying merely to ensure that the child is visually oriented towards the correct object to attempting to establish for her child what precisely he is to look for.

The type of clues offered does not stay at the same level throughout the search sequence. Mothers adjust the level of sophistication of the clues they give in the light of the feedback they receive from their listeners. A comparison of the clues given immediately before and immediately after breakdowns in the searches for unfamiliar objects (i.e. when the child picked up an unwanted object) revealed that in seven out of eight cases, mothers restarted the search by repeating the same type of clue they had used immediately before the breakdown, or by offering assistance of a more explicit kind. In other words there is evidence of mothers systematically altering the relative sophistication of the clues they give as the conversation proceeds. The feedback they receive from their children during the course of the interaction modifies their expectations of their children's capabilities and helps to indicate the appropriateness of various clues.

Mother–child interactional exchanges, such as those of the retrieval task, offer us an opportunity to examine the many different ways in which adult speakers attempt to enhance understanding in their child listeners. Earlier in this section, we described some of the main conversational moves that occur in search sequences, and in the preceding paragraphs we have seen how the type of informational clues that are offered to children differs overall as a function of the listeners' maturity, and is modified during the course of search sequences in response to momentary lapses in communication.

Searching either in imagination, in memory or in reality for a named object, establishing reference and ensuring joint attention are basic but complex communication skills on which listeners have to draw continually. 'Getting the message across' can be a problem and, with a young child as a partner, the cognitive and linguistic immaturity of the listener constitute considerable obstacles to easy communication. But, as we have seen, adults routinely adapt their message presentation in ways that serve to accommodate the limited receptive language skills and cognitive/inferential abilities of their listeners. In doing so, adult speakers invite children to participate in talked-about activities, and make it possible for them to contribute as conversational partners from a very early age. Syntactic simplification is one level of adaptation which may encourage understanding, but as much of the more recent literature shows, it is only *one* aspect of an interlinked system of constraints and considerations that operate on conversational exchanges and that serve to enhance the likelihood of a child understanding and/or responding appropriately to the utterances he hears. The cognitive and social bases of communicative interchange need equally to be borne in mind if an adequate description of children's language-learning achievements is ever to be realised.

In the retrieval task, the children were being helped to understand which object was being referred to by their mothers' continual modifications and prompts. For some objects, though (e.g. 'car' and 'dog'), 2- and 2½-year-old children need little or no help: they know enough of the meanings of these words to respond appropriately without their mothers' intervention.

But what do children understand of the rest of the language addressed to them? How do they manage to 'break the linguistic code' and attribute meaning to the words, phrases and sentences they hear? What is entailed in the process of integrating conceptual knowledge with linguistic knowledge? This is the topic of the next section.

Early word meanings

The development of understanding of language is a process of coming to know what meanings to assign to utterances in their contexts. The focus of this section is upon the psychological processes involved in children's development of understanding of word meanings, rather than upon the rules for combining grammatical or semantic categories. Miller & Johnson-Laird (1976) have coined the term **psycholexicology** to denote the study of word meanings: this section is about developmental psycholexicology.

Meaning is by no means a simple concept, and the 'meaning of meaning' has been a subject of dispute by philosophers, linguists and psychologists since antiquity. The simplest naive theory of meaning holds that words 'stand for' objects or object classes, so that, for example, the meaning of the word 'book' is simply the set of all objects to which the word refers. This is a simple 'referential' theory of meaning, in which meaning is identical to reference.

But consider some of the problems involved. In the first place, one thing or entity may be referred to by a variety of different words. 'John', 'the postman', 'Mary's husband', 'the captain of the darts team' are all referring expressions which might appropriately be used to described the same person. The way in which we select the appropriate word or phrase to refer to a person or thing depends upon our purposes in making reference, and upon the context within which the utterance is produced (Brown, 1958). In other words, **reference** should be seen as a psychological and communicative act on the part of a speaking subject. It is an attribute of the *use* of language, rather than a property of words in themselves.

The philosopher Frege (1892) distinguished between the **sense**, or meaning (*Sinn*) of a word, phrase or proposition, and its **reference** (*Bedeutung*). If, for example, I say 'The author of *Pride and Prejudice* also wrote *Sense and Sensibility*', I am not uttering a tautology, for the expression 'the author of *Pride and Prejudice*' does not mean the same as the expression 'the author of *Sense and Sensibility*'. The two expressions share a common referent, but their sense is different. Recall the discussion of the **given–new contract** in chapter 1 (p. 53). As was said there, if we wish to convey information to somebody, we have to establish a common *point of reference* to which the new information can be added. So we can see that the ability to apply different meaning expressions to the same referent is, in fact, a fundamental and very important property of linguistic communication. For example, if I say 'Deirdre's new baby is a boy', to a mutual friend who has not seen Deirdre for a year, or heard from her, I am in effect combining in one utterance a series of different meaning expressions (or propositions) relating to a single referent. We could expand this utterance to the following string of propositions:

(i)   There exists a baby
(ii) The baby is 'new'
(iii) The baby is Deirdre's
(iv) The baby is a boy

Formal logic systems provide notations for the description and combination of such 'atomic' propositions, and linguistic theories of reference attempt to explain how grammatical devices allow speakers to select particular 'bits' of information as the given and others as the new, in the context of discourse.

So, as we can see, the act of reference is itself a highly complex linguistic and psychological problem to be explained, and cannot serve as a simple explanation of 'meaning'. But the problems do not end there. If meaning is not reference, what then is it? Commonly, it is held by linguists that the sense of a word is a *relation* which it contracts with other words (Lyons, 1977). Intuitively, some sets of words are more closely related than others – 'uncle/aunt' vs. 'church/tyre'. These relations between words can be formalised for specific limited portions of the lexicon of a language – **semantic fields**, as they are called – by means of **tree diagrams**, as in figure 3.1.

In principle, a limited number of **semantic features** such as [4-wheel] or [animal drawn] can be employed to account for the various distinctions drawn in the lexicon of a particular semantic field. This type of analysis is called **componential analysis,** because meaning is here broken down into its simple components. One advantage that this approach has over referential theories of meaning is that it locates meaning within the linguistic system itself, rather than importing it from the world of 'objects'. Obviously, many of the words in common currency in any society do not have concrete referents – think of words like 'liberty', or the names of deities; but this does not deprive these words of cultural meaning.

In fact, this neatly illustrates the point that words do not actually stand for objects as such, but for *concepts*. In talking to others, we make reference to particular things, people or events, but we do so by classifying them as members of general classes which are similar to or different from each other. Componential analysis is a formal method by which these dimensions of similarity and difference can be specified for a particular universe of discourse. In essence, it is a taxonomic enterprise: just as a zoologist may divide the subject matter of her discipline into genus, species, variety, etc., and attempt to account for these divisions by specifying the attributes shared, for example, by one species but not another, the componential analyst will analyse her data base – the lexicon of a language – by recourse to certain rules for specifying the attributes shared by the concepts denoted by words. Within particular semantic fields, and especially in the field of anthropological linguistics, this type of analysis can

Figure 3.1. Tree diagram of part of the semantic field of vehicular transport

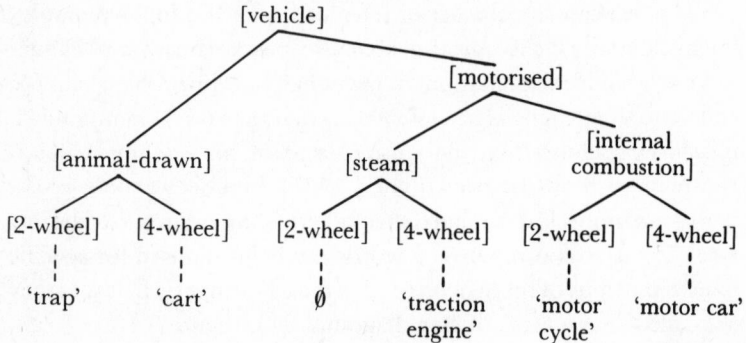

yield important insights into the conceptual structures used by a particular culture.

However, there remain several problems. Firstly, there is always a degree of arbitrariness in making one sort of classification rather than another, and in the end the analysis which one selects is the one which is most appropriate for one's analytic purposes. For example, the Chinese are currently reclassifying their flora according to the culinary, medicinal and other uses to which plants are put, in contrast to the Linnaean classification based upon morphological criteria. Secondly, although the analysis is purportedly to do with semantics, the distinctions it yields are actually *conceptual*. As we have said, words *refer* to actual things, but they *denote* concepts.

Traditionally, philosophers have distinguished between the **extension** and the **intension** of concepts. The extension of the concept consists of all the objects, actual or hypothetical, which are instances of the concept, or to which one might refer by using the word denoting the concept. The intension of the concept consists of the set of all attributes which all the members of the extension class hold in common. Thus, the intension might be seen as the set of all the semantic features which one encounters on the route 'down' a tree diagram to a particular lexical item.

To give an example: the extension class of the concept DEMOCRACY consists of all past, present and future, real or imaginary, political systems with some form of elected representative government. The intension of the concept might include attributes such as: universal equal suffrage, guaranteed secrecy of ballot, right of recall, decision by majority verdict, etc. Depending on which criteria are included in the intension set, one may then argue about whether or not the extension class 'democracies' should include the slave societies of Ancient Greece, the peoples' democracies of the present, or any historically known society. This is not 'just semantics': the point is rather that there is no such thing as 'just semantics'. We cannot guarantee meaning, in any formal analysis, against the kind of objections which would be raised against any attempt fully to define the concept DEMOCRACY. Concepts, and word meanings, are not wholly stable, and the boundaries between what is and what is not to be considered part of their extension are 'fuzzy', as Lenneberg (1975) has pointed out.

In the last analysis, the meaning of a word or utterance is largely dependent upon the use to which it is put in a particular context. This is the point made by the philosopher Wittgenstein, whose point of view we shall briefly return to below. This instability of meaning is well exemplified by choosing a politically and emotionally charged concept like DEMOCRACY, but the point applies to 'simple' everyday concepts as well. For example, if someone who is staying with me asked to borrow a book, it would be odd for me to offer a book of stamps. Yet it is difficult to think of a more appropriate English term for 'books' of stamps, since the stamps are sold in 'pages' between 'stiff covers' in the same sort of way as books for reading. However, although we may be unable to agree upon a full specification of 'democracy' or 'book', we will most likely share a common 'core' meaning.

What is the best means of representing these 'core' meanings? Rosch, in a series of articles (e.g. Rosch, 1977), has pointed out that some members of a class are 'better' instances of exemplars than others – for example, a magpie is a more typical bird than an emu. She suggests that the way concepts are stored in memory is generally in terms of 'best exemplars', or **prototypes**. As she says, 'many experiments have shown that categories are coded in the mind neither by means of lists of each member of the category nor by means of a list of formal criteria necessary and sufficient for category membership but, rather, in terms of a prototype of a typical category member' (Rosch, 1977: 213).

Rosch claims that concepts are most readily stored in memory at a certain particular level of abstraction, and she calls concepts at this level of abstraction 'natural categories'. At this level, objects are classified together which (a) have a maximum number of attributes in common, (b) are recipients of common motor movements and (c) are maximally similar in appearance. This 'basic' level of concept formation is the level at which children first tend to name objects (Anglin, 1977). Further, in accordance with Rosch's prototype theory, children learn the names of 'good' category members before they learn the names of 'poor' exemplars. To illustrate the point, consider one of Rosch's examples: 'table' is a basic-level concept, whereas neither 'furniture' nor 'kitchen table' are.

It seems, then, that, while the boundaries between concepts are fuzzy, any given basic-level concept has a **core meaning** which can be represented in terms of a prototypical class member. This core meaning encodes not only the appearance of the prototypical class member, but also information about how a person typically interacts with it. Nelson (1974) has proposed a theory of conceptual development in which the core of a concept consists of a specification of the dynamic **functional relations** which class members contract with people and with other objects. According to this theory (the **functional core concept theory**), what defines, say, a chair, is not only, and not even predominantly at first, the attributes that chairs have in common, but the way that chairs function in everyday life in relation to other objects. According to Nelson, concepts are not formed by children through breaking things down into their component attributes, and then classifying them on the basis of these attributes, but by classifying objects first on the basis of how we interact with them and later abstracting their common attributes. Of course, things which function similarly often also appear similar: and Nelson suggests that while concepts may be first formed on the basis of function, new members of the concept class are subsequently identified on the basis of their perceptual similarity to the **prototypical** member. But this similarity, as Bowerman (1978) points out, may combine different features together in 'noncriterial' ways, so that the eventual form of the concept is a set of items linked by general resemblance.

Wittgenstein (1953), too, talked of the way in which participants in a common 'form of life' classified objects, events and situations less in terms of a formal list of criterial attributes, and more in terms of 'family resemblances' between them. These resemblances, he said, have their origin in our common experience, as human beings in a particular culture, of the way in which we interact with the world, and this is what he meant by a 'form of life'.

Nelson's functional core concept theory also has affinities with Piaget's concept of the sensorimotor scheme, for she proposes that :

'Piaget's sensori-motor schemes provide an important principle of similarity for the young child to operate with: those things are similar that can be acted upon in the same way. With some modification, this can serve as the foundation stone for a complete model of the child's early concepts and can help to illuminate both his word learning and his sentence construction.' (Nelson, 1974: 274)

She notes that the salient features of the world for the young child are its dynamic properties, rather than its static perceptual attributes: the child attends to his own actions upon objects and towards people; other people's practical and communicative actions; the movements, appearances and disappearances of people and things – in other words, their general functional properties. Those properties of the immediate universe which are stable and unchanging are essentially merely a background for the child's growth of knowledge about the dynamic, but rule-governed, relationships *between* the constant elements – they are the 'ground' upon which the 'figure' of knowledge is articulated (to borrow the terminology of Gestalt psychology).

However, this does not entirely solve the problem, for even if we grant that the core of a concept – for children as for adults – consists of dynamic, functional, relational knowledge, this still does not tell us how the child is able to recognise any given *instance* of the concept's extension class. As Huttenlocher (1974) has pointed out, the way this problem is experienced by the child in language comprehension is slightly different from the way it is experienced in language production. If the child hears the word 'ball', he has to *recognise* that particular acoustic pattern as being related to the functional core concept BALL – as *denoting* it. He then has to search in the immediate array to find the appropriate referent – that is an instance of BALL. The 'functional core' of the concept BALL may be specified as something like [rolls and bounces when thrown/moved]. But supposing that the ball is actually stationary? Clearly, in order efficiently to recognise a ball as being a BALL, the child must also attach further perceptual information features to the functional core – in this case [round, soft texture] or whatever. The child must *recall* these criterial attributes in a mental process mediated through the functional core, and then *recognise* an object which satisfies their specifications.

In speech production, on the other hand, the child must *recognise* these attributes of an actual object as relevant coded 'features', then *recall* the acoustic pattern 'ball' through a mental process which is again mediated by the functional core concept. However, this raises further problems, for the experience of a young child, compared with that of an adult, is limited, and the child's knowledge is even more limited. As adults, we are aware that the condition for a ball adequately to fulfil its function is that it should be (within certain vaguely specifiable limits – think of rugby or American footballs, or cricket balls) round and bouncy. The rest is strictly irrelevant. The child does not, however, automatically know this. In his experience, balls may also always have been on the floor, be blue with yellow stripes, furry, inflatable, attached to a bit of string, thrown by Mother, have a particular taste, or whatever. The child's task is to isolate the strictly relevant – that is, criterial – features for the instantiation of the object class BALL from those that are merely contingent. The achievement of this state of knowledge takes time, and the child is liable to make mistakes.

It has long been known (e.g. Leopold, 1939) that young children make many mistakes in naming objects, and the most common type of mistake is the **overextension** of early word meanings, as when the child incorrectly and consistently refers to an object using the name of another object, usually similar in some way. Bowerman (1978), for example, reports that her daughter Eva, at the age of 15 months, used the word 'moon' to refer to the real moon, to a half-grapefruit seen from below, flat shiny circular green leaves she had picked, a ball of spinach she was about to eat, mounted steering 'horns', slices of lemon, a chrome dishwasher dial, crescent-shaped pieces of torn paper, a magnetic capital letter D, and various other things. This is a clear case of a perceptually based overextension, grounded in the perceptual rather than functional similarities between the objects referred to as 'moon'. Functional overextensions, too, have been observed, as in the case of the child who labelled various objects (a bucket, a bunch of keys, and a newspaper page) when on her head as 'hat'.

Other types of naming mistake made by children include **under-extension**, in which a word is used to refer only to a limited subset of the adult extension class, and **overlap**, in which the child uses a word to refer to, again, a subset of the adult extension class plus some things not included in the adult class. Overlap is thus apparently a mixture of overextension and underextension. For example, one child that we studied used the word /bələ/ to refer to flying birds, butterflies and other insects, and the word 'bird' to refer to birds on the ground – especially chickens. There is, additionally, another type of overextension in which the child will refer to a wide set of dissimilar referents using a word, but only in certain restricted contexts: Piaget (1962) reports that his daughter Jacqueline's first use of the word 'dog' was to name a dog seen from the balcony; subsequently, 'dog' was applied to any other moving object seen from the balcony.

Some theorists (Bierwisch, 1970; Clark, 1973a, b) have proposed, on the basis of their observations of child language overextension, that children acquire word meanings 'bit by bit', through the gradual addition of semantic features. It has further been proposed that these semantic features – of the type that we have illustrated in the discussion of componential analysis–directly correspond to the sort of perceptual features referred to in the discussion of functional core concept theory. In other words, so the theory goes, the child is innately equipped with a perceptual system which segments the perceived world into isolated abstract features which are then directly mapped onto the linguistic system. But since these features are incorporated into the language system only gradually, early word meanings are only partial or limited subsets of the full semantic feature specification of the adult word. As Eve Clark (1973a) puts it: 'as soon as [the child] has attached some feature(s) of meaning to [the word] it simply has that meaning for him' (p. 72).

It is further supposed by the proponents of this hypothesis – the **semantic feature hypothesis** – that the first features which are attached to the word are the more general or abstract ones, as opposed to the more concrete ones. The hypothesis has more recently been modified (Clark, 1973b) to a **partial semantics hypothesis** in which linguistic semantic knowledge (i.e. coded semantic features) is contextually modified by 'nonlinguistic rules', which again are based upon direct perceptual features, but which map not onto the language system – at an early stage of development – but onto nonlinguistic responses, so that the child's responses are determined by both linguistic semantic (feature) knowledge and by direct perceptual evidence. However, this modification does not substantially affect the basic hypothesis, since both versions assume a direct link between perception and language or action. In this assumption, the semantic feature hypothesis directly contradicts the functional core concept hypothesis, which assumes that the relationship between language – specifically, word meanings – and perception is mediated by a separate, functionally based conceptual system.

Both theories are intended to account for the phenomenon of

referential overextension in early child language development, but they do so in different ways. The semantic feature hypothesis supposes that the perceptual properties or attributes of objects are mapped directly onto word meaning, bit by bit building up an intensional-attribute list which specifies the extension class for each word. Thus, the word 'doggy' might initially be specified only in terms of the feature [four-legged], and thus the child will refer to all four-legged animals as 'doggy'. The functional core concept hypothesis, on the other hand, while equally according an important role to the perceptual properties of the object, sees this role in terms of rules for identifying and referring to *instances* of an object class (or concept), which is based not directly on perceptual criteria, but upon dynamic, functional, relational properties. In this theory, it is not the case that all the word 'doggy' *means* for the child is 'something that is four-legged', but that the child possesses a concept DOG, a word to label it – 'doggy' – and certain rules for identifying instances which satisfy the criteria for class membership of DOG. These rules may be called **instantiation rules**. Therefore, according to the functional core concept hypothesis, it is not the concept of DOG which is impoverished relative to the adult system, or the meaning of the word 'doggy', but simply the instantiation rules which have not yet fully developed – in this case, the rule may be of the form:

Objects which have four legs are instances of DOG

As we have stressed, this does not mean that this is *all* that the concept DOG consists of – the various other components may be:

Functional core information
Instances of DOG run, bark, wag their tails, lick children, etc.
Perceptual information
Instances of DOG have fur, tails, four legs, etc.
Linguistic information
Instances of DOG are called 'doggy'
My dog is called 'Marmaduke'.

In a sense, rules for instantiating the concept are rather like reversed rules for defining it, and children's errors may be based on simple reversal of the terms: 'dogs have four legs' becomes 'creatures with four legs are dogs' – but this simple error does not allow us to conclude that there do not exist other definition rules which might equally, in a different context, yield a different overextension. We have observed a young child examine a piece of wire shaped ⌒(and say 'doggy'. It would be absurd to conclude that this child's meaning entry for dog was restricted to bent wire shapes! In fact we can see from this example that children use extraordinarily complex and creative strategies for making the best use of their limited linguistic resources in a wide range of contexts.

We can now see why Rosch's concept of a prototype, or best exemplar, fits naturally with the functional core concept hypothesis, rather than the semantic features hypothesis. As we noted earlier, Rosch contends that natural concepts or categories – that is, the concepts we use to classify real world objects, states, and events – exist at a particular level of abstraction. So, although the same object may be referred to in several different ways, at different levels of abstraction – e.g. stripped-pine dining table, dining table, table, piece of furniture – there is one particular level of abstraction in classification 'at which the organism can obtain the most information with the least cognitive effort' (Rosch, 1977: 213). As she says:

> 'real world attributes, unlike the sets often presented to laboratory subjects, do not occur independently of one another. Creatures with feathers are more likely also to have wings than creatures with fur, and objects with the visual appearance of chairs are more likely to have functional sit-on-able-ness than objects with the appearance of cats.'
> (Rosch, 1977: 213)

Thus, prototype codings of categories will tend to occur at the level of abstraction at which as many attributes as possible are predictable from the fact of possession of any one attribute, while still coding the fewest and most 'separate' different categories. This is the level of basic-level categories and, as noted earlier, categories at this level are amongst the first named, most easily recognised, etc., and are the most abstract level of category at which a name can generate a visual image in an adult.

Rosch suggests that 'it may be through prototypes that the efficiency of basic level categories in providing the most information for the least cognitive effort can be translated into an actual cognitive code' (1977: 225). It would seem, then, that human beings, including children, encode objects not as abstract feature lists, but as stable complexes of features clustered together in such a way that they can usually be predicted to cooccur in a particular functional context.

The concept of a stable object is not, it appears, innate, but takes time to develop. The object concept and its development in infancy has been the subject of extensive investigation by Piaget, and Piagetian descriptions of sensorimotor development and its stages are closely tied to the stages of development of the object concept. One aspect of the object concept is referred to as **object constancy**. Piaget & Inhelder (1969: 31) say this about it:

> '[Piaget] has observed a relationship between certain constancies of form and the permanence of the object. When he handed a baby of seven or eight months its bottle backwards, he observed that the infant turned the bottle around easily if it noticed part of the red rubber nipple in the background, but that it did not succeed in making this correction if it did not see any part of the nipple and only the white base of the milk-filled bottle was visible. This child, then, did not attribute a constant form to the bottle.'

One might say that the concept of BOTTLE was not yet represented for this child by an efficient prototype. Indeed, it is questionable whether a 'concept' of bottle existed at all, for the child had not yet come to understand that a constant function could be fulfilled by an object whose apparent form was subject to change and variation. Usually, object constancy emerges at around 9 months of age. But if we examine the issue more closely, we find that there are still more complexities. Granted that a bottle with its nipple pointed away from the mouth is still a bottle, or an upside-down cup is still a cup, they are nevertheless not very 'good' bottles or cups. An upside-down cup is still a cup, but in that orientation it will not, as anyone can find out, perform its normal function of containing liquids very efficiently. In order for it to do so it must be righted to its normal – 'canonical' – orientation. Freeman, Lloyd & Sinha (in press) have shown that 9- to 10-month infants, at about the age that Piaget says they are acquiring object constancy, do better in tasks where they have to find an object *in* one of two upright cups, than when they have to find an object *under* one of two inverted cups. These experiments demonstrate that children's early concepts encode both functional and perceptual relational information, that is, cups are recognised by infants as 'better' containers when upright than when inverted.

It seems, then, as if the child's early knowledge of relational concepts, such as IN, ON and UNDER, emerges from the same source as his knowledge about object classes. Walkerdine & Sinha (1978) reported an experiment in which 2-year-olds and 2½-year-olds were asked to place an object *in* or *on* a cup; half the time the cup was upright, half the time it was inverted. The younger group of children almost always put the object *in* the cup, regardless of its initial orientation and regardless of the instruction. It seemed as though they were unable to conceive that the cup might act in any way other than as a container. For these children, any object only served one function, and any functional relationship could only be produced with objects which normally (canonically) are placed in that functional relationship. So, although they could not place the object *on* a *cup*, they could quite readily place the object, upon request, *in* the cup or *on* a table.

By contrast, the older group of children tended to respond by placing the object in the cup if it was upright, and on the cup if it was inverted. They seemed to have realised that cups, when inverted, can serve as supporting surfaces instead of as containers, but had not yet coordinated this awareness with their developing understanding of the language of spatial relations. By the age of 3 years, children successfully completed both these tasks.

What can such experiments tell us about the way in which young children's early word meanings develop? First, they point to the importance of considering the growth of the child's understanding of language against the background of his developing cognitive abilities – his conceptual systems for classifying objects, events, actions and relationships. Second, they highlight the way in which such knowledge is rooted in everyday activities and routines, in which the child interacts with objects in contexts which enable him to classify them on the basis of the functions which they serve within the culture. Third, they demonstrate very clearly that, in attempting to understand an utterance, the child draws upon his knowledge of the predictable characteristics of the context in order to make sense of the language.

Similar points can be made with regard to the early productive use of words. Braunwald (1978) noted that her subject, Laura, used the item 'ba' multi-functionally, to apply to various aspects of the 'drinking' situation. The use and development of this early form reflected complex interrelations between communicative function, cognitive categorisation and context of utterance, and all of the latter factors were involved in determining the ways in which, later on, Laura's vocabulary widened and differentiated. The important point to note is that a single, routine, interactive context – requests for drinks – provided a rich and structured source of information about both the referential categories and the communicative functions embodied in early words.

The study of early word meanings has been a fruitful source of hypotheses concerning both the linguistic and the cognitive capacities of young children. We are far from understanding the full complexities of the process of early vocabulary acquisition, and we have not been able to present more than a small part of what is currently known. However, it is a safe generalisation to say that learning to understand the meaning of words is not an all-or-nothing process, any more than is acquiring a concept. A great deal of the development of both understanding of language and understanding of concepts consists of the gradual extension of what is already acquired to new contexts, and in this process children are aided both by their own understanding of the characteristics of the context, and by the attempts of adults to render more salient the relevant aspects of the context to which the child should pay attention.

Situated comprehension of syntax

The suggestion that young children's attempts to understand the utterances addressed to them are the result of specifiable interpretation **strategies**, is an inviting and exciting one. It is an idea, moreover, which can be applied not only to the development of early word meanings but also to syntactic development. The nature of some of these strategies is only now becoming understood. In this section of the chapter, we shall be describing some of these interpretation strategies in the order in which they apply to a developing child.

Primitive responses

The majority of pre-school children respond to the request to 'Show how the boy pushes the girl' by selecting the named objects and making one of them act on the other in some way. There are some 2-

and 3-year-old children, though, who consistently fail to make one toy act on the other. Even after repeated presentation (and demonstration too sometimes) these children persist in responding in an 'intransitive' way.

The most detailed analysis of these early responses comes from Sinclair & Bronckart (1972), but they have also been recorded by other researchers (e.g. Bridges, 1980; de Villiers & de Villiers, 1973): (a) **Intransitive responses**, with one or both of the named participants performing an intransitive action. So, for example, when asked to act out the event described by the sentence 'The dog chases the cat', these children may pick up just one toy and move it about the table top or may take both toys and act out an event in which neither toy is the clear recipient of the action: the toys may be made to race side by side, for example. Similar problems may arise with requests to 'Show how the car hits the lorry' or 'The girl kisses the boy', where reciprocal actions may be portrayed (i.e. the vehicles collide head on or the boy and girl dolls are brought together to kiss).
(b) **'Child as agent' responses**, where the child acts on one or both of the named participants himself. That is to say, one or both of the toys becomes the patient of the child's own action. Asked to act out the sentence 'The boy pushes the girl', a child responding in this way would knock one or both toys down himself. De Villiers & de Villiers (1973) reported that there was no tendency for the children to prefer the first or last named participant as the patient of their actions.

It is not clear why young children respond in either of these ways. It could be that children of this age fail to acknowledge the transitive nature of verbs such as 'to push', 'to chase', or 'to kiss', or it may be that they are incapable of simultaneously treating a toy as the patient of their own actions and the agent of a portrayed event. Interestingly, studies of children's spontaneous play have found that children may be 3 years old before they make one toy act on another in a make-believe scene (Lowe, 1975). Chapman & Kohn (1977) have also suggested the possibility that the children's failure derives from a limited memory span.

Probable-event strategies
Not all events relating two or more objects have an equal likelihood of occurrence. For example, a statement about a boy, a ball and the activity of kicking is more likely to convey the relation described by

the sentence 'The boy kicks the ball', than the highly improbable and bizarre relation 'The ball kicks the boy.' In contrast, 'The boy kicks the donkey' is termed a reversible sentence because the actor and the patient can be interchanged and still leave a semantically plausible sentence.

The effect of the plausibility or probability of the event described by a sentence on young children's interpretations is well documented in the research literature (Bever, 1970; Strohner & Nelson, 1974). If they are presented with reversible sentences such as 'The baby feeds the girl', or 'The mouse chases the bear', 2- and 3-year-old children tend to reverse the relationship between the referents and make the girl and the bear act as agents of the actions (the feeder and the chaser respectively) and make the baby and the mouse the objects of the actions. That is, the children draw on semantic and conceptual knowledge rather than on syntactic considerations to decide about participant roles. In other words, these young children are relying on their knowledge about the usual relations between particular objects to guide their interpretations of sentences; they are not drawing on the syntactic structure (or the word order) of the sentences they hear to tell them what those sentences mean.

How will a child of this age respond when there are no strong semantic constraints operating to make one interpretation more likely than another? Will word order then assume importance for the way children interpret sentences? One way of investigating this suggestion is to examine children's interpretations of active and passive sentences.

Word order strategies

The comprehension of contrasts between grammatical constructions, such as that between active and passive sentences, has often formed the basis for tests of children's syntactic development. Typically, when pre-school children are asked to act out reversible sentences such as 'The girl chases the boy' and the corresponding passive 'The boy is chased by the girl', they perform less well on sentences in the passive voice than on active sentences; it is only when children approach school age that there is any appreciable convergence of the performance figures for the two types of sentence.

Several investigators have been tempted by such data to suggest that pre-school children generally assume that the first mentioned participant in a sentence is always the agent of the described action. Bever (1970) for example, attributed the poor performances of the 4-year-olds in his experiment to the overgeneralisation of a strategy of the form:

'Any NVN sequence with a potential internal unit in the surface structure corresponds to "actor–action–object" '.
(p. 298)

An interpretation rule of this sort, if applied to an active sentence, would generate an appropriate response but, if applied to a passive sentence, it would produce a reversal of intended meaning because the first mentioned participant in a passive sentence refers to the object of the action, not the actor.

There are several reasons, though, why we have to be cautious about this suggestion. A major problem is that researchers in the past, such as Bever (1970) and Strohner & Nelson (1974), have tended to base their arguments on the evidence of generalised age trends in comprehension test performance (i.e. how 3-year-olds as a group respond on average to a set of passive sentences). To assume a direct correspondence between group and individual patterns of behaviour, however, may be quite misleading. An analysis which requires data about the performance of a group of children to be averaged may therefore conceal important information about the coexistence of two or more response strategies. This point was demonstrated clearly by Sinclair & Bronckart (1972), in one of the earliest studies to be analysed at an individual, rather than a group level. French-speaking children (aged 2 years, 10 months–7 years) were asked to use toys to act out the meanings of three-word strings (e.g. 'boy–push–girl', 'boy–girl–push', 'push–boy–girl'). By comparing the response profiles of individual children across test items, Sinclair & Bronckart found that the children were very consistent in the way in which they interpreted the three-word strings, but that not all the children of the same age interpreted the word strings in the same way. There was evidence of at least six distinctly different response patterns: some children, for example, treated the noun nearest the verb as the agent of the action whilst others treated the noun nearest the verb as the patient. Yet other children treated the first mentioned noun as the agent or the last-mentioned noun as the patient, regardless of the position of the verb. This important information about the existence of different response patterns would have been lost if the data had been expressed in the more common form, in terms of the percentage of correct responses per age group. Dewart (1975, cited in Cromer, 1976) carried out a similar study of young children's interpretations of (English) sentences such as 'Send the cat to the dog' and 'Hit the cat with the dog' and their variants (e.g. 'Send to the dog the cat', 'To the dog the cat send') and also found consistent but different patterns of response at the individual level. The most popular strategy was one that could be characterised as 'the first referent is actor/instrument/direct object'.

Dewart's and Sinclair & Bronckart's analyses share one characteristic with many other comprehension studies however; they start from the assumption that children look to the surface structure of an instruction sentence or word string in order to establish which of the referents is meant to be agent and which is to be made the object of the action. The notion that linguistic cues (and, in particular, word order) constitute the primary source of information for children when they are interpreting spoken utterances is implicit in the way most investigations of syntactic comprehension have been designed and analysed (e.g. Baldie, 1976; Bever, 1970; Fraser, Bellugi & Brown, 1963). Typically, results are grouped not only across individuals within a particular age group but also across test items of the same sentence type, and elaborate experimental procedures are invoked to ensure that other factors (e.g. the physical arrangement of the toys in front of the child) are randomised. Unfortunately, there is no reason to suppose that randomising the positions of the toys has ever actually prevented children from relying on extralinguistic variables, although it may well have had the effect of rendering less obvious to adult experimenters any response patterns that were based on extralinguistic considerations.

However, two recent studies (Bridges, 1980; Chapman & Kohn, 1977) have sought to determine the extent to which children draw on a variety of sources of information when they interpret sentences, by examining the regularities in individual children's patterns of response, not only in terms of the linguistic (word order) characteristics of the instruction sentences, but also in terms of the extralinguistic cues inherent in the testing situation (and, in particular, the relative positions of the referents). Chapman & Kohn (1977) reported that all the 3½-year-olds they tested (n=7) consistently made the first mentioned object the actor in active sentences. In contrast, only 60 per cent of the 3½-year-olds in Bridges' (1980) study responded correctly to active sentences – of which only 12 per cent assigned participant roles in both active and passive sentences on the basis of word order. The reasons for this discrepancy are not clear, but it may be attributable to differences in the design of the two studies.

Situational variables

Just how much might pre-school children's language interpretation be influenced by situational or contextual factors? Consider the situation in which a young child is given a green Dinky car to hold and is shown a red car already in position on a road, and is then asked to 'Make it so that the red car pushes the green car.' Many young children, when faced with this situation, consistently respond by making the green car (or whichever toy is in their hand) act on the red car (which is 'in place'), and thereby systematically reverse the meaning of the sentence by interchanging the roles of the referents (Bem, 1970; Bridges, 1980; Dewart, 1975). Even in a standard acting-out task in which neither of the toys is already in position, as many as 30 per cent of children aged 4 years or under may respond consistently by treating whichever referent is nearer their pushing hand as the agent of the action (Bridges, 1980). A similar positional bias has been reported amongst 2½-year-olds by Chapman & Kohn (1977). The form of the instruction sentence (i.e. whether it is active or passive) does not modify the responses of these children at all; it is the physical arrangement of the toys in front of them that determines how they respond. Positional preferences are also to be found in the response patterns of 3-year-old children in tasks where they are asked to select which of two pictures or arrays matches a given sentence. Over half of the children of this age either repeatedly choose the same array or regularly alternate between the two arrays, without regard for the form of the sentence or the order of mention of the referents (Bridges, 1980).

Despite their differences, the 'first referent is actor strategy and the 'car nearest my pushing hand is actor' strategy have one important point in common: neither differentiates between active and passive sentences. Children using either of these strategies act as though they are not aware of the significance of differences in form as a cue to differences in meaning. Instead, they seem to operate on the assumption that information about participant roles is to be found elsewhere, in the way the toys are already arranged, for example, or in the order in which the toys are mentioned in the instruction sentence. Participant roles are consequently assigned on the basis of the children's interpretation of the physical and social context in which the utterance is perceived rather than on the basis of syntactically conveyed information. To suggest that 3-year-old children do not pay attention to what is being said would be unwarranted; young children clearly do take heed of what is being referred to – at a lexical level, at least. Beyond this, though, their linguistic analysis does not seem to extend. Faced with the following sentence, 'The car pushed the lorry', most 3-year-olds seem to acknowledge that a car and a lorry are involved and that the activity they are engaged in is pushing, but which vehicle is actually doing (or going to do) the pushing is something which they look to the situation to tell them.

Under more normal circumstances, of course, this level of analysis may be all that is necessary for successful communication, especially in a situation in which all the referents are visible to both speaker and listener. After all, once a listener has successfully found the referents of a speaker's comments, the two of them will have managed to establish a joint focus of attention and the conversation can continue. Children's 'interrogation' of the situation in front of them rarely (if ever) needs to go beyond ascertaining which objects, events or people are being discussed. As soon as the participants have been identified, the relationship between them, literally, 'goes without saying' because it can be discovered from the situation itself.

To a certain extent, therefore, it is unnecessary for a child to draw on information about participant roles to understand the nature of someone else's comments. It is not until he is put in a comprehension test situation that it becomes apparent that in interpreting speech he does not yet subscribe to the conventional (adult) way of extracting meaning from grammatically contrastive sentence pairs such as 'The car pushes the lorry' and 'The lorry pushes the car' (or, at least, it seems that such rules are not yet fully consolidated, for he is prepared to relinquish these considerations very easily in favour of extra-linguistic ones).

By the age of 4½ years though, the majority of children demon-strate that they can consistently respond to active and passive sen-tences in an adult manner. This is not only true for acting-out tasks and selection tasks (Bridges, 1980), but, interestingly, this is the age at which children have first been reported to correct syntactically deviant sentences in terms of word order rather than semantic adjustments (de Villiers & de Villiers, 1974). This is the age too, when most children first demonstrate their ability to verify active and passive sentences accurately (Bridges, 1980).

The basis on which young children interpret sentences and assign participant roles (such as those of the agent or the object of an action) thus undergoes change during the pre-school years. 'Child as agent' and intransitive responses in which no attempt is made to make one referent act on the other are common amongst 2-year-olds. Primitive responses of this type, however, are less frequent in the behaviour of 3-year-old children and are replaced by patterns of response consis-tent with event probability, word order, or referent-position interpretation strategies. Most of these comprehension strategies, as Chapman (1978) has pointed out, can be characterised by lexical understanding (i.e. the comprehension of individual words) with context or past experience determining sentence meaning and role relationships. Only after the age of 4 years do most children come to draw consistently on syntactically conveyed information to assign participant roles and thereby respond in a completely adult-like way in a comprehension test.

Conclusion

What general conclusions can we draw from the studies and approaches to the development of children's language comprehen-sion that we have outlined in this chapter? First, comprehension is not an all-or-nothing phenomenon; there are degrees of understand-ing. Second, even where children appear not to understand utter-ances in the way that adults do, this does not mean that they are unable to use their own strategies to derive a meaning from what they hear, although this meaning does not always correspond with what an adult would understand. Third, and conversely, the pro-cesses involved in a child's comprehension are not necessarily the same as those of an adult, even where there is an appearance of comprehension. What is more, there are considerable differences between individuals in the strategies which they employ, and one of the most fruitful ways of studying language comprehension is the careful analysis of protocols of individual children's response patterns. We know very little about the sources of individual differences in children's language development, and future study will surely address this issue in a more satisfactory manner.

None the less, there are also regularities to be observed in the development of comprehension. Initially, young children's comprehension seems largely to be based upon their appreciation of certain fairly standardised routines which adults utilise for drawing the children's attention to particular aspects of the interactive context. Whatever structures of representation are available to the young child do not at first seem to be systematically linked to their understanding of language. By the age of 2 years or so, however, the child has developed a set of rules for linking word meanings to conceptual representations. A consequence of his limited productive and receptive vocabulary, as compared with the richer structure of categorisation and classification used to guide his nonlinguistic activities, is that there are often mismatches between word and meaning at this stage of development. But a shift from purely pragmatic to both pragmatic and semantic understanding does take place before the end of the third year.

Next, the child must learn to understand the structure of syntax independently of the force and meaning to which it is one means of giving expression. As we have seen, this development continues late into childhood. However, learning to comprehend the significance of syntactic structure is also related to the child's developing knowledge of interpersonal relations and the structure of the social and physical world.

When the child enters full-time schooling, he will in normal circumstances be assumed to have developed an adequate mastery of the basic structure of his native language. It is often thought that major qualitative changes in children's language comprehension abilities have, by this time, given way to a quantitative process of filling out already acquired abilities. However, as we shall see in chapter 5, the relation between understanding an utterance and understanding its context remains a central problem area for the child during his early years at school. School as a context of learning not only provides new opportunities for developing knowledge and language; it can also be the occasion for mutual lack of comprehension between teachers and children.

Before taking up these issues, however, we shall consider some aspects of the child's productive use of language and his interaction with his parents at home.

4

Context, meaning and strategy in parent–child conversation

PETER FRENCH and BENCIE WOLL

The previous two chapters have been concerned firstly with the development of language from its earliest beginnings in mother–infant interaction and secondly, and more specifically, with the development of comprehension. In the present chapter we shall be considering the relationship of language to the social context, and the role which context plays in the child's productive mastery of meaning and interactive skills. The view of language which we take here is a **constitutive** one: not only do participants rely upon context in making sense of one another's utterances but, in quite important ways, that context is brought into being or constituted through the use of language. From this position, social settings and relationships are not seen as independent or external variables which operate upon the child to determine his language development. Rather, they are established and maintained by the concrete interactional behaviours through which the child enacts them in collaboration with those around him. The means by which they are enacted are largely linguistic: it is through the use of language that the child, his parents and his peers constitute and display their social relationships, one with another. In this sense, then, we may look upon social settings and relationships as interactional achievements. As such, their existence is as much dependent upon the participants' use of language as that use of language is dependent upon them.

In the first part of this chapter we shall be expanding and illustrating these ideas by reference to transcribed excerpts of conversations between children and their parents and peers. Then, by further reference to transcribed recordings, and by recasting some recent research into the terms of this constitutive approach, we shall attempt to demonstrate one side of an equation: how it is that the child's experience of interaction and his social relationships with others may serve as a context for his learning to mean.

The final part of the chapter is devoted to a consideration of the other side of this equation. That is, we shall be looking in some detail at the ways in which children are able, through their knowledge and use of language, to enact and manage their social relationships with their parents.

Context and meaning: some developmental opportunities

To the novice student of linguistic and interactive learning it may appear somewhat strange that we should choose to emphasise the socially situated aspect of meaning development: after all, where and how else could the child gain mastery of interactive skills other than in and through his encounters with others? Whilst we fully share the assumption upon which this question rests, we make no apology for the direction taken here. For, as Wells points out in chapter 2, a great deal of the earlier psycholinguistic research began from the implicit premise that the development of competence in this respect is an essentially 'private', psychological activity on the part of the child. And, even though more recent work would *seem* to have reinstated the growth of linguistic learning within its social–interactive context, in practice this reinstatement has often amounted to little more than a few prefatory remarks on the importance of context as resource for interpreting problematic or ambiguous utterances, the body of the argument being taken up with an attempt to formulate context-independent trends. As Mishler (1979) suggests in his critique of the 'context-stripping' research methods which he himself had previously practised, 'Our ideal in theoretical work is the formulation of general laws, laws that we hope are universal. The essential feature of such laws is that they be context independent, free of the specific constraints of any particular context and therefore applicable to all' (p. 2).

Further, even where research has been more modest in its objectives, and more explicit attention *has* been paid to the context in which communication occurs, the relationship between context and meaning frequently remains ill-conceived or poorly formulated. Indeed, quite often the term 'context' is used only to refer to ongoing nonlinguistic activity which may accompany language and to aspects of the physical setting in which an utterance is situated. These features are then assumed to have an identity which is, to a large degree, independent of the language itself. The relationship between linguistic meaning and context, on this view, is postulated as one of one-way determination: spoken words do not in themselves contain sufficient information for participants to grasp one another's meanings, but, by making reference to aspects of the setting, which have a stable identity, one may achieve a sense of what it was that one's interlocutor intended.

To illustrate what is entailed in this position, we might reconsider the well-known example in Bloom's (1970) study (cf. chapter 2, p. 82). On two separate occasions in one day a child under observation produced the utterance 'Mommy sock.' Bloom argues that the child's intended meanings on the two occasions were widely divergent – on the first occasion 'Mommy' is taken as the possessive modifier of 'sock' (gloss: 'This is Mummy's sock') and on the second 'Mommy' is agent, and 'sock' object (gloss: 'Mummy is putting on my sock') – yet the surface forms of the two productions are identical. In order, then, to disambiguate the utterances, to arrive at a formulation of their semantic content, Bloom suggests that it is necessary to make reference to the extralinguistic context: on the first occasion the child is helping mother with the laundry, and on the second mother is dressing the child.

However insightful this mode of reasoning may seem, it can, in the last analysis, only provide us with a partial and somewhat one-sided picture of the role of context in meaning development. This will become clear if we examine for a moment the longer conversational sequence in which one of these productions (the first) was embedded[1]:

> Mother: Here's mommy's dirty socks. Wash. We'll do a laundry and we'll wash 'em. We do the laundry on Thursday too. You help me do the laundry?
>
> (Kathryn pointing to Mother's socks)

---

[1] Dore (1979: 340–1) also provides a reanalysis of these data, which similarly urges us to examine the conversation as the context of the utterance. However, in our view, Dore's analytic separation of the 'context-of-ongoing activity (involving people, objects and events)' from the 'context-of-conversation (involving utterances as descriptions, evaluations, acknowledgements and repetitions)' is misleading. The reciprocally constitutive relation of talk to other activity is obscured by such a distinction.

Kathryn: Mommy sock. [də] – dirty.
Mother: Yes. They're all dirty. I know.

(Bloom, 1970: 47)

Now let us consider that rather than features of a setting having an identity which remains stable across interactional episodes, an object may be differently constituted and described on different occasions. This phenomenon arises from the fact that descriptions of objects are potentially inexhaustible, and therefore any actually occurring description must, by necessity, be selective in character. As Drew (1978) suggests:

> 'the description of any person, object, scene, etc., is indefinitely extendable, because there are always further features of the object etc., which may be added to the description. This ensures that any empirical description is essentially incomplete, and is constructed from a selection of the features (categories) which might be invoked about the person or object etc. Thus for members an initial problem in depicting persons [or objects] in a setting is the selection of *relevant* categories with which to describe . . . [them] given that some selection(s) might not be relevant for the task in hand, but may lead to misunderstanding, may not enable hearers to recognise whatever the description intendedly depicts etc.' (p. 8; original emphasis)

To give but a crude example, while a particular object may be described as an 'empty margarine tub' when disposing of kitchen rubbish, it may, on other occasions, be differently described as, say, a 'plant pot holder', a 'container for marbles', or maybe a 'half-pint measure'. The point is that descriptions, rather than being mere disinterested encodings of stably identifiable features of the environment, are selected for particular interactional purposes, and depend for their sense upon the context in which they are produced. However, their contexts are in turn also interactionally constituted. So, to return to the example cited, we may observe that the context of the utterance in question is constituted, in part, through the mother's utterances 'Here's mommy's dirty socks. Wash. We'll do a laundry . . .' It is within this context that the child's subsequent description of the object as 'Mommy sock. [də] – dirty' – ('Mommy('s dirty) sock') – rather than, say, 'dust rag' or 'mask' – can be seen as both a relevant description, *and* as further contributing to the ongoing constitution of the context itself.

The relationship of language to context which we are proposing here, then, is one of *reciprocal* constitution: not only does language gain its sense from the context or setting in which it occurs, but settings in turn take on their particular meaning for that occasion *via* the language that occurs.

Although such observations may appear self-evident, they significantly affect our conception of the process of meaning development. For rather than seeing this process as simply one of learning to express an independent reality in terms of pre-established lexical categories, a reciprocally constitutive conception of language leads to a view of the child as an active participant in the social production of that reality. It is through the child's progressive mastery of his native language that he is able to participate in the construction of order and meaning in his environment. The psychological import of this process has been documented both by Wells (1975; in press c) and by Bruner (1964), who suggests that 'Once the child has succeeded in internalizing language as a cognitive instrument, it becomes possible for him to represent and *systematically transform* the regularities of experience with far greater flexibility and power than before' (1964: 4; our emphasis).

This transforming, or reality-constituting aspect of language is perhaps most dramatically demonstrated in the imaginative play of the child. For here the identities of participants and objects may be constituted in ways which radically transform their previous status. In the following interaction, two girls, Susan and Joanna (both aged 4½ years), are able, entirely through their use of language, to assign to themselves and one another identities which are meaningful only within the framework of the game itself:

> Susan: Can I be a baby?
>   Can we play a game?
> Joanna: Mm
> Susan: Ga ga guh
>   When shall I watch?
> Joanna: No darling(v)
> Susan: Ga
> Joanna: Sit here with all the big girls

Here we can see in quite sharp relief that it is by means of language that the context is given its particular meaning ('S: Can I be a baby? Can we play a game? J: Mm'), and that context then both provides a backcloth against which subsequent utterances may be rendered meaningful ('Ga ga guh') and is further constituted by means of the production of those utterances. It is in this sense, then, that Bruner conceptualises the mastery of language as setting its user free from the constraints of the here-and-now, as 'a progressive release from immediacy', as a medium which permits 'operations in the absence of what is represented' (1964: 14). And to be purely speculative, we might hypothesise that the opportunities which this reality-constitutive aspect of language provide for children may in themselves be a significant impetus for their meaning development. So, far from being a stable reference point against which one participant may establish the meaning of another, it again becomes clear that context is both established through the use of language and has a reciprocally determining influence upon the meaning of what is said. And it is in this sense that we may begin to consider the conversation itself as the context for the development of meaning.

One further specific way in which children's conversations with their parents may in themselves constitute an important context for the development of meaning becomes apparent when we consider the sorts of skills which conversational participation requires. As Wells points out in chapter 1, conversations may be described in terms of the operations which one participant's talk performs upon that of another. It is clear, moreover, that conversational moves are far from randomly chained together. Rather, participants must constantly monitor one another's productions in order to produce next moves which are, in finely tailored ways, appropriate in relation to current ones. It is through this process of monitoring and production that understanding is constantly displayed over the course of conversations (Sacks, Schegloff & Jefferson, 1978). In other words, we might say that conversationalists are continuously engaged in the giving and receiving of 'immediate feedback' (Dore, 1979).

The developmental importance to the young child of engaging in this form of interaction with his parents is clear: it is only through attempting to express his meanings linguistically to competent speakers of the language that he can receive information on the communicative efficacy of his developing skills. If his meanings are expressed in ways which depart radically from social and linguistic convention, then they are likely to occasion either a request for clarification:

> Jonathan: Do you * things up at
>   play — at play-
>   school playschool?
>
>   Mother: Pardon?
>
> Jonathan: Did you wake things
>   up at playschool?
>
>   Mother: Did you break what
>   things up at play-
>   school?
>
>   . .
>
> Jonathan: No
>   Did they WAKE you —
>
>   Mother: Did you wake the
>   people up at play-
>   school?
>
>   . .
>
> Jonathan: Did you wake them
>   up?
>
>   Mother: Yes you did didn't
>   you?
>   (Jonathan, 2 years, 9 months)

an invitation to 'self-correct':

>   Father: Want some more?
>   [P. and F. are having lunch]
>
> Philip: No
>
>   Father: No what?
>   (Philip, 4 years, 3 months)

or perhaps even an outright correction:

>   Mother: What does that look
>   like?
>
> Jonathan: A eight
>
>   Mother: It looks like a square
>   doesn't it?
>
> Jonathan: Square
>
>   (Jonathan, 1 year, 9 months)

Alternatively, such an utterance may receive a response which, without making an issue of the child's own utterance, nevertheless makes it clear to him that he has been misunderstood.

One conversational practice that may be particularly relevant in providing the child with feedback, and which is remarked upon in this respect by Dore (1979), is that of **formulation**. Formulations first received attention in the work of Garfinkel & Sacks (1970), who point out that:

> 'A member may treat some part of the conversation as an occasion to describe that conversation, to explain it, or characterize it, or explicate, or translate, or summarize, or furnish the gist of it, or take note of its accordance with rules, or remark on its departure from rules. That is to say, a member may use some part of a conversation as an occasion to *formulate* the conversation . . .' (p. 350; original emphasis)

Such formulations are in fact a recurrent feature of parents' interactions with young children, and the following examples from our data are not untypical of the form they may take:

(1) Tony: Mummy (v)
                              Mother: Yes
     Tony: Here papa cat
                He – here papa cat
                              Mother: Grandpa's cat
                                      Yes
                              (Tony, 2 years, 3 months)

(2) Tony: There minnig car
                There minning car
                              Mother: Mini car
                                      Yes
     Tony: ⟨Minnig gone/
                mini car⟩
                              Mother: Mini car's gone
                              (Tony, 2 years, 3 months)

(3)   Mother: What do you want
                                      darling (v)?

Stella: [əbɪs]

                              Mother: A biscuit
                                     I gave you one and
                                          you didn't want it
                                     (Stella, 1 year, 9 months)

In each of these examples, the parent's formulating utterance can be seen to operate upon the previous utterance of the child. Further, the parent's formulation involves some *reshaping* of the child's utterance at the lexical or syntactic level. So, in (1) we find 'T: Here papa cat → M: Grandpa's cat'; in (2) 'T: There minnig car → M: Mini car', and 'T: ⟨Minnig gone / mini car⟩ → M: Mini car's gone'; in (3) 'S: [əbɪs] → M: A biscuit'. This reshaping of previous talk is a very general feature of formulations. And it is by this means that speakers are able to exhibit to one another in a strong form their understanding of what has already been said. For whereas 'repeat utterances are equivocal as demonstrations of understanding ... unequivocal displays can be achieved by producing a transformation or paraphrase of some prior utterance' (Heritage & Watson, 1979: 129). However, in producing such rephrasings or transformations parents may be able not only to demonstrate their understanding of what the child meant, but also progressively to remodel for the child his meanings in terms of the adults' systems of lexis and grammar. Consider the following in this respect:

Gerald: There the –
            ⟨a picture of flowers⟩
            ⟨a picture of flowers⟩
            ⟨a flower⟩
            ⟨a picture of flowers⟩

                              Mother: Yes
                                     There is a picture of
                                          flowers on the cup
                                     (Gerald, 2 years, 3 months)

Jonathan: Edwards
            Edwards

                              Mother: Edwards
                                     What about
                                          Edwards?

Jonathan: Edwards out

Father: Edwards has gone
out
(Jonathan, 1 year, 9 months)

Gerald: Mummy (v)
⟨No⟩
⟨No⟩

Mother: You don't want to do
that do you not?

. .

All right
(Gerald, 1 year, 9 months)

In these examples, the child's utterance is either syntactically ellipsed or incomplete, and the parent's formulation of that utterance involves its expansion into a grammatically complete sentence. It was in view of this that Brown and his colleagues (e.g. Brown, Cazden & Bellugi, 1969) suggested that children begin their syntactic development using a kind of truncated or 'telegraphic' speech (i.e. their utterances contain only 'content' words) which is systematically expanded and filled out by their parents. These expansions then provide a model from which the child may gradually induce the rules of syntax. Whilst this claim has come under some criticism in its details, we might still take the general point that parents frequently do take the opportunity to formulate their children's utterances in ways which provide them with feedback on their forms of meaning expression. In this sense, then, the conversation itself provides a context for the child's learning to mean. As Dore (1979) has put it: 'It is rather obvious that adults introduce children to the community's shared meanings for words, but somewhat less obvious that they display for the infant how others interpret the intention motivating the choice of words on any particular occasion' (p. 344). It is through sustained participation with adult partners in such conversational contexts, then, that the child gradually comes to modify his forms of expression and eventually to express his meanings in the terms of the adult system.

So far we have considered in a general way some aspects of the role played by social settings and conversational contexts in the development of meaning. What we have not yet considered in any detail is the bearing that the social relationships in which the child participates may have upon this process. Whilst a general examination of such features of adult–child conversation as formulations may give us some insight into how the child's meanings become progressively differentiated, it leaves unanswered the question as to why these meanings emerge in the particular order in which they do. By extending our conception of context to encompass the child's social relationships, some light can be shed on this question. However, we must bear in mind the point which we made at the outset. Not only do social settings and objects take on their specific identities through the use of language, but participants in those settings also display their *own* identities in the act of speaking. In this sense, then, social relationships too are interactional achievements. So, for example, the relationship of parent to child may be achieved by, among many other things, displays of concern over the child's well-being, by the giving of advice or the issuing of reprimands. It is, in fact, against this background that Edwards (1978) locates the development of the linguistic expression of possession. Certain objects are 'out of bounds' because they are 'Daddy's', 'Lucy's', etc. This same sort of social relationship of parent to child also provides opportunities for the learning of negation: 'Don't touch', 'You can't have that', etc. It is because such forms as these figure saliently in the linguistic enactment of the parent–child relationship that, it is suggested, they occur early in the child's development.

Similar suggestions are made by the Bristol team on the basis of their investigations of the order in which particular linguistic systems emerge in children's speech. In developmental studies both of sentential meanings (Wells & Woll, 1979) and of the auxiliary verb system (Wells, 1979b), the order in which terms within the systems emerged was found to be more highly correlated with the relative frequency of the same terms in the adult speech addressed to the children than with their relative syntactic or semantic complexity. Furthermore, the adults themselves did not use the various terms with a constant frequency over the period of acquisition: in a substantial number of cases a clear pattern could be discerned, with a peak in the adult frequency being systematically related to the emergence of the particular term in the children's speech. An adequate theory of language development, they therefore conclude, must take account of the social functions that language serves as well as of the formal and cognitive complexity of the semantic and syntactic systems that are being learned. It can be seen from this evidence that there are clear patterns of interconnection between the child's expanding experience of interaction with the world and the meanings and forms that he learns in order to communicate with others about that experience.

The parent–child relationship as conversation

In the second part of this chapter we shall consider the enactment of the parent–child relationship through conversation in much more detail. That is, we shall be looking at some concrete interactional practices through which children manage their unequal status in relation to adults. However, we should point out that this competence involves much more than simply enacting a set of abstractly specifiable procedures; the parent–child relationship (in common with all other facets of social life) must be *locally* managed: what either participant says, and how he behaves, are subject to the constraints of the particular occasion, including what has happened in the course of the interaction up to that particular point. Further, children are quite resourceful in the management of interactions with their parents: not only do they manage successfully to display a respect for the conversational restrictions which their parents may place upon them, but they can do so while at the same time circumventing those restrictions. The strategies which children use in this respect have important consequences for the view we take of the interactional learning process. For although we pointed out earlier that, over time, the child's modes of expression approximate more and more closely to those of the adult system, it seems clear to us that to conceive of the entire social learning process solely in terms of becoming more 'adult-like' is to remain insensitive to features of children's conversational practice. In fact, we would argue that the particular strategies we shall consider here are developed as solutions to the problems children face *as* children.

Specifically, for example, children may quite regularly find themselves having difficulty in engaging their parents as conversational partners. In order to bypass these problems, however, they enter into engagement strategies which are, in some respects, distinctive to them as children (cf. French, 1980). These strategies, we shall maintain, are all related to elements of language structure, and are (a) learned at some early point in children's interactional careers and (b) discarded, or at least used less frequently, at later points, as the child gradually achieves a more equal interactional status with his adult interlocutors. However, our knowledge of children's interactional strategies is, as yet, rudimentary: the ones we discuss here derive specifically from and build upon some fairly recent and, for us, exciting developments in the field of conversational analysis (see chapter 1 for an account of this approach). And it may well be that as our knowledge of adult–child conversation increases, the defects just outlined in the traditional view of socialisation will become even more apparent.

Children talking to adults: participant asymmetries

If one were asked to provide two general characteristics of the research on conversational interaction, one might mention firstly the focus upon rather 'special' types of social relationship or social setting. Even though the aim of much of this work has been to extract generalised, or even universal, interactional processes and structures, researchers have nevertheless been led into considering the distinctive features of relatively unusual interactional contexts. Thus we find in the literature accounts of how, for example, turn-taking in conversation is organised in courtrooms (Atkinson & Drew, 1979), or of the manipulative quality of talk between psychiatrists and their patients (Labov & Fanshel, 1977). As a second characteristic one might point to the fact that a great many settings which have been studied are constituted not by participants of equal interactional standing, but by speakers who 'take on', for the purposes of the occasion, unequal conversational rights. So, for instance, in order to get through the business of a court, the judge may, at his discretion, interrupt a line of cross-examination and question its relevance to charges against the defendant. He may sustain an objection raised by one counsel, and thus terminate a series of questions to the defendant already begun by the other. And, of course, he is responsible both for opening the proceedings and for deciding if and when to adjourn. None of these rights pertain to other participants in courtroom interaction, and because of this we may say that conversational rights are **asymmetrically distributed** among those present.

This general point is applicable to a great many social occasions when adults convene for 'formal' or 'official' interactional purposes;

it also applies to the much more spontaneous, interactions between children and adults. As Speier (1976) points out:

'The manner in which . . . [children] can participate in conversations with adults is internally controlled by an asymmetrical distribution of speakers' rights, wherein adults claim rights of local control over conversation with children, and children are obliged to allow them that control. Children's failure to do so can be met with the sanctioning power of adults.' (p. 101)

Despite the parallel we have drawn between the asymmetrically distributed conversational rights of adults participating in 'official' transactions, and those in operation for adult–child talk, there is an important difference. This concerns the fact that, as adults go about their daily business and 'move' from one social setting to another, they may, and in many cases they are expected to, change their social identities accordingly. These changes in identity are displayed to us, for the most part, through their conversational activities. So, for example, to return to our hypothetical judge, though he may well exercise his interactional rights as a judge whilst sitting at the bench in a courtroom, he would soon find that he was required to account for himself if he were, for example, constantly to interrupt the conversation between two of his colleagues during a lunch engagement, or attempt to adjourn a dinner party at the home of a friend. Adults, then, do not have preferential rights or restrictions in conversation that operate across all the situations in which they partipate; rather, these change depending upon whom they are interacting with and to what end. On the other hand, children's conversational rights tend to be rather more stable across settings.

Generally speaking, *whenever* they interact with adults, they may be expected to display their identity or position as children by observing the convention that their interlocutors assume conversational rights over and above their own. These rights include at least the following:

(i)   to refuse to engage with a child in conversation
(ii) to veto a child's attempts to introduce some topic into the conversation;
(iii) to 'protect' a conversation already in progress with someone else against interruption from a child;

(iv) to enforce silence upon a child or to disengage from conversation with him;

(v) to dismiss or remove a child from the conversational setting;

(vi) to sanction or override a child's protest against the exercise of any of the rights cited in (i)–(v) above.

These restricted conversational rights are not confined to children's interactions with adults; an adult may also 'step in on' and curtail a child's interaction with his peers. As Speier (1976) suggests, 'Much parental work is of a sort that calls for monitoring of children's activity from a distance, and that work is specially entitled with the right to intervene if deemed necessary' (p. 101). The issue of restricted conversational rights thus affects the child's interactional life in more pervasive ways than it does that of the adult. However, this is not to suggest that the child will necessarily experience this as a *problem*. As we mentioned earlier, it seems clear that they develop and deploy strategies for forestalling or bypassing many difficulties which might arise from their inferior status.

The following discussion is devoted to a consideration of the forms these strategies may take. In order to focus this discussion more clearly, we shall first of all consider the strategies available to children for engaging a reluctant, unwilling, or otherwise engaged adult in conversational exchange. Some passing comments made by Sacks (1974) offer a preliminary illustration. He notes that, around the age of 3 years, many children begin conversations with an adult in a similar way. They use openers like: 'You know what, Daddy?' or 'You know something, Mummy?' (1974: 229). One interesting feature of such questions is that, unlike most questions, they constrain their recipients to produce an answer which is also a further question – i.e. 'What?' They thus carry some guarantee that the floor will be almost immediately returned to the first speaker, who will then be able to proceed with whatever topic or purpose he had in mind when initiating the conversation. As Sacks (1974) says, the child

'is thereby provided with the opportunity to say whatever it is he wanted to say in the first place, not now, however, on his own say-so, but as a matter of obligation.

In that case then ... we may take it that kids take it that they have restricted rights which consist of a right to begin, to make a first statement and not much more. Thereafter they

proceed only if requested to. And, if that is their situation as they see it, they surely have evolved a nice solution to it.'
(p. 231)

To relate this to the conversational privileges appertaining to parents set out above, we can see from (ii) that a parent may, at her discretion, attempt to prevent a child from introducing a particular topic into a conversation. However, by means of a strategy like 'You know what, Mummy?', the child is not only able to introduce his topic, but is able to introduce it in response to the parent's invitation. In this way, then, the child not only 'gets his way', but in doing so is also seen to respect the superior interactional rights of his parent – i.e. by 'displaying his recognition of who's in charge' (Hustler, in press).

Our own data reveal a rather similar strategy. Given that a parent may, if she sees fit, make it clear to a child that other matters are to take priority over his wish to engage her in conversation (cf. (i) above), one way of overcoming this problem may be to direct some question to her which will require clarification. Should the parent then make an issue of the question's terms of reference through a request for clarification, the child is then in a position to reproduce that question in a more explicit form, and thus set up a constraint for the parent to take part in conversation with him through providing an answer to it. Indeed, this strategy for gaining conversational access may be seen to operate in the following interaction between Tony and his mother:

[Mother is busy washing the table. Tony has been asking questions about what she is doing]

Tony: It dirty is it?

                                    Mother: That's right
                                                'Cos it's dirty

Tony: Mummy (v)
            Off these Mummy
                (v)?

                                                . .37. .
                                            [T. plays with cutlery]

Tony: Why Mummy (v)?
            Why?

                                    Mother: Why what?

Tony: Why throw that in
          dustbin lorry (=
          pedal bin) Mummy
          (v)?

                              Mother: It's rubbish

Tony: Oh
          More haw haw (=
          horses) please
          Mummy (v)   ['haw haw' = horses.
                                        Mother has been
                                          playing horses
                                          with T. and he
                                          wants to play
                                          again]
                              Mother: * * * * *
                              (Tony, 2 years, 9 months)

Having successfully engaged his mother in one interchange through the initial question in the sequence, his subsequent attempts to re-engage her ('Mummy Off these Mummy?') fail to elicit a response. However, after quite a lengthy pause, we find Tony again attempting engagement by means of the elliptical questions 'Why Mummy? Why?', for which there is no apparent referent. However, in her attempt to clarify what it is that Tony is referring to, his mother simultaneously and unavoidably invites him to re-present his question in a form which is comprehensible to her. In so doing, Tony is able both to fulfil his initial aim of gaining conversational access to his mother ('T: Why throw that in dustbin lorry Mummy? M: It's rubbish') and to do so at her request, as is the case with the 'You know what?' type of question.

A further occurrence of this engagement strategy occurs the same day when Tony and his mother have gone out into the garden. Mother is dozing in the sunshine while Tony plays on the lawn:

Tony: That could go like that Mummy (v)
          . .6. .
          Mm   [sounds like a car]
          . .14. .
          Why Mummy (v)?

Why?
. .12. .
Is this for *?
Mummy (v)?
Get up Mummy (v)
* *
Hello took took (v) (= tortoise)
Why Mummy (v)?
(hums a tune)
. .28. .
No!
No   (Tony, 2 years, 9 months)

There is little in the transcript to which we can refer in order to render any of Tony's questions comprehensible. Moreover, since Tony's mother is (or has been) dozing, she too might be expected to have problems in locating any nonlinguistic object or event to which his questions might constitutively refer. We could therefore expect that the type of reply elicited by the questions would once again be a request for clarification, and hence an invitation for him to re-pose his questions in a form which will be understandable and which will then constrain her to answer him. Indeed, that it is some form of engagement or attention of a 'come what may' kind that Tony has in mind would seem to be borne out by his more direct 'Get up Mummy' following the failure of his 'Why Mummy? Why?' to secure him conversational access. Again, then, by exploiting the procedure of posing a question which has as its response a further question, Tony may be seen as, at one and the same time, attempting to overcome the problem of his restricted status as an interactant *and* also observing it. (This may explain why some children are perceived by adults to be always asking 'Why?' Such children have perhaps discovered that to ask such a question, even when 'conversationally inappropriate', is likely to provide them with an opportunity to give an extended response or explanation.)

The two strategies for gaining conversational access that we have considered so far would seem to require a firm grasp of conversational sequencing rules. The first involves having some idea of how questions like 'You know what?' solicit more or less open invitations to introduce whatever topic one has a mind to introduce in the turn after next. And the second involves some knowledge (a) of the general formats in which speakers routinely resolve problems arising from unclear utterances, and (b) that the outcomes of bringing such a format into operation may be an invitation to produce an utterance which will constrain one's interlocutor to engage in further talk. In addition, we might say that a successful performance of the second type of strategy depends minimally upon the child's capacity to gauge the (in)ability of his parent to contextualise and render his talk meaningful.

In this sense, then, we are crediting the child with both a fair degree of knowledge about linguistic communication, and the ability to apply that knowledge in the development of strategies for overcoming problems he faces as a child. Of course, when we speak of 'knowledge' in this context we do not mean that children know the rules of conversational sequencing in the sense that they could tell you them if asked, but merely they behave *as if* they know the rules. We would further point out that in seeing these strategies as being typical of (though not peculiar to) children's communicative practices, we are presenting a challenge to most traditional conceptions of social and interactive learning. Rather than viewing the progression from infancy to adulthood as a process of incrementally learning more and more adult-like interactive behaviours, we are suggesting that, because of children's restricted rights to talk with adults, they may first go through a period in which they develop and put to use interactive strategies which are sensitive to their status as children. On this analysis then, communicative development would consist not in treading some straight and steady path to adult competence, but in learning first of all how to cope with being a child.

Indeed, it would seem that children are quite resourceful in this respect: the strategies discussed above are only two from a wider and more varied set which has been identified. Not all of these involve the child in asking questions. If we return for a moment to the case of the 'You know what?' utterance, we can note that this type of question shares features with the sorts of utterance which speakers perform prior to imparting news or telling a story. In fact, a well-tried way of introducing a story or news into conversations is by means of utterances which likewise solicit invitations to proceed. On the whole, however, these utterances – usually termed 'story-prefaces' (Sacks,

1968) – would not be functionally identified as questions. Utterances of this kind, such as 'An amazing thing just happened . . .', signal to their recipient that what the speaker has in mind is worthy of mention and solicit replies such as 'Oh, yes' which act as the go-ahead to bring the story into the conversation.

Much of children's talk to their parents concerns matters which, from an adult point of view, are of a taken-for-granted or obvious nature. In other words, we frequently find children wishing to raise topics or comment upon features of the setting which an adult might let pass without mention. However, because they seem intuitively to recognise that talk about self-evident features of the current situation is of interest and importance to their children (cf. chapter 2, p. 98), many parents are willing, and sometimes even eager, to cooperate with them in discussing otherwise mundane matters. Thus we find Gavin's mother actively encouraging his talk about the passing traffic:

		[Gavin is standing on a table looking out of the window]
Gavin:	Lorry	
		Mother: Lorry out there?
Gavin:	There	
	Out there	
		Mother: Lorry?
Gavin:	Another one	
		Mother: Going is he?
Gavin:	[ə]	
		Mother: Mind you don't fall
		(Gavin, 1 year, 9 months)

There are, however, as we have mentioned, occasions when parents may wish to give other matters precedence over discussions of this order. They may, for example, wish to continue a conversation among themselves without interruption from children, and hence they may refuse their children's attempts at conversational engagement (see (iii) above). An instance of this occurs in the following transcript, in which Sally attempts to break into a conversation between her parents:[2]

---

[2]   We are indebted to David Hustler for permission both to reproduce this example and to represent his analysis of it.

Mother: That was all really –
oh she was talkin
about – erm Julie
and
(1 second pause)

{ Sally: <u>Mummy</u> (v)

{ Father: Julie – Julie and <u>who?</u>
{ Mother: <u>Chris</u>

{ Father: <u>Julie and who?</u>

{ Mother: <u>Julie and Chris</u>
(1 second pause)
<u>and – and</u>

{ Sally: <u>Got to tell</u> you some-
{ thing

Father: <u>Julie</u>
Mother: Julie SMITH 'n Chris
Father: Mm

{ Sally: THIS is funny

Mother: 'n Pat 'n
($\frac{1}{2}$ second pause)
Just a minute Sally (v)
<u>I've told you before</u>

{ Sally: (inhales noisily)
Erm – Mummy have
you got any of that
decorated paper
what's under the
Christmas tree?

(Sally, 4 years, 10 months;
quoted from Hustler, in press.
Braces denote which utterances
occur simultaneously)

Bringing together our comments on story-prefaces and the fact
that children frequently raise in their talk matters which adults might
see as being of a non-noteworthy kind, we shall suggest that a further
strategy for engaging a reluctant parent may take the form of the
child beginning his talk with an utterance which conventionally

marks what is to come as worthy of mention or significant. Looking
at Sally's attempts to engage in conversation with her mother, we can
see 'a progression from what might be viewed as less powerful to
more powerful starters' until, upon her third attempt at engagement,
she produces what would appear to be a story-preface and, as such,
'seems to promise more news of the sort that parents might be
interested in' than either her previous attempt or her earlier
'Mummy' (Hustler, in press). As we mentioned earlier, as with 'You
know what?' questions, what characteristically follows a story-
preface is an invitation to proceed, and the pause in the conversation
which follows her third attempt might well be regarded as such an
invitation. Significantly however, it becomes clear when Sally eventually does gain the floor that her concern is not to impart significant
news, but to pose to her mother a request.

So far, then, we have considered both the use of questions which
solicit further questions in return and the use of story prefaces as
examples of strategies that children employ in order to get reluctant
parents to talk with them. Before concluding this topic, let us consider one further example of interaction which illustrates yet another
strategy.

> [Frank and Louise (brother and
> sister) are playing on the floor.
> Mother is cutting out a sewing
> pattern]

Louise: * * * * *

..7..

Frank: * * to put that <u>one</u>
truck

Mother: <u>Nan's</u> * * * (dinner)
So ⟨you⟩ don't get
them all out every-
where
Do you?

Frank: After we're ⟨going⟩
to Nan's

Mother: Nan's coming over I
said
Nobody's going out

> [I.e. because of the recording
> equipment being in the home]

> [Frank is wandering in and out of
> the lounge, Louise playing on
> the floor, TV is on and Mother
> is watching]

Louise: (noises)

. .6. .

Louise   Er ⟨get⟩ the red ⟨one⟩
          (=toy)

Frank: I'm not doing it ⟨with
          you⟩
          I'm going out the
          back

. . . .

          I'm doing something

. . .

          I'm doing something
          Ma (v)

Mother: What you doing?
        Come in and shut the
        door

. .

Frank: I'm going out the back

Mother: Get in here and ⟨see⟩
        that door's shut
        (Frank, 4 years, 3 months)

In addition to having rights to refuse children conversational cooperation, we may note that adults also have rights to censure certain
topics. Indeed, Mother's reply to Frank's initial attempts to raise the
issue of 'going out' ('Nan's coming over I said Nobody's going out')
might well be heard as decisively putting an end to that topic. Later,
though, Frank raises the topic again, this time in the course of
withdrawing from a game with his sister ('I'm not doing it ⟨with you⟩
I'm going out the back'). Despite the fact that his mother is present at
this utterance, however, she does not take it up and, after a silence of
four seconds, Frank produces what might be heard as *less specific*
reformulations of his intent: 'I'm doing something I'm doing some-

thing Ma'. It is after the second of these productions that his mother requests a more explicit statement on the matter ('What you doing?') and thus invites him to re-introduce the censured topic. In this way, then, the child manages to override a conversational restriction set up by his parent, and does so, once again, in response to her request.

A further aspect of this sequence which is of interest to our discussion concerns the design of Frank's utterances 'I'm doing something . . . I'm doing something Ma'. As Wells points out in chapter 1, different utterance types set up different degrees of expectation for a response. So, for example, whereas what are usually termed first parts to **adjacency pairs** (questions, invitations, etc.) place their recipients under an obligation to produce relevant second parts (answers, replies) in return, other utterance types such as statements and answers seem to allow greater latitude, i.e. acknowledgements of statements and answers may be optional (Wells, MacLure & Montgomery, 1979). Looked at in these terms, Frank's first 'I'm doing something' perhaps does not place his mother under any particularly strong constraint to reply. However, as recent work by Wootton (in press) suggests, 'one technique for transforming an utterance, at its potential completion point, into one which carries a stronger constraint on its recipient to take a turn' is to append to it a term of address. Thus, having failed to engage his mother in conversation upon his first production of the utterance, after a three-second silence, Frank re-presents it, this time with the appended address term 'Ma(v)'. It is, then, through the use of this technique, in conjunction with a nonspecific formulation, that Frank is able to secure an invitation to resurrect the topic, earlier vetoed, of his wish to 'go out'.

Again, then, we can see that children are extremely adept at devising strategies for getting round the conversational restrictions their parents set up for them, and that these strategies are designed in ways which give the impression that the asymmetries of the parent–child relationship are being preserved.

We shall now conclude by pulling together the various lines of analysis we have followed in this chapter.

Conclusion

We began by outlining one view of the relationship between

language and social context. This view is a constitutive view. It suggests that rather than language merely relying upon context for its meaning, there is an important sense in which contexts are actually produced by the language of participants. By taking this view, we have, we believe, secured firm theoretical grounds for taking the conversation itself as the context for the child's developing mastery of meaning. One aspect of conversational practice which may be extremely important for this development is the 'formulation' of the child's utterances by his adult interlocutors. Through this practice, parents are able to remodel the child's meanings in the terms of the adult systems of lexis and syntax. Further, it is suggested that, because certain meanings figure saliently in the conversational enactment of the parent–child relationship (e.g. 'prohibitions' from parents), the linguistic forms through which these meanings are expressed emerge at an early point in the child's communicative career.

In pointing to these trends, however, we must be careful not to represent the child's relationship with his parents as something which exists independently of him and which determines his interactive practices. For, in our constitutive view, social relationships are brought into being and displayed through the concrete communicative behaviours of participants. It is, then, at least in part through the child's development of language that he is able to enact his relationship with his parents. This enactment, however, consists of much more than merely following through some programme or set of rules of a 'once-learned-never-forgotten' kind. The child must be able to tailor his behaviour in accordance with the specific 'needs' and opportunities presented in the interaction at any particular point. Further, he may, whilst appearing to respect the requirements and restrictions his parents place upon him, attempt to circumvent those restrictions. His strategies for so doing display both detailed knowledge of conversational sequencing rules, and an ability to bring that knowledge to bear upon the needs of the occasion. The picture which begins to emerge, then, is one of the child as an active, resourceful, and even occasionally cunning, conversationalist. In this respect, his interactive behaviour is an extremely adaptive response to his social situation and should not be considered as an impoverished version of adult behaviour. The view of the child's communicative competence we wish to convey here is one in which rules are invoked and manipulated in accordance with unique situational features – a view for which Widdowson (1979) has found an elegant analogy:

> 'We may claim that we know how to play the game of chess if we know the moves it is permitted to make with different pieces, that is to say if we know the constitutive rules of the game. But when we are actually engaging an opponent, we do not merely move our pieces in accordance with these rules: we *use* these rules to create openings, to develop a plan of campaign, to make a game of it.' (p. 63; original emphasis)

Parents' conversational practices which are now recognised as likely to promote communicative competence in general (Wells & Robinson, in press) may well facilitate this development, but it is also facilitated by practices that are seemingly restrictive. After all, it is only through facing problems that one can ever have the experience of constructing solutions.

5

Developing linguistic strategies in young school children

VALERIE WALKERDINE and CHRIS SINHA

Introduction

In recent years considerable attention has been paid to the way in which the primary school might foster the linguistic and cognitive development of young children. In this chapter we shall examine the assumptions on which such a view of 'aiding development' is based, in the light of work carried out in Bristol and by a group of practising teachers engaged on small-scale research projects.

Very often, language and cognition are seen in terms of 'skills', 'concepts', 'operations', and so forth, which the children can be led to practise in the classroom. In such models, the content of the task is usually taken to be irrelevant, as long as the task is seen to embody the generalisable skills or operations it was designed to foster. We would suggest that there are serious problems with such an approach, which separates the process of enquiring, discussing, remembering, etc. from the content and context for and in which the skill or operation takes place. We want to show in this chapter that the way children make sense of the context around them is crucial to an understanding of their performance in school.

Let us begin by recalling some of the recent work on the development of very young children described in earlier chapters. The lesson of this work will be that children make sense of their surroundings by generating categories which are meaningful, yet, because they differ from our own, we adults often fail to recognise their meaning. We view them as simple, not advanced; concrete, not abstract; demonstrating understanding in adult terms or failing to demonstrate such understanding. Such evaluative categories as these do have their uses, but they often blind us to the way in which children make their own sense in order to act consistently on the world. And this may easily lead to inadequate techniques of educational intervention.

Early child development

What could be more innocent than a new-born baby? Babies, some might say, are natural beings and the main task of the adult is to socialise them – to make them into social beings. However, in a sense, babies are already social before they are born. For although they may appear 'biological animals', we treat them as social before they are born since we already have a set of social categories to define their actions. We read manuals of baby care, we listen to old wives' tales, we wonder whether it will be a boy or a girl – we think about the baby as a person. The point is that *we* have to make sense of our baby from the beginning and impute meaning to its actions in order for us to know how to act in relation to the signals it gives us – for example, its cries. In this way, we act in relation to the social framework in which we make sense of ourselves and we use the same framework to interpret the actions of our children, in order to be able to act in relation to them.

Recall from chapter 2 the work of Colwyn Trevarthen on interactions between mothers and young babies. In one study (Sylvester-Bradley & Trevarthen, 1979), a mother explains and responds to her 3-month-old daughter using the very social categories with which she makes sense of her own actions and mental states. These categories are those of the emotions, intentions and rationality of adult mental life. She describes Sarah's behaviour as 'grumpy', 'cheeky', 'pensive', and responds to behaviour which she considers anti-social by mirroring it verbally. For example:

> You're telling me off, aren't you?
> You're not going to have a chat today?
> Are you bored with Mummy? . . . talk all the time

In this way we understand young children's actions and vocalisations in terms of social categories which pre-exist them. When we pick out certain actions, sounds, etc. and fit them into categories, it is because only some of them 'signify' for us; that is, they stand out because we can locate them within a system of categories of meaning, a system which, as we pointed out in chapter 3, is embedded in a set of social practices common to our culture. The same mode of operating is also used by the children themselves. As we have seen, children's conceptual systems do not always coincide with those of adults, because they, unlike us, are trying to *construct* the system from a particular place within it. None the less, adults and children are co-participants in what we earlier called a common 'form of life'. Both adult and child are generating and using categories; their mutual influence on each other leads both participants, when a breakdown occurs in communication, to change their systems to bring them more into line with the expectations which each has about that of the other. Not only do adults guide children towards adult meanings, they sometimes reformulate their own system to accommodate the childish meanings. There are many examples of this kind of adjustment in previous chapters, but let us briefly focus on two studies.

Bruner (1975) relates many instances of adults picking up vocal and gestural signals and integrating these into their own responses to the child, in order to facilitate cooperative understanding. He and his colleagues found that children did initiate interactions themselves, despite their limited gestural and vocal resources:

'We early observed that mothers seem themselves to "standardise" certain forms of joint action with the child – mostly in play but also in earnest. This usually consists of setting up standard action formats in which the child can be helped to interpret the mother's signals, her gestures, her intentions. They are recurrent occasions that provide the child with an opportunity not only of predicting the mother's intentions, but, so to speak, calibrating his attention with hers. These episodes also permit the child to develop more or less standard ways of signalling his intent, whether it be to refer to an object or to signal his desire. At this stage of development of communication, the establishment of illocutionary effectiveness is paramount, the object being to develop means for operating mutual consent.' (Bruner, 1975a: 12)

Here we can see that both adult's and child's actions signify for each other in a coherent and organised way. However, it is not surprising that these systems of organisation are often different for adult and child. In Ferrier's (1978) study of her daughter's early utterances, referred to in chapter 2, recall that the child interpreted the mother's habitual utterance 'Phew' successively as a form of greeting and as a reference to nappies and their associated containters. The child's interpretation was coherent and rational – but, being based on limited experience, it was incorporated into a different system or framework of categories. It is in this light that we should interpret the **overextensions, underextensions** and **overlaps** in early child utterances which we discussed in chapter 3.

Sometimes the results of children's idiosyncratic operations upon linguistic input can be amusing. Take the case of 3-year-old Alice, in conversation with her mother:

Alice: What are you doing, Mummy?
Mother: I'm watching you
Alice: Don't be silly, I'm not a television

School-age children, too, are prone to misinterpret teachers' utterances: as on the occasion when a small boy came home from school and told his mother that the playground was going to be flooded and there were going to be boats – and please could he take a coat-hanger. It turned out that he had been told that there was going to be a school sale. The charm of this example should not distract us from the central point, that children's interpretation of adult's utterances often have consequences which lead teachers to believe that they are being either wilfully stupid or 'developmentally delayed'. Our argument is that occasions of 'erroneous interpretation' are strategically vital points in children's intellectual development and, as such, are of central importance to educators. Children's errors, in this view, are not stupid; rather they are intelligent and adaptive. They appear as mistakes because they are based on inadequate or incomplete evidence, or use a frame of reference which is different from that of adults. When children make such errors it does not necessarily mean that they need more practice. It may indicate rather the need for the teacher to get inside the child's own framework in order to move forward.

Language, context and cognitive development

Chapters 3 and 4 have emphasised the central role of context in children's language comprehension. Here, we want to look more generally at the interactions between language and context in children's problem-solving, with a view to drawing out the implications of these for classroom practice. We shall start by examining some of the work we did as part of the Bristol study (Sinha & Walkerdine, 1978; Walkerdine & Sinha, 1978).

In a number of related investigations we explored how 3- to 8-year-old children, when faced with a problem task in the laboratory, operate upon the context in order to work out how to solve the problem, in just the same way as the younger children referred to in previous chapters. Put more generally, we set out to examine the relationship between semantic and cognitive development. We started with the assumption, long held by Piaget, that semantic and cognitive development would run in parallel, word meaning building on concepts previously acquired through action. However, as our work progressed, it became clear that whatever the task presented to the children, whether intended to test semantic or cognitive development, it was impossible to understand the children's responses without reference to their active categorisation of features of the context. The strategies adopted by the children to solve the particular problem at hand depended largely on which features signified for the children and in what way.

For example, we used a task which we called the **locative orientation test**. In this task, the children were asked to place a toy car either 'in front of' or 'behind' a toy lorry on a model road. There were four conditions, illustrated in figure 5.1. A Piagetian explanation would suggest that, in each condition, there should be a progression from egocentric to decentred responses. An egocentric response to 'in front' in condition 1, for example, would be one in which the child placed the car between himself and the lorry (see figure 5.2).

Figure 5.1. The four conditions on the locative orientation test

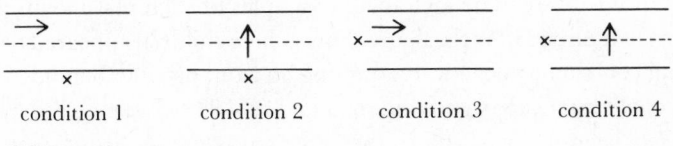

| condition 1 | condition 2 | condition 3 | condition 4 |

KEY
  × Orientation of the child
  → Orientation of the reference object (lorry)
  ⟹ Orientation of the placed object (car)

Figure 5.2. An example of an egocentric response on the locative orientation test

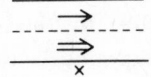

Furthermore, some work on semantic development, notably that of Clark (1973a, b), posits on the basis of the **semantic feature hypothesis** (cf. 142 above) that children acquire the term 'in front of' before they acquire 'behind'.

But is acquisition such a simple and straightforward matter? The results of the locative orientation test do not support either the decentring model or Clark's order of acquisition. We gave the task to 32 $3\frac{1}{2}$-year-olds and to 30 5-, 6- and 7-year-olds. The responses of the $3\frac{1}{2}$-year-olds seemed, at first sight, to be very confusing. Certainly there were no clear response patterns of the sort that would be called egocentric; neither was there any tendency for 'in front of' to be better understood than 'behind'. If we look carefully at the term 'in front of' we can see that it might require different placements of an object (in this case the car) depending on what aspect of the context signifies, by fitting into the existing categories of the child. For example, we often use the term 'in front of' to include a 'facing' element – paying the milkman at the front door, talking to a class of children, etc. We may also note that the objects in a given situation impose their own constraints; in this case cars and lorries have recognisable fronts and backs. Moreover, vehicles move on roads according to definite rules – embodied for us in the Highway Code. But these constraints have to be learnt, and if we put ourselves into the place of the child we can begin to understand that 'in front of' may be based on a category system in which only a limited set of features signify. In fact none of the $3\frac{1}{2}$-year-olds managed to co-ordinate all of these different features governing the situation, but they all made consistent, if idiosyncratic, responses in which stable categorisations can be identified. Examples of such placements are given in figure 5.3. As the figure shows, these children appeared to be using consistent rules for interpreting 'in front of' and 'behind', but the contextual cues signifying road and vehicle axis seemed to have no salience for them, and so they apparently used a 'front' feature without fully understanding its implications for mutual direction of movement.

Older children's responses were more similar to each other. By the age of 5, children consistently used the 'front/back' axis of the lorry, regardless of their own position. A few children over 5 gave what we called 'road user' placements; by this we meant that they gave responses which took into account the direction of the traffic flow along the road. This is something that no children below the age of 5 did, and seems to reflect an increasing awareness of road usage rules. Examples of such placements are given in figure 5.4.

Thus we can see that the same context signifies differently for different children depending on their existing category systems. It is

Figure 5.3. Examples of 3½-year-olds' responses on the locative orientation test (from Walkerdine & Sinha, 1978)

(a)   Parallel placement strategy responses given by one child

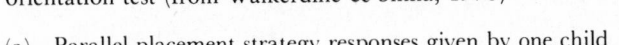

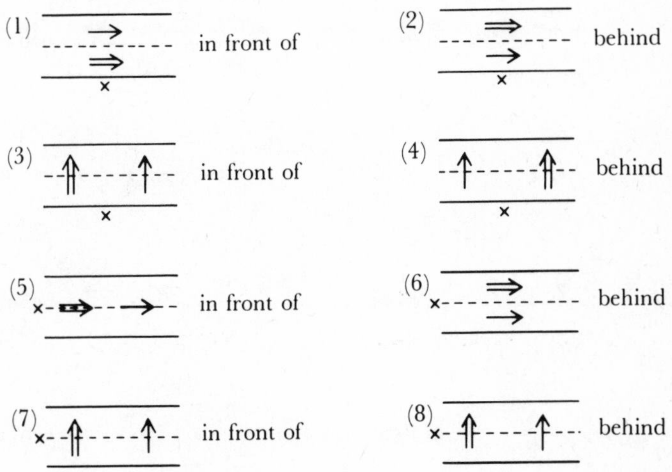

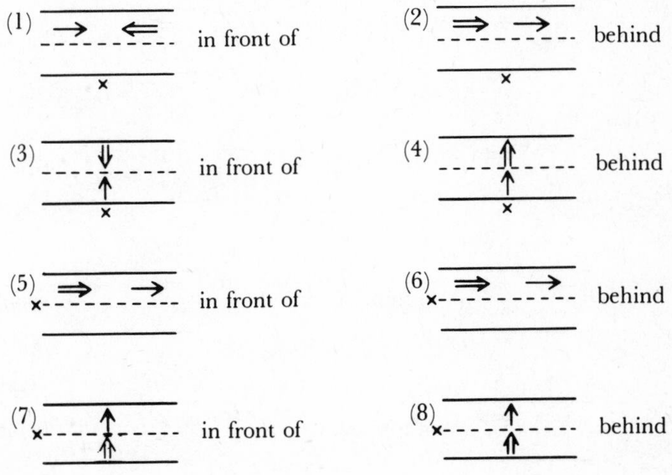

(b)   Use of a 'facing' feature for 'in front of' (responses given by one child)

true that the categorisations of the children do progressively stabilise and cohere with those of the cultural practices of the community. However, giving this task to a group of adults made it clear that adults also vary in their responses: the same context signifies differently for different adults depending on what they pick out as salient.

Figure 5.4. Examples of locative orientation placements used by children aged 5 years and over (from Walkerdine & Sinha, 1978)

(a) Consistent use of axis of lorry

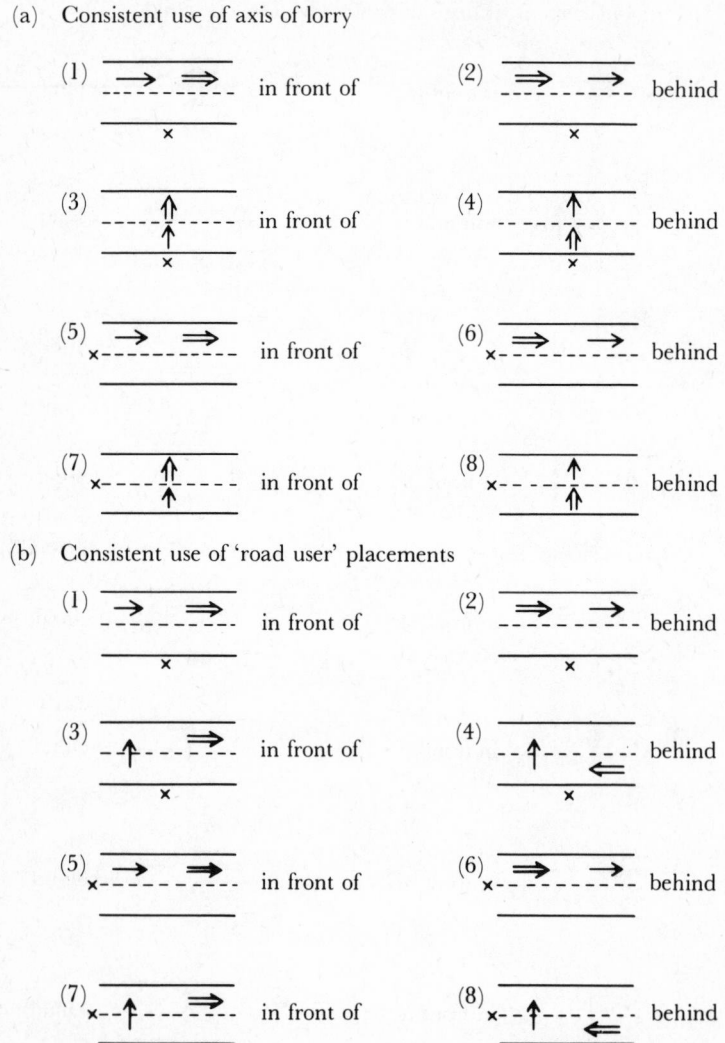

(b) Consistent use of 'road user' placements

We administered the same task to 16 adults: of these, only 5 used the 'road user' strategy; 9 used the axis of the lorry; 1 used the axis of self; and 1 produced strange configurations which she explained as 'trying to avoid crashes'.

If we go on to consider the kind of tasks that are given to children as tests of their 'cognitive development', we can see the same phenomenon at work. We have noted in chapter 3 that, for very young children, in order to be able to act upon an object, the object has to signify, and how it signifies will determine how the child acts upon it. This means fitting it into an existing system of categories which produces a framework for action and which makes possible a particular sequence of actions. We have seen that the different ways the same term signifies for children and adults in the locative orientation test is crucial to their responses to the problem. Similarly, in Piagetian experimental tasks, children are confronted with a problem in which action upon certain objects is required in the framework of certain instructions given by the experimenter, and these instructions are by no means unimportant.

A view which explains children's responses solely in terms of the acquisition of either a set of skills or general cognitive structures minimises the importance of procedures of signification. Our own work, and that of several other recent studies, shows how such processes are crucial in the understanding of children's performances in tests of cognitive development. One particularly interesting study is that by McGarrigle & Donaldson (1975), which demonstrates the importance of the way in which the child categorises and understands the nature of the task itself. They gave a **conservation of number** task in two different ways: the standard Piagetian presentation and their own variant. In the standard format children were presented with two rows of counters. They were asked if there were the same numbers of counters in each row. Then the experimenter transformed one of the rows so that it was more spread out and the question was posed again. At this point many children said the number in the two rows was different. McGarrigle & Donaldson point out that normally if an adult, for example a teacher, asks a child a question about something (particularly if the teacher is assumed by the child to have greater knowledge than he has), then does something to change the thing that is being talked about, and then repeats the question, it is a safe bet to assume that the action is relevant to the question. So the child naturally assumes that a different answer is called for in response to the second question. They suggested that, if this action were made apparently accidental, children's categorisations of the nature of the task would be changed and more children would reply correctly. What they did to test this was to introduce a 'naughty' teddy bear whose object was to spoil the game. After the first set of questions was asked, in swooped the teddy bear and transformed one of the rows. The experimenter re-posed the question after the 'accident' had occurred. In this condition, significantly more of the 4- to 6-year-olds conserved than in the standard test condition.

They argued that, in the 'teddy bear' condition, the children were given a coherent framework for understanding the second posing of the question 'Are they the same?' That is, an accident had occurred and there was a need to check the counters. In the 'standard' condition however, the framework which was set up was more likely to alert the children to difference – even though there was none – there being no other reason to ask the question twice. So, in this case, the social logic of the context – that is, the rules and conventions governing everyday discourse – signified more strongly than the *formal* logic of the problem. When teachers ask questions of children, then, what do the children think is being required of them?

In the Bristol study two more experiments serve to throw light on the same topic. In the first experiment we can point to the problems of the way in which the term 'same' signified in conservation tasks. In this case the test was one of conservation of liquid, in which the children were given two identical beakers each containing exactly the same amount of squash. The experimenter asked if there was the same amount to drink in each beaker and then poured the squash from one of the standard beakers into a tall, thin beaker and repeated the question. As expected, children below the age of 5 generally gave classic non-conserving responses, saying that the 'transformed' beaker did not have the same amount of liquid. However, we were surprised by the children's responses to an additional task which was supposed to check the conservation responses. In this task we took the standard beaker of squash and put the empty, tall, thin beaker next to it. We then took a jug of squash and told the children that the experimenter would pour squash into the tall beaker and they were to shout 'stop' when 'we both have the same to drink'. In fact, the results were quite unexpected. At the age of $3\frac{1}{2}$, 14 out of 19 children shouted 'stop' at the correct point, although all of them had given nonconserving responses to the first task. By the age of 4 this response type had almost disappeared – in other words, children appeared to have lost a previously acquired ability. Why should this be so? Our attempt to understand this phenomenon focused on the significance of the relationship of the instructions to the task.

The term 'same' is used to denote a set of relations as complex as those we have observed in terms such as 'in front of'. For example, it is possible to say that two different things are the same as each other, if they look similar or are functionally identical, e.g. 'I'll have the same again!' But there is also the 'identity' sense of 'same': 'I am the same person today as I was yesterday.' These different interpretations can only be learnt in context, as we have already explained. In the conservation task, children are faced with a confusing situation in which one part of the task – the action part – makes them focus on one interpretation, and the other part – the perceptual part – focuses them on another. It is not surprising, therefore, that as they get older and learn more interpretations, they may become more and not less confused. With this view in mind, we devised another task in which the word 'same' did not occur at all, to see what difference this would make to the children's responses.

A large toy horse and a small toy dog were placed in front of the child, who was told: 'Here is a big horse, he likes a lot to drink; here is a little dog, he likes a little to drink.' A standard beaker of squash was then placed by each animal's mouth so that the horse's beaker contained more than the dog's. The squash from the dog's beaker was then poured into the tall, thin beaker and the horse's drink into another standard beaker. After this transformation, the level of squash in the tall beaker was higher than that in the standard beaker (although it contained less). The child was then told: 'Remember the big horse likes a lot to drink and the little dog likes a little to drink. Now give them their drinks.' Here the task focuses on the actual actions to be carried out and not the perceptual attributes of the beakers of squash, their similarity and difference. We predicted that if the problem was merely one of perceptual confusion, then children should fail this test; but if our linguistic hypothesis was correct, then those children who failed the earlier test should now pass this one. Indeed this is what happened: 6 out of 9 $3\frac{1}{2}$-year-olds passed, as did

20 out of 23 4-year-olds. However, at $4\frac{1}{2}$ an interesting switch again happened, where 6 out of 11 failed the task, but this time several children spontaneously recoded the quantities of 'big' and 'small'! This coding makes the beakers signify in a different way and therefore focuses on the wrong attributes. We would not claim that this task is 'the same' as the conservation task, but we do feel that it highlights the crucial role of signification and categorisation. Sinha & Carabine (in press) have discussed some of these issues in greater detail.

Another example, from the work of a primary school teacher (Stanford, 1978), highlights a further aspect of the signification problem in relation to conservation tests. Such tests are commonly used in many primary schools as part of the mathematics curriculum (e.g. Nuffield Mathematics Project, 1972). In this case the teacher, Sheila Stanford, was using a test of conservation of area, in which sets of five squares representing houses were arranged in various ways on boards representing fields. After the original arrangements of the houses had been transformed, the children were asked whether the amount of space the farmers had left was 'the same' or 'not the same'. To Stanford's surprise, some of the children failed the test, so she questioned these children further to discover their reasons for responding that the amount of space the farmer had for building was 'not the same' after the transformation. As the following example reveals, the children's responses related to the practical problems of building:

'T: What do you think about the amount of space the farmers have left in their fields. Do they have the same amount of space left or has one more or less than the other?

K: This one has more space than the other [where the houses were built close together].

T: Why do you think that field has more space than the other?

K: Because he has built them close together and the other farmer has left gaps.

T: They have built the same number of houses haven't they, and the fields are the same size aren't they?

K: Yes, I know, they have the same amount of space left in the farmyard but this one has more space for building. Look! (pointing to the gaps) he couldn't build houses

between the gaps. If he wanted to build houses he should build them close together. He must be a silly farmer to build his houses scattered all over the field like that.'
(Stanford, 1978: 6)

K. has made sense of the context; it is the kind of sense described by Donaldson (1978) as 'human sense', in that K. was invoking the 'real world', and the intentions of the farmer were being used as criteria for answering the test. Her sense is based on a refusal to accept the terms in which the problem is posed and to act deductively upon a set of parameters. That this is so can be seen by her final comment. She implies that houses are normally built close together and that anyone who does not follow this 'rule of building' is effectively rendering this space not equivalent for the purposes of building: 'he couldn't build houses between the gaps'.

A strictly Piagetian view of this task, on the other hand, would be based upon the 'ideal world' of mathematics, in which one acts logically on what is theoretically correct, rather than on what is practically possible. A basic premise of this view is that such a task is an 'application' of a logico-mathematical principle. However, this ignores the very process of signification which calls into question those aspects of the problem that are open to deductive reasoning. Typically, a child's failure on such a task would lead the teacher to assume that he is 'not ready' for more advanced work and to suggest more practice of the same kind of task. However, given the process we have seen in operation here, it does not follow that more practice with different examples and contexts would necessarily allow him to see 'beyond the social'. Indeed Walkerdine & Corran (1977) showed how such practice in an infant school mathematics lesson can lead to frustration rather than to improvement.

Before going on to consider more school examples and their implications, let us look at one more experiment from the Bristol study which reinforces the argument being put forward here, that the ease with which children and adults can solve a logical problem is related to the words and objects used in the task. In this case, the task consisted of a set of syllogisms or three-term series tasks of the form:

Put X in front of Y but behind Z

There were also several variants of the task involving 'before' and 'after', (full details may be found in Walkerdine, 1975), but here we will deal only with those involving 'in front of' and 'behind'. These made use of a toy car, bus and lorry on a road, and a set of green, blue and red blocks on a board. The task was given to children aged from $4\frac{1}{2}$ to 8 years and to a group of adults. Regardless of age, everyone was more successful on the 'road' items than on those involving the blocks. Analysis of the errors made suggested that the categorisation procedure into which the road task could be fitted allowed the subjects to remember the sequence more easily, because it made sense to them in terms of 'road and vehicle' categories. This is not true for the blocks. For example, in the problem:

> Put the red block in front of the blue block but behind the green block

there are no cues to suggest categorisation procedures: the blocks have no intrinsic fronts and backs. Here, even what counts as the front is a problem – in other words, the task is difficult precisely because little contextual support is available to help subjects make sense of the instruction. Indeed some adults reported that such difficulties led them to misrepeat the instruction, as they frantically tried to remember in a situation where nothing supported their memorising. Thus, for example, 'behind the green block' became 'green block behind'. Too many tests of 'reasoning' or intelligence are like this blocks task – they do not signify for the subjects taking the tests.

From these examples, it is clear that the contexts in which problems are encountered, far from being peripheral, are crucial to an understanding of the solutions that children produce. It is in this sense that 'context' must assume a central position in our understanding of children's development, from the very beginning.

The school context

In the previous sections we have tried to show that, in order to understand the rationality of children, we need to be less tied to traditional dichotomies such as 'simple' and 'complex', 'concrete' and 'abstract', 'child' and 'adult'. This is not to claim that there are no processes to which we can appropriately give the label 'development', but that we should not look from inside out to a set of skills or structures needing action or practice, but rather from the outside in, in the sense that it is 'the social' which defines what we are and provides the means for understanding all action and interaction.

But what of teachers? We suggested earlier that existing models of children's school performance provide little on which to base a strategy for intervention. How can we better understand the relationship between children's strategies and school performance? In order to begin to explore this question we will outline some examples of children's strategies from one infant school classroom (Coghill, 1978).

If we examine Coghill's notes on the children in her classroom, we can begin to see the rationality of their categorisations. In the first example the children are playing with a balance beam:

'On a recent occasion I was watching a group of five year olds at play in school. They had a rather old balance-beam which they were using in their game of "shops". This was a conventional beam with twenty hooks – ten on each side of the fulcrum. The original washers were lost and the children were using some Formica pattern tiles to hang on the hooks, there were enough of these so that even with the beam full there were plenty of spare tiles. One child acted as shopkeeper: he was in charge of the balance-beam. This he used alternatively as display shelf and till. A child would come to the shop holding some spare tiles as money. He'd say something like "I want potatoes". The shopkeeper then asked "How much money have you got?" The customer then counted out a number of his money tiles and handed them to the shopkeeper. The shopkeeper took them, counted them and put them down on the table and turned to his display shelf, took that number of tiles off the hook, handed them to the customer, "Here's your potatoes", picked up the money tiles from the table and hung them on the beam on the hooks vacated by the goods; the beam now appears to be functioning as till. The shopkeeper then turned to the next customer. This game went on for many minutes. Finally another child took over as shopkeeper. He played for a few minutes in a similar manner. Then, during one transaction he merely took the tile money from his customer, and without going through the motions of counting it, placing it on the table, taking the goods from the shelf and then putting the money in the till, he just handed the original money tiles back to the customer as goods. There were immediate cries of "It's not fair", "You're cheating".' (Coghill, 1978: 2)

It is interesting to note the way in which the rules of the game are generated here. The game was certainly not being played in a haphazard way, but rather specific rules were formulated by the participants, which utilised the particular 'props' that were available in the situation.

Another example relates to the problem of the interpretation of the words 'odd' and 'even'. Coghill describes how she was working with a young girl who came across these two words in her reading book:

'On this occasion she had no idea what the text meant, "1, 3, 5 and 7 are odd numbers. What is the next odd number?" To help her understand I told her that to find out if a number was an odd number or an even number we could take that number of things, share them between two people and if each person had the same amount it was an even number and if there was one left over it was odd. We did this with several sets of things, books, pencils, bricks etc. She seemed quickly to grasp the idea. A little later in the book she read, "What is the number of your house? Is it an odd or an even number?" She said, "Mine is number 15 and it's even. We share it with the people upstairs."' (Coghill, 1978: 3)

Given the data on which the young girl was operating, her conclusion seems perfectly reasonable.

Let us look at how she arrived at it. Firstly, Coghill introduced the notion of *sharing things* as a way of explaining the consequence of having two as a factor. This led the girl to think of her house as a 'thing' to be shared. We then see her presented with the problem of the number *of* her house. In this case 'of' is referring to the ordinal properties of the house in a sequence of houses, but she ignores this in favour of the fact that her house divides into two – that is into two parts with no remainder as Coghill had mentioned. So, she shared the 'things' and not the number. Her mistake lay in the way in which she based her logical inference on that which signified for her. Her error was, specifically, a confusion over the ordinal and cardinal properties of number, which must be taught, and not a failure to make a logical deduction.

At another time Coghill was confronted with the way in which the categorisation into which a term fits in other contexts 'got in the way' of what she was trying to teach:

> 'When I give out the milk to my class I require, for safety reasons, that they sit at a table. Because they do not have assigned seats, the number of children at each table varies each day. I use this opportunity to "count in twos" and to "discover" which numbers are odd and even. There is one boy who always has a quick count-up and moves to a table where he makes it into an even number because he doesn't like being the "odd one" . . . I have in fact heard children refer to odd numbers as "bad" and even numbers as "good". One day recently we were playing a game in school where we drew numbers out of a box, ascertained if they were odd or even and then chalked up the points on a graph. The children cheered when "evens" got a point and booed at "odd" numbers. When I questioned them about this one child said: "We like evens better" and there was a chorus of assent.'
> (Coghill, 1978: 7)

In this case the terms 'odd' and 'even' were located for the children at the intersection of two different category systems: the same term or sign, in this case 'odd', signifying in two different bodies of knowledge, one being part of a system of moral order, the other part of mathematical discourse. For the children, the first is more common and more pervasive, the one into which they are initiated first. Hence, when they meet the second, it seems strange, because the significance of the one cannot be removed by the other meaning. Indeed the second meaning may not even have been acquired by some of the children, such is the force of the block. It is important to note here that children often find this juxtaposition of two meanings funny. Their jokes are often based on precisely this notion when the embodiment of a term in one discourse is juxtaposed with that of another.

However, the occurrence of a signifying term in very different contexts of discourse can be a problem for many children when they come to learn mathematics. In order to tackle many mathematical problems we have to 'repress' the contextual details and work on the mathematical signs alone. For example, we have to learn that in the sum 'There are six apples. Four girls ate one each. How many are left?', the fact that apples, girls and eating are being described is totally irrelevant in the solution of the problem, which can be expressed as '6 − 4 = ?' This is very difficult to learn, because it means that all the signifying elements set up by the mention of girls, apples and eating 'get in the way' of the mathematisation of the problem. A vivid example of such a problem comes from one teacher's discussion of her work in secondary school science (Powell, 1978) Powell describes a group of girls having trouble with classification:

'The generic term "Man" found the pupils unable to place him correctly during a small exercise when previously they had classified themselves within the mammals. "He doesn't have babies" was their flawless logic or as Jean wrote in her notebook, "You don't see a male going round with a bun in the oven". The word "behaviour" seems to have had a bad press in the past, for this biologically neutral term was regarded only in terms of naughtiness and when applying it to tadpoles there was a request that it should be changed to "habits".' (Powell, 1978: 6)

In a similar vein, the girls in another lesson suggest that 'evaporation' is the process of thickening milk and that 'perforations' are tea bags. It is now possible to begin to see how the problem of the intersection of a term which signifies in two different areas of discourse may provide a problem of transition from one to another which is likely to be particularly common in school. Such a problem cannot be adequately conceptualised by explanations of children's performance which minimise meaning and context in favour of disembodied structures or skills alone.

What are we to make of the picture built up by these examples? How can it help the teacher? We hope, at least, that the inadequacy of clichés such as 'practice makes perfect' or 'she's not ready for this yet' will now be fully apparent. Intervention by the teacher is clearly needed but what form this intervention should take is much less clear. For the interpretations constructed by individual children in school are varied and complex and should not be underestimated. If a particular child does not appear to make sense, we suggest that it is because we have not been able to gain access to the categorisation procedures in operation, rather than because the child is making non-sense.

Understanding children understanding

In this final section, then, we shall explore some of the ways currently available for gaining access to children's own processes of understanding and make comments and suggestions which may enable interventions to be more effective.

Traditionally, psychological and educational practice has employed tests of one sort or another to answer questions of the kind: 'How much comprehension ability does a particular child possess?' From our arguments, however, it should be clear that we do not see these sorts of questions as very fruitful. Neither do we see the majority of testing instruments as useful for gaining insight into the real processes underlying intellectual development or classroom learning.

The most pervasive form of educational testing remains the traditional IQ test. This sort of test was, of course, never intended to provide answers to the sort of problems we have been discussing. Rather, such tests were intended, from their inception, to be used as instruments for classifying individuals according to the requirement placed on the educational system to grade children in preparation for the demands of the labour market. A central feature of most tests currently in use is their reliance upon normative data. Such tests define the 'thing' which they purport to measure – 'language', 'intelligence', or whatever – exclusively in terms of the extent to which individuals or groups of individuals differ from each other in the distribution of their scores within a 'normal' population, defined as a statistical entity. Because such tests can only yield information in terms of the extent to which a person's score deviates from the norm, they can tell us nothing about the strategies or processes he or she employs in order to answer the questions. And so they cannot be used as a basis for intervention at an individual level. Indeed, Piaget recognised this many years ago, when his dissatisfaction with the methods of one of the founders of the intelligence test, Binet, led him to his early research into the language and thinking of young children.

Of course, there are other criticisms of the IQ test, and much has been said about the social, political and scientific issues involved (Kamin, 1974; N. Rose, 1979; S. Rose, 1978). However, what we wish to emphasise here is that the practice of testing is always carried out with some purpose in mind and so tests cannot be considered to be politically neutral. Furthermore, for the children who are tested, they are frequently mystifying and socially divisive, serving to perpetuate and reproduce inequalities of wealth, power and opportunity. However, simply removing the IQ test will not of itself change the relationship between school and the labour market, nor will it remove the constant demands for assessment.

What we wish to consider here, therefore, is a different conception of 'testing' – one which might provide access for teachers to those processes of understanding that we discussed earlier. This, indeed, was what Piaget had in mind when he devised his well-known experiments of conservation, seriation and so forth. Many teachers now use tests of this kind to assess the level of children's understanding, or as a guage of their 'readiness' to move on to new kinds of work.

However, although there are clearly positive and progressive aspects of Piaget's theory, the experimental methods he uses are in some respects open to the same sort of criticism we have made of IQ tests. That is to say, the model of development they are based on relies overmuch on logico-mathematical reasoning and neglects the way in which children make sense of context. For this reason, tests based on his developmental theory may have a harmful effect when used as a basis for curriculum planning. If there is to be a place in the curriculum for testing, it should be conceived of as a way of systematising the process of observation and diagnosis which is the cornerstone of all well-planned teaching. In this sense, testing should be integrated with all other classroom activities. In particular, tests can be devised by teachers to examine more closely what is going on in a child's mind when a specific error is seen to occur in dealing with a particular task. Below, we list some points which we believe should be borne in mind by anyone who wishes to test children's understanding – for educational or experimental purposes.

(i) No test can provide us with pure, privileged access to mental or social processes. We always have to do interpretive work on data, whether this be gained by observation or by experiment. Obtaining data is a process of production, not of collection. In this process, theory and hypotheses play a crucial role in setting up a framework within which to interpret the data. No test or testing practice is without a theory, but all too often the theory which informs the test is left implicit – indeed it is often assumed that the person administering the test does not need to know the theory. We believe, on the contrary, that theory is a vital tool for the teacher.

This means that any test, to be of value, must possess two features. First, the theory on which it is based must be coherent and explicit. Second, the theory must take account of the strategies and processes that lead to the responses that are observed. There is a still further implication – for the tester rather than the test. The person who is doing the testing is not simply collecting facts, but is using the child's responses to construct an interpretation. Testing itself should be an interactive process, in which the teacher actively tries to match his perception of the child's responses to the hypothesis that he is forming about how the child understands the task.

(ii) The tester must be aware of the importance of context. This point is forcibly made in Donaldson (1978). In interpreting an action or an utterance made by a child, we must always keep in mind the possibility that there is an aspect of the situation to which we are not currently paying attention that is influencing the response. Indeed, we cannot know in advance all the aspects which may come into play, for we cannot know the child's total biography.

(iii) The relationship between the tester and the child is of crucial importance. Adults are very powerful figures and, as we said in chapter 3, power is a crucial dimension of the communicative situation. The adult should not forget that his 'communicative potency' is usually greater than that of the child, and should not equate silence or passive assent with either understanding or failure to understand.

(iv) The approach which we advocate is extremely demanding, because it rests upon the assumption that one is continually learning and relearning to interpret another person's discursive frame for understanding. Such a difficult task cannot be undertaken in isolation, and certainly cannot be mastered just by reading a book or a manual. Cooperation and communication between all those who figure in children's lives is essential: parents, teachers, psychologists, social workers, speech therapists, doctors and all other workers need to pool together their experience and information. Teacher workshops and joint research groups can provide an invaluable aid and stimulus to such cooperative and collective understanding.

In the view which we have been advocating, testing need not be a separate activity from other classroom practices. Vygotsky (1978) gave us some insight into what might constitute a 'science of pedagogy'. He wished to produce a theory of how the development of the child might be integrated with a teaching practice in such a way that children progressively internalised cooperative understanding in order to represent for themselves ways of mastering new domains of learning. He used the concept of the 'zone of proximal development' to index those critical areas of a child's cognitive and communicative development in which what the child could now do with the help of an adult might point to what he would next be able to accomplish alone. The role that this implies for the adult, of supporting and extending the child's meaning, was seen to be a major influence on the early stages of language development. It has been the argument of this chapter that the same sort of role is also required of the teacher, insofar as this is possible, so that the strategies the child has developed for making meaning at home can provide a firm foundation for the sort of learning that will be required of him when he goes to school.

6

A comparison of talk at home and at school

MARGARET MAcLURE and PETER FRENCH

Introduction

In this chapter we shall bring together the two contexts of home and school and attempt some comparison of the types of interaction that are typical of the two settings. In doing so we shall draw extensively on transcripts of actually occurring interaction, as one of our major aims will be to provide a firm grounding for such a comparison in systematically collected empirical data. Such an empirical basis for comparing the language of home and school is long overdue, particularly since, over the last fifteen years or so, a considerable amount of educational, sociological and political energy has been invested in the study of language in relation to social class and educational disadvantage (see chapter 7 for a discussion of these issues). Yet much of this work has exploited claimed differences between home and school language, without any *systematic* examination of naturalistic data from either setting. As a result, certain widely held positions have emerged, whose claims to validity are almost impossible to evaluate, but whose sociological and political effects have nevertheless been considerable.

Advocates of these positions can be very broadly (and with over-simplification) divided into two groups. Firstly there are those who claim that there is a (usually class-based) difference in the form or use of language in the home, such that for some children there arises a 'mismatch' between their prior experience and use of language and the particular linguistic demands of the school, with resultant implications for differential educational success. This position in turn gives rise to two outcomes. If the class-based difference in pre-school language experience is taken to be fixed and irremediable (as some interpretations of Bernstein's early works, for example, would claim), language difference comes to serve as a scapegoat for the perpetuation of class-based inequalities. Harold Rosen (1972), in his critique of Bernstein's early research and the uses to which it has been put, makes the timely observation that language has thus come to replace 'intelligence' as a rationalisation for the continuation of educational and social disadvantage.

If, on the other hand, the claimed language differences are seen as susceptible to change, then optimistic remedial programmes of linguistic 'enrichment' for the disadvantaged are devised and implemented, with the aim of eradicating or reducing systematic educational inequality (cf. Blank's (1973) diagnostic and remedial routines for teachers of 'poorly-functioning' children).

Such **mismatch theories** generally take the interactive context of the school as 'given', and speculate about its fit with the interaction typical of home.

The second (usually sociological) approach, on the other hand, focuses mainly on the language of the school, and the comparison with the home (and other nonschool contexts) remains largely implicit. In contradistinction to some – often vaguely defined – notion of how 'ordinary' interaction works, school talk is identified as having special properties, which are then often characterised as manipulative and oppressive, and related to the regulative function of schools in perpetuating the social status quo.

Despite the differences between these two types of approach, they do have one feature in common, in that they presume some discontinuity between the types of language which occur in the two settings. The second type, which lays emphasis upon classroom-specific forms and uses of language, probably embodies this proposition in its purest form. However, mismatch theories, in maintaining that middle class children undergo a home-based experience of language more closely attuned to the linguistic demands of the school, than is that of their working class counterparts, make a similar assumption. The language of classrooms is still held to be distinct from that found in homes – only *less* distinct from the language of some homes than from that of others. A fundamental aim of this chapter is to subject this claim to scrutiny.

Drawing upon actually occurring examples of parent–child

interaction representing a wide array of social backgrounds we shall address such questions as: How far is it feasible to suggest that infant classroom encounters with language are a new and strange experience to the novice pupil? In which *specific* ways may the language of teachers and pupils be seen as aligned or unaligned with that of parents and their children? At what level do school and home language, irrespective of social background, share properties in common?

Given the educational and political significance of these issues, we must therefore be particularly attentive to two things. The first concerns the nature of what it is that we compare. As Wells points out in chapter 1, language has many facets, and it is essential that we make clear from the outset which 'level' of language use we choose to base our comparison upon and what our reasons are for selecting it. The second point of concern is that each comparison we make between home and school language should be firmly grounded in empirical data which is, within our experience, representative of the two settings. First of all, then, we must consider where to begin to look, in comparing the ways that language is used in the home and school settings.

It is now well established that, by the age of about 5 years, the great majority of children have achieved control of the basic grammar and phonology of their language (Wells, in press a), though it has been argued that there are residual areas which are not mastered until somewhat later (cf. Chomsky, 1969). However, it is clear that by the time they enter school most children are capable of constructing most of the sentence types of their language, of encoding complex semantic relationships and so on. In school, then, they are not going to encounter many unfamiliar syntactic constructions or phonological units, and we can say with some confidence that there is no significant 'transition' involving grammar, phonology or even lexis (though children will of course encounter new vocabulary items at school, they already have quite an extensive vocabulary on which to draw for most of their everyday interactions). Recent thinking tends to the view, therefore, that substantive differences between the home and school contexts, if they occur, are more likely to reside in the nature of the interaction which takes place in each.

It is now a commonplace of the sociolinguistic approach to language that observable features of the language used on any particular occasion will be related to who is doing the talking, for what purposes, by what means etc. (cf. Hymes, 1972). School and home obviously differ on many of these parameters, and it might be expected that the language used in each setting would therefore reflect these differences. However, the identification of context-specific properties of interaction is by no means a simple procedure and, despite the early optimism which predicted that a set of closely specified registers could be isolated for speech in different social contexts (cf. Halliday, Mackintosh & Strevens, 1964), actually occurring interaction has always proved to be more fluid and flexible than the sociolinguistic 'variables' set up to categorise it.

In fact, classroom language intersects with talk in other settings on a whole range of dimensions. Firstly and most obviously, it must be carried out in accordance with the interactional prerequisites for any sort of communication. For example, participants must use general interpretive procedures, such as those identified by Cicourel (1973) – for example, the 'wait and see' principle, a method by which one participant construes the sense of another's utterance by reference to what he says next. However, in addition to these generalised 'ground rules' for interacting, which obtain across all contexts, talk between teachers and pupils is likely to have features in common with talk from other settings and between other sorts of participants. For example, one might expect to find properties of classroom talk which are 'like' features of television discussions, where there are several participants, one of whom has overall responsibility for the direction of the conversation. We might also find shared properties with doctor–patient interviews, where one member 'diagnoses' and advises the other. And significantly, with reference to the specific comparison of home and school, the fact that in both settings the inter-action takes place between adults and children may give rise to yet other significant areas of similarity, as compared with inter-adult talk.

The problems of establishing contrasts between talk from one type of setting and another are complicated further by the fact that there is at present no fully worked-out theory of interaction which specifies exactly which features of conversation are *common to all settings*, and which can guide the search for significant differences. As differences are *presupposed* by the mere fact of attempting a comparison, this means that analysis may start from a predisposition to find them, with the risk of underestimating those interactional features which are found in all, or almost all, settings. Given that interaction is, inescapably, a socially embedded activity, we cannot avoid studying it in particular contexts. What must be avoided, however, is the conceptual error of assuming that, because features X, Y and Z can be identified in instances of, say, classroom talk, it therefore follows that these features are 'properties' of classroom talk, as opposed to other sorts of talk.

In the remainder of this chapter we shall select some dimensions of interaction on which to compare the home and school, basing the comparison on transcripts of tape recorded conversations in each setting. As home talk and school talk cannot be counterpoised as distinct monolithic entities, our aim is not to provide an overall characterisation of 'the language of the home' versus 'the language of the school'. Nor, obviously, could we hope to cover all aspects of conversational organisation in one chapter. In being necessarily selective, therefore, we shall deal in most detail with the organisation of question and answer sequences, as these are central to classroom interaction. The analysis will deal with two broad areas; firstly, we shall look at general conversational structure – the ways in which participants link their utterances together to form extended sequences of interaction. Secondly, we shall consider the ways in which participation in conversation is organised and distributed among participants.

The sequential structuring of conversation

When we come to consider the sequential–structural properties of conversation, it immediately becomes evident that 'home' talk and 'school' talk share many conversational properties. Greetings are exchanged, requests are made and either complied with or refused, information is given and acknowledged, and breakdowns in communication are noted and overcome. Any one of these types of conversational sequence involves characteristic structural patterning (cf. chapter 1) that would repay further investigation across the two settings. However, here we shall concentrate mainly on the ways in which sequences involving questions and answers are handled by the participants in each setting.

Three-part structures

To begin at a very general level, it has often been pointed out by analysts that, in classroom talk, question–answer sequences tend to have a three-part structure[1] (rather than a simple two-part question–answer structure) consisting of:

(i)   (Teacher) question
(ii) (Pupil)   answer
(iii) (Teacher) evaluation

(cf. Mehan, 1978; Sinclair & Coulthard, 1975; Stubbs, 1976) as in the following examples, where there is a sequence of such three-part structures in a discussion about the seasons.[2]

(1) Teacher: And after spring will be —?
    Betty: Summer
    Teacher: Summer
              And after summer will be —?
    Betty: Autumn
    Teacher: Autumn good girl
              So altogether there are —?
    Betty: Four
    Teacher: Four good
                        (Betty, School Recording, 5 years, 7 months)

This question–answer structure is also commonly found in the home data, as in the following:

(2) Father: What's that?
    Jonathan: 'abbit
    Father: A rabbit that's right
                        (Jonathan, 1 year, 9 months)

Moreover, just as in the classroom, it is not uncommon to find extended stretches of conversation in the home data given over to these structures, where the adult asks a question, assesses the child's reply, then instigates another question:

[1] See chapter 1 for a different structural analysis of such sequences. We are not concerned here with a detailed formal analysis, and use the term 'three-part' simply for convenience.
[2] This structure is not tied to questioning sequences, but is also displayed with teacher-initiated directives: e.g.

Teacher: Put your book away now
   Child: (does so)
Teacher: Good girl

(3)   [Mother and Samantha are
                                looking at a picture book]

Mother: What's that?
Samantha: Boat
Mother: A boat yes
           What's that?
Samantha: Spider
Mother: A spider
           What's that?
Samantha: Rabbit
Mother: Yeh
           What's that?
Samantha: Birdie
Mother: Birdie

                                        (Samantha, 2 years)

It can reasonably be claimed, therefore, that the three-part question structure is one with which most children are familiar before starting school.

'Pseudo-questions'

An associated feature of questions and answers in the classroom, which many analysts have identified, is that they are typically 'pseudo-questions' (Barnes, 1969), where the questioner is not asking for information unknown to her at that time, but for a display (cf. Labov & Fanshel, 1977), by the addressee, of knowledge already available to the questioner. Much sociological significance has been attached to the fact that teachers 'set up' and monitor children's contributions by means (amongst others) of the three-part structure and pseudo-question strategy. It has been argued that this is a major method by which the socialising function of the school is achieved, since children's knowledge and experience are defined as relevant and valid only within the teacher's frame of reference (cf. Edwards & Furlong, 1978; Hammersley, 1977; and many others). The point that we would wish to make here is that, in any event, these conversational strategies are also very common in adult–child talk in the preschool years. Pseudo-questions also occur, for example, in (2) and (3) above. As far as discontinuities between the two settings are concerned, then, it seems that most children are already acquainted with the pseudo-questioning three-part structure by the time they get to school. Additional evidence for this comes from the fact that new pupils seldom seem to misinterpret teacher's pseudo-questions as 'genuine' requests for information. In fact the following example is the only clear instance we have identified of this happening:

(4)   [Teacher and group are looking at
                                       slides]

Teacher:	What can you see?
Rosie:	And they're going in the sand
Teacher:	Mm?
Rosie:	You have a look
Teacher:	Well you have a look and tell me
	I've seen it already
	I want to see if you can see
	(Rosie, School Recording, 5 years, 2 months)

Interestingly, when the child above misinterprets the teacher's first question, the teacher makes quite explicit the grounds on which it was asked.

In describing the typical structure of three-part question–answer sequences in the classroom we have oversimplified somewhat. There are instances where the evaluative element by the teacher is only interpretable implicitly from what follows, and, depending on its sequential environment, it will be heard as either positive or negative evaluation. However, without going into the details of these alternative mechanisms, it seems to be the case that they are also displayed in the home data.

Differences in question sequences between home and school

Despite the similarities we have outlined, there are some differences between the home and school data. Firstly, the proportion of pseudo-questions is much higher in the school data. Though teachers do ask children questions to which they do not know the answer themselves, this tends to occur in a restricted range of settings. Firstly, they occur in management phases of the day's activities (cf. Edwards & Furlong, 1978), where teachers are checking on whether certain procedural matters have been accomplished (e.g. 'Have you had your milk yet?'). Secondly (see p. 235 below), they are used for turn-allocation purposes where the teacher establishes candidate answerers for a next question, for example:

(5)[3] Teacher: When I woke up this morning –
   →   Who looked out of the window when they woke up this morning?

                                      [Children raise hands]

    Teacher: Only – only 1 2 3 oh 4 of you
              Now who can tell me what they saw out of the window this morning?
              Jackie (v)?

              (Jackie, School Recording, 5 years, 3 months)

Thirdly, as (5) also illustrates, they are used to set up 'topics' for such activities as copy-writing, 'news-time' or discussion, where children are asked about some event or activity which happened outside school, as a basis for further activities.

A second difference between question–answer sequences in the home and at school concerns who does the questioning. As many analysts have pointed out (cf. Barnes, 1969; Flanders, 1970), not only do teachers do by far the largest part of the talking in class, they also ask most of the questions. Questions from pupils are much less frequent and usually concern procedural matters (e.g. 'Do I need my word book?', etc.). By contrast, child-initiated questions are much more frequent in the home. In some instances they have the three-part structure outlined above:

(6)   [Mother and child are watching TV]

    Samantha: Mummy (v) what's those?
    Mother: Clapperboard
    Samantha: Clapperboard

              (Samantha, 2 years, 6 months)

One difference between child-initiated and adult-initiated question sequences is that the third part is not heard as evaluative, but rather as some sort of acknowledgment, or even in the early stages as a 'mimic', of the adult's utterance. Such child repetitions of adults' utterances are extremely common in the data, especially between ages 2 and 3 years.

---

[3] In this and subsequent examples, → indicates an instance of the point at issue.

Children's strategies for answering questions

So far we have looked in general terms at the structure of
question–answer sequences in the two settings, and identified a
broad similarity in their properties. Turning now more specifically to
children's answers and the means by which these are produced, we
again find some continuity across the 'transition' from home to
school. In a previous study of infant pupils' strategies for answering
teachers' questions (MacLure & French, 1980), we found that a
central group of strategies involved the use by children of abstract,
a-contextual categorisation operations performed on some element
in the original question. For example, we noted that a possible
answering strategy was to identify some item presented in the
teacher's question as a superordinate term for a class of items, and to
select answers in terms of their membership of that class. This can be
seen in (7) and (8):

(7)   [Teacher holds up book with
                                 picture of a squirrel on front
                                 cover]
  Teacher: What is the squirrel looking for?
  Children: Nuts
  Teacher: Paul (v) what sort of nuts?
→ Paul: Acorns
→ Children: Acorns
  Teacher: Yes
              Any other nuts Karen (v)?
→ Karen: Coconuts
  Teacher: Not coconuts no
→ Child: Hazelnuts

(8)   [Same lesson]
  Teacher: Here's some birds you don't see very often
                        [Holding up picture of pheasants]
              Can anybody tell me what they're called?
  Child 1:   Parrots
  Child 2:   Parrots
  Child 3:   Parrots
  Teacher: No they're not parrots
  Child 4:   [kətʊz]
  Teacher: Cockatoo <u>no</u>

Child 4:	<u>Peacocks</u>
Child 3:	Peacocks
Teacher:	Pheasants

(from MacLure & French, 1980)

In (7) children seem to be selecting from the general class 'nuts' and in (8) from the class 'birds you don't see very often', in each case ignoring the topically defined elements – for example in (7), nuts *which squirrels eat*. Nevertheless, children using this strategy may produce what are heard as right answers. For instance, those whose selection of a class member of the set 'nuts' also happens to fall within the topically defined sub-set 'which squirrels eat' will be seen to have produced a correct answer to the question in (7). So 'right' answers such as 'acorns' in (7) above *may* in some instances be the outcome of this generalised a-contextual method, and not the result of the pupil having taken on his teacher's framework of relevance.

Turning now to the home data, there is evidence that preschool children operate this same abstract categorisation procedure to come up with answers. In (9), for example, the child's answers seem to be drawn from the general set of colour terms.

(9)   [William is about to begin drawing]

Mother:	Are you doing the elephant or not?
William:	Yes I'm doing a elephant
Mother:	What colour?
William:	Red
Mother:	You don't do elephants red
William:	No it's blue
Mother:	You don't do elephants blue either
William:	No it's purple
Mother:	What?
William:	It is purple
Mother:	No it's not purple
William:	It's white then
Mother:	It's not
	Shall I tell you which colour?
William:	What is it?
Mother:	Grey

William: And colour?
Mother: What?
William: Grey and colour
           . .
           Grey and colour

                          (William, 2 years, 6 months)

In addition to the categorisation strategies, we also found other strategies which depended on group participation to provide a pool of previous answers from which to generate new answers. These, predictably, are seldom found in the home data, as the number of participants involved is almost always much smaller.

At least in their earliest years at school, then, children can and do use this categorisation strategy for generating answers: a strategy which they have already used in similar interactive situations at home. Although this type was only one from a larger set of strategies identified (MacLure & French, 1980), all had one element in common: they represent a mode of reasoning which teachers (and probably most parents too) would not wish to encourage. The interchange of speech between teachers and pupils involved in class discussions, however, is perhaps necessarily busy and rapid: prolonged exchanges between the teacher and any one pupil would surely result in losing the attention of the many. We shall return to this issue later in the chapter, but at this point we shall simply say that we see little opportunity for teachers to probe deeply into the modes of reasoning pupils are using to generate their answers in the context of multi-party discourse. Because of this, the surface forms of children's answers are often taken to reflect competencies or knowledge they may not yet have acquired.

To sum up so far, then, it would seem that, by the time they enter the infant school, most children will be familiar, to some degree, with both the 'pseudo-questioning' techniques and the conversational formats routinely associated with this type of questioning. Further, it is possible that they will also be equipped with a set of 'unofficial' resources for answering their teachers' questions when faced with the realisation 'I don't really know.' It would seem, therefore, that there is no very fundamental discontinuity with regard to questioning and answering between the language of the home and that of the school.

Corrections

Quite obviously, however, not all questions posed to children – or anyone else for that matter – receive an immediate answer which is satisfactory to the questioner. Sometimes the recipient of the question either provides an answer which is not acceptable to the questioner, or fails to give an answer at all. Following an unacceptable answer, a correction may be attempted, and we shall now turn to the ways in which correction is handled in the home and school data. Given the pedagogic purpose underlying much school talk, the ways in which teachers attempt to elicit correct answers from pupils is of immediate interest to educationalists, and it is important for comparative purposes to see how their methods for doing so compare with those in other contexts. As we shall show, it again proves impossible to identify school-specific conversational methods, as there is substantial overlap in the ways in which corrections are handled in each setting.

Before starting to look at the various ways in which corrections can be handled, however, we should point out that correction need not, of course, be done at all: questioners may opt *not* to correct, but to 'let it pass'. And while a great deal of correction does take place in classrooms, it is not uncommon to find teachers passing over errors, particularly in those instances where two or more chldren are giving different answers, one of which is the 'correct' one. In these cases, teachers often respond to and endorse the correct answer and ignore the incorrect one(s), as in (10):

(10)   [Teacher and class are talking
                                   about apples]

Teacher:	What colour are the pips?
Child 1:	<u>Brown</u>
Child 2	<u>Black</u>
Child 1:	<u>Brown</u>
Child 2:	<u>Brown</u>
Teacher:	Yes they're dark brown that's right
	(Betty, School Recording, 5 years, 2 months)

When corrections *are* instigated, it has been noted (cf. Schegloff, Jefferson & Sacks, 1977) that there are two broad alternative formats for correcting. The first is for the *recipient* of the utterance which is identified as incorrect (i.e. the questioner) to supply the correct answer for the other person (usually termed **other correction**) as in (11):

(11)   [Teacher is pointing to words as
                                           Rosie reads]

  Rosie: I . am . tall . said the . . tower
  Teacher: Chimney
  Rosie: Chimney
                         (Rosie, School Recording, 5 years, 7 months)

The second is for the recipient of the utterance to withhold the correction but to invite the speaker to **self-correct**, for example:

(12)   [Teacher and class are talking
                                           about seasons]

  Teacher: Now when winter is over a new season will start
                  Do you know the name of that season?
  Betty: January
  Teacher: No that's the name of the month
                  What season will it be?
                  After winter will be s——?
  Betty: Spring
  Teacher: Good girl springtime
                         (Betty, School Recording, 5 years, 7 months)

As Schegloff et al. (1977) and Drew (in press) have pointed out, sequences involving self-corrections and those involving other-corrections are not equivalent structures: they differ in their turn design, in their sequential implications and in their preceding sequential environment. Conversational analysts describe this non-equivalence as a **preference organisation**, where other-correction is a **dispreferred** activity. Its dispreferred status is argued on the grounds that corrections are not done by recipients of 'erroneous utterances' at the first possible opportunity – i.e. interruptively, at the point where the error occurs nor, often, at the first possible indication that the first speaker's utterance is complete; invitations to *self*-correct being offered instead. Furthermore, where other-corrections *are* done, they are designed in such a way as to display their dispreferred status: for example, they may be presented as (partial) acceptances (e.g. 'Yes, but . . .'), or they may be softened in their force. We shall present examples of most of these correction formats below.

When we come to compare the organisation of correction sequences in the home and school settings, a first point to note is that other-corrections are relatively infrequent in the school data. There may be special reasons, over and above their generally dispreferred status, why this is so. As we have argued elsewhere (French & MacLure, 1979), the requirements for pupils to provide correct answers with minimal aid or input from the teacher is at a premium in present-day classroom interaction, since this is one way in which – in the absence of more formal assessment procedures – teachers can monitor children's progress and their own teaching effectiveness. Other-corrections, therefore, tend to be done subsequent to (unsuccessful) invitations to *self*-correct, such as the successive reformulations of the original question in (13):

(13)   [Teacher and class recalling story 'Elmer the Patchwork Elephant'. They have reached the point where the other elephants said 'Good Morning Elephant' to Elmer, in contrast to the beginning of the story where they said 'Good Morning Elmer']

Teacher: What did they say that was different?

Child: The – um – he wasn't patched any more

→ Teacher: Yes but what did they . the . the other animals say to him that was different?

            . .

→   They said 'Good Morning Elephant' didn't they?
              (Stella, School Recording, 5 years, 2 months)

It looks, then, as if other-corrections are tied to diagnoses by teachers that pupils do not have the resources to accomplish self-correction.

When we look at the home data, we find first of all that other-corrections by parents in the turn immediately following the error are more common, for example:

(14)   [Mother and Samantha are looking at pictures in book]

Mother: What's that?

Samantha: Lorry
→ Mother: It's a tiger

(Samantha, 2 years)

(15)   [Adult and Thomas are playing
with plastic letters]
Adult: What's that Thomas (v)?
Thomas: What's that that's [ə] letter Tom [='T for Tom']
→ Adult: That's letter F
Thomas: That's letter F

(Thomas, 2 years, 1 month)

(16) Mother: What does that look like?
Jonathan: A eight
Mother: It looks like a square doesn't it?
Jonathan: Square

(Jonathan, 1 year, 9 months)

In these home examples, as in example (11) from the school data,
other-corrections are done in the turn immediately following the
error. However, as in the school data, we also find other-corrections
being withheld until invitations to self-correct have proved unsuccessful, as in the following (cf. example (13) above from the school
data):

(17) Mother: Where did you go today Tommy (v)?
. .
Where did you go this morning?
Thomas: What – what?
Mother: Where did you go this morning?
Thomas: What?
Mother: You went to nursery
Thomas: Yeah!

(Thomas B., 2 years, 7 months)

Other-corrections can be done – as in (11), (14), (15) and (16) above
– by an immediate citing of the correct item (with or without an
appended tag (cf. (16)) whose interactional significance may be to
mitigate in some sense the force of the correction). Alternatively,
they may be preceded by an explicit rejection of the incorrect item:

(18) Mother: Who did we see for dinner Thomas (v)?
    Thomas: Joanne
→ Mother: No we saw Joanne this morning
             We saw Daddy.

                               (Thomas, 2 years, 1 month)

It seems, therefore, that the various formats for corrections are habitually displayed in both the home and school settings.

However, we can identify some differences associated with corrections in the two settings which do not lie in their sequential–structural features, but in who instigates the correction. Pupils' corrections of teachers are extremely uncommon, but we do find children correcting *parents'* utterances in the home data:

(19) Mark: Where man gone?
    Mother: In his house
    Mark: Uh?
    Mother: Into his house
→ Mark: No, no, gone shop Mummy (v)

                                 (Mark, 2 years, 1 month)

In other words, as we also find with reference to the three-part question–answer–evaluation structure, there is an **asymmetry** in the school data in terms of participants' rights to initiate the sequence, these generally being the prerogative of the teacher alone; the home data, on the other hand, indicate a greater symmetry of participation with regard to correction. Additionally, we again find differences in the frequencies with which the particular structures occur across the two settings.

Despite these differences, however, it is still the case that the various methods of instigating corrections occur across the two settings. We cannot investigate in detail here the interactional significance which may attach to the selection of one correction format rather than another. Drew (in press), however, suggests that particular forms of correction may be associated with 'instructional' talk: for example, both correction of the child's error in the turn immediately following the turn in which the error was made, and outright rejection of the error seem to occur more frequently in the context of 'instructional' talk. Having compared some home and school data on correction, he makes the general point which we emphasise throughout:

'Such sequences [i.e. of 'instructional' talk] occur in both the school and the home data, so that it is not that one should investigate the talk as though it were setting-specific, but we should begin to ask whether there are systematic features of the sequences in which adults instruct children, wherever.'

Again, then, we would suggest that, with the qualifications set out above, there is a strong continuity between home and school inter-action in terms of the ways in which correction activities are managed. This continuity directs us once more to question the premises of theor-ists who either conceptualise the home–school transition as interaction-ally problematic for children in some degree, or who characterise the school in terms of a set of context-specific conversational practices.

Question prefaces

So far we have been looking at some general conversational struc-tures and strategies associated with question–answer sequences, and the ways in which 'breakdowns' in these sequences – through chil-dren's inability to provide acceptable answers – are repaired by means of different types of corrections. Through correction, the eventually successful outcome of the question–answer sequence (i.e. the 'correct' answer) is achieved *post hoc* – that is, *after* some-thing has 'gone wrong'. But there are other ways in which speakers can attempt to set up interactions so as to increase the likelihood of a successful outcome, for example by taking prefatory measures before the particular question is asked. It seems clear that teachers quite frequently do this to avoid having to engage in repairs follow-ing a breakdown in interactions with their pupils. As McHoul (1978: 201) suggests, 'having someone without an answer (not wishing to answer) forced into providing one may be a lengthy and complex business involving . . . rephrasing and repeats'. Teachers use a number of prefatory strategies for this purpose but each works by directing the pupil towards the area of experience which he will be required to draw on in order to answer the question successfully, as in the following examples:

(20)   [Teacher and pupils are doing number work with coloured shapes]

→ Teacher: Let's look at the last one Daniel (v)

Now look at Rachel's
What colour has she got in her set?
(Joan, School Recording, 5 years, 2 months)

(21)   [Teacher and children are looking
                              at photographic slides of India]
→ Teacher: Can you see the Indian Ladies?
             What are they wearing?
(Rosie, School Recording, 5 years, 2 months)

(22)   [Teacher is directing attention to a
                              wall-chart]
→ Teacher: Now look at the wall
             See there's the hungry caterpillar
             And what does it turn into?
(Elspeth, School Recording, 5 years, 2 months)

In each of these examples the questions require the pupils to give an interpretation of some feature of the immediate physical environment. In cases like these, the prefatory utterances are usually of a type which does not require any verbal response from the pupils – in other words they occur *directly before* the question itself. Further, the only implications which they appear to carry for the recipients are ones of perceptual action, by drawing on a highly restricted set of verbs of perception ('look', 'see', etc.).

A second set of question prefaces, on the other hand, explicitly requires pupils to provide a verbal response before the question itself is posed. These tend to be used when teachers' questions, rather than requiring children to draw on features of the immediate environment, require reference to more general experience, or prior school learning, as in (23)–(25):

(23)
Teacher: Now you remember yesterday afternoon when we
               went to the puppet theatre
           Do you remember?
Child: Yes
Teacher: I wonder if you can remember the name of the story
           Who can remember the name of the story
           Those two children we saw
(Benjamin, School Recording, 5 years, 4 months)

(24)   [Teacher asking about a character
                              in a story just read]

⌐ Teacher: Was he pleased to take the shoes?
| Children: Yes
            No
  Teacher: Why not?
                              (Penny, School Recording, 4 years, 10 months)

(25)   [Teacher asking about a room in
                              the castle the class had visited]

⌐ Teacher: Did you have a look inside Stella (v)?
| Child: Yes
  Teacher: What did you see?
                              (Stella, School Recording, 4 years, 10 months)

In this set of examples two question–answer exchanges occur in sequence. The second question, in each case, depends upon the first gaining a specific outcome. In (25), for example, the teacher's second question, 'What did you see?' presupposes that Stella has in fact looked inside the room – something which has been established via the first question. These examples are similar to those in the first set in that the prefatory strategies focus for the pupil the experience which he will have to mobilise to answer the subsequent question successfully, but they also serve as a *check* for the teacher. As the prefatory utterance is in question form and therefore requires a response, that response indicates to the teacher whether or not the pupil has achieved the focus the subsequent question will require, and hence also whether it is likely to be answered successfully. Additionally, from the pupil's point of view, answering the first question sets up a certain *commitment* to answer the second. In (25), for example, having indicated by her 'yes' response that she has seen inside the room, Stella may reasonably be expected to answer the teacher's subsequent question.

Again, however, these prefatory strategies do not discriminate school talk from talk in other settings in any clear-cut way. Indeed, the second type of prefatory structure, in seeking commitment from recipients, closely resembles the **pre-sequences** identified by Sacks (1968) in inter-adult conversations. These occur sequentially prior to a variety of conversational activities in addition to questions and, like examples (23)–(25), entail the use of the prefatory question–

answer format. The following (from Sacks, 1968) shows a **pre-invitation**:

Jack: Say what're you doing?
Judy: Well, we're going out. Why?
Jack: Oh! I was just gonna say come out an' come over here and talk to the people. But if you're going out you can't very well do that.

Thus there are close parallels between the sorts of question prefaces found in teacher–pupil talk and those found in wider conversational contexts. And though pre-sequencing is far less common in the pre-school data, there does seem to be some continuity across the two settings, as we can see from the following home examples:

(26) Mother: Do you want me to carry you down? [i.e. the stairs]
     Samantha: Carry me down
     Mother: All right then come on
                                    (Samantha, 2 years, 6 months)
(27) Mother: You're not going to read your book?
     Simon: No
     Mother: What you carrying it about for?
                                    (Simon, 4 years)
(28) Mother: Have you finished with this Fanny love (v)?
     Fanny: Yes
     Mother: Well put it back then
                                    (Fanny, 4 years, 6 months)

In these examples the parent's final question or directive can be heard, as in the classroom examples, as strongly dependent on the child's having given a particular answer to the preceding question.

One possible reason for the comparatively low frequency of such prefatory sequences in the talk between parents and children might lie in the fact that mothers, compared to teachers, already have considerable access to their children's stock of experiences and do not, therefore, have to engage in measures designed to learn about those experiences. A second reason may be related to an additional purpose such sequences have in classroom talk. In addition to directing pupils' attention to relevant material on which to draw in order to answer, and checking that this has been achieved, these sequences can also be used to accomplish orderly, nonproblematic transitions from one speaker to the next, by identifying candidate answerers from amongst the class as a whole, for example:

(29) Teacher: What about a face
                Did any of you give your snowman a face?
     Children: Yes
     Teacher: Jackie (v) what did you use?
     Jackie: (some) buttons
                        (Betty, School Recording, 5 years, 7 months)

In this example the teacher's prefatory question operates in a similar way to those discussed above, in that it secures agreement on some point on which the second question depends. Here, however, the prefatory question is addressed to the class as a whole, while in the previous examples the teacher had already singled out one pupil to answer both questions. This last type of prefatory question, then, serves the additional function of establishing a 'pool' of potential respondents for the next question, thereby diminishing the risk of selecting pupils who are unable or unwilling to answer. We shall deal in more detail with this last type of question preface in the final section, when we come to look at the ways in which participation is organised in the classroom.

As far as pre-sequencing is concerned, then, we again find that there is no absolute distinction between home and school: similar question-prefatory structures are found in both settings. However, as with the three-part structures and correction sequences examined above, we do find distributional differences, and in the case of pre-sequencing they are fairly marked. This seems to be partly explicable in terms of the wider range of interactional purposes which pre-sequencing serves in school.

General comments on conversational structure at home and at school

Most of what we have had to say about conversational structure has, for reasons of scope and space, been restricted to an examination of how sequences involving questions and answers are handled in the home and school settings. But such sequences of course comprise only a tiny part of the complex structuring of interaction, and their analysis presents only one small fragment of a total picture which no one, as yet, has been able to complete.

The most that can be made of such a partial description, from the point of view of a comparison of interaction in the two settings, therefore, is to draw some tentative conclusions, pending further investigation. And also, as we suggested right at the outset, to provide at least some empirical corrective in specific instances to the speculation which has surrounded putative 'mismatches' between home and school language.

Firstly, just as previous work has demonstrated with reference to syntax and phonology, children most certainly do *not* enter a culture of unfamiliar interactional routines when they enter school. They have already encountered and participated in the majority of se-quence types they are likely to be expected to share in at school. This holds not only for the specific structures we have looked at – ques-tions and answers, corrections, pre-sequences – but for a wide range of interactional activities. In fact, as far as conversational *structure* is concerned (as opposed to the organisation of participation, which we shall examine below), the school setting may, if anything, present children with a *more limited* set of conversational options than they have become familiar with at home. This is most noticeable in the asymmetries we have observed above in the distribution of rights to initiate sequences. For instance, although similar structures for ques-tioning and correcting were found in both settings, child-initiated instances with teachers were seldom found in the school data. Other, more general, asymmetries can also be identified. Just as the child at home has more latitude to ask questions and evaluate and correct his adult interlocutor, so also he has more opportunity to introduce new topics and to attempt to change the topic of conversation. Such opportunities are much less frequently available to children in school – firstly, because much of the talk is done for pedagogic purposes, and therefore topical development remains largely the prerogative of the teacher and, secondly, because of the com-plexities involved in handling conversations involving large numbers of participants.

Furthermore, although we found a general overlap in the sequence types occurring in both types of interaction, there are some general indications that these may have a different interactional significance in each setting. For instance, as we noted in the discussion of pre-sequences above, although the structure comprising two linked question–answer exchanges, i.e.:

$$\left[\begin{array}{l} \left[\begin{array}{l} Q \\ A \end{array} \right. \\ \left[\begin{array}{l} Q \\ A \end{array} \right. \end{array} \right.$$

is found in both settings, in school talk it may carry additional interactional purposes, such as *facilitating* answer-production, *checking* on potential contributors and soliciting *commitments* to answer. Such additional dimensions are traceable to particular priorities in classroom interaction which do not hold for home talk: firstly, its general pedagogic purpose and, secondly, the problems of handling large groups of participants – a facet of classroom interaction which we shall now consider in more detail, as this is one dimension of conversation on which school and home can be clearly distinguished.

The organisation of participation and turn-taking

Although there is considerable overlap in the types of conversational structures found in the home and school, there is one obvious difference between the two interactional settings – namely the number of participants who habitually engage in conversation. In many infant schools it is not unusual to find the teacher addressing a class of thirty or more pupils, while in the home, of course, such large groupings rarely occur. The maintenance of conversational order (the allocation of turns at talk, the avoidance of overparticipation, etc.) therefore, presents particular problems in classrooms, and these are reflected in specific properties of classroom talk which distinguish it quite clearly from talk at home.

Nevertheless, the participant structures found in each setting are not totally distinct. Conversations involving much smaller groupings of participants also take place in the classroom, ranging from one-to-one talk between teacher and pupil, to groups of three, four, five and upwards; on the other hand, children also engage in multi-party talk in the home, with siblings, both parents, other relatives, friends and neighbours, in different permutations.

However, we shall focus here mainly on those occasions in the classroom where the teacher and class or large group are jointly engaged in one single conversation, rather than in overlapping conversations between individuals. The activities which take place on these occasions are of course varied, ranging from such practical matters as taking the register or dinner money, to those which we might describe as pedagogically or educationally oriented: 'news time', 'story time', 'having a discussion', etc. We shall deal mainly with the latter, particularly teacher–class discussions, looking quite closely at such matters as how they come to proceed as orderly events. In doing so we shall place some emphasis on how the teacher 'manages' the conversation. However, this is not to relegate the pupil to a purely passive role for, as we shall see, these discussions can only be accomplished through collaborative action – through pupils' displays of willingness to participate in situationally appropriate ways. Thus, although the teacher may take responsibility for opening and closing discussions, for introducing and ending topics and for allocating turns of talk to particular pupils, it is only by virtue of teachers and pupils acting in collaboration that infant classroom discussions take on their orderly and largely unproblematic character.

One obvious requirement for teachers is the securing and maintenance of the attention of their pupils, not just from an 'educative' point of view, but for the more practical reason that it diminishes the possibility of more than one conversation happening at a time. As Sacks, Schegloff & Jefferson point out, gatherings of more than three parties run the risk of the 'schism of one conversation into more than one conversation' (1978: 23). With thirty or so children participating, conversational schism is an ever-present possibility, which would impede the progress of the lesson. Joint attention to the topic of the lesson is therefore a basic requirement.

On occasion we find teachers explicitly making an issue of a pupil's inattention by asking some questions to monitor his engagement, but this is not very common in our infant classroom recordings. Rather, it seems that infant teachers have strategies for securing and maintaining attention which forestall the need to remedy *in*attention. One way of doing this is by addressing the class as a collectivity or **cohort** (cf. Payne & Hustler, 1980). By setting up the situation as 'one against many' through speaking to the class as *a whole*, the teacher requires the pupils to act collectively as *one party* to the interaction.

This, however, would be unlikely in itself to sustain the interest of pupils for any length of time, and in fact might have the reverse effect. For the longer the time spent by the teacher in addressing the class, the higher the chances of individual pupils' attention beginning to wander. It is important, therefore, for teachers also to engage the pupils individually as contributors to the official talk of the lesson. One very effective way of doing this is through the asking of a series of questions addressed to individual pupils in the manner described on p. 226 above. To answer a question successfully demands attention both to the question itself and to the prior talk on which the question might depend for its sense. Thus, because the teacher may exercise prerogative over whom she calls upon to answer her questions, it is necessary for all pupils to attend to the official proceedings of the lesson. As McHoul (1978: 201) suggests, by having the 'burden of "discovering" knowledge distributed among those assembled . . . any party present will have to attend to the lesson's ongoing course in order to be able to answer any question put his/her way'. In these ways, then, the requirement for joint attention in class discussion teaching is secured by features internal to its design.

Such problems of establishing joint attention seldom arise in the home, firstly and most obviously because of the smaller participant groupings usually engaged in talk, and secondly because, in any case, it is often not an overriding requirement that all present should attend to a *single* topic. Additionally, collaboration on topics among more than two participants most frequently involves one child and two or more adults, and the establishing of attention is not at issue.

Returning to classroom discussions, it is clear that the mechanisms for establishing attention cannot in themselves entirely provide for the orderly nature of the conversations, for in addition to possible under-attention, there is also the possibility of overparticipation. As Hammersely (1974) has put it:

'From the point of view of the teachers, the classroom encounter as an interaction system, focussed on and co-ordinated from the front, can just as easily disintegrate as a result of "over-participation" as it can by escalating inattention.' (1974: 356)

Because of this possibility, then, teachers may, on occasion, make an issue of overparticipation, and take steps to reorient pupils to what Sacks et al. (1978) have termed the 'one speaker at a time rule':

(30) Teacher: Can anyone tell me what comes after February?
    Child 1: March
    Teacher: Again
    Child 1: March
    Teacher: Good girl that's right
    Child 1: My Daddy in March
    Child 2: It's my birthday ⟨in March⟩
    Teacher: Some of you have birthdays in March yes
    Child 1: My-my-my Daddy's birthday in March
          on a sa-Sunday
                     [Several voices calling out]
    Teacher: Is it? Good
→   Don't call out Paul (v) there's a good boy
          (Betty, School Recording, 5 years, 2 months)

(31) Teacher: Claire (v) why weren't we here . . ?
          Why didn't we come to school yesterday?
    Claire: ⟨****⟩   [Some children with hands up,
                           others calling out]
→ Teacher: Sh sh sh don't call out please
          (Betty, School Recording, 5 years, 7 months)

Again, however, we would stress that although instances such as (30) and (31), where the teacher temporarily digresses from the immediate business of the lesson in order to reinstate an orderly system for turn-taking among pupils, are not uncommon in our recordings, they do not constitute a *primary* basis upon which interactional order is established. Indeed, in many of the teacher–class discussions we have observed, there are no examples of the teacher acting in this way at all; yet, despite the potential for disorder inherent in thirty-party conversation, it still happens that the discussion proceeds in an orderly fashion without, by and large, too much simultaneous or overlapping talk. In order to understand how this is achieved, we must first consider the usual procedures which hold for turn-taking in casual conversation involving small groups of participants, and then the way in which multi-party classroom conversation is organised to avoid the problems which such procedures would create.

There are potentially two ways in which a speaker may gain the 'floor' from another: (a) he may be selected as next speaker by the current one (e.g. by having a question directed specifically to him), or (b), if the current speaker has not selected a specific next speaker, it is open to any participant to **self-select** (Sacks et al. 1978). Obviously, with thirty possible contributors, such a system could result in chaos. Firstly, if pupils were continually to select option (a) – i.e. to select at will a next speaker – it might be a long time before the teacher achieved a turn, and discussion would stray a long way from her projected lesson. Secondly, if under option (b) anyone could begin to speak on completion of the last speaker's turn, then many speakers would frequently attempt to talk simultaneously.

To forestall such situations, classroom discussions are organised on rather different lines. Far from consisting of a random ordering of speakers (as in desultory conversation), most transcripts of teacher–class discussions tend towards the pattern TPTPTP . . . , where a turn from one or another pupil is followed by one from the teacher. Rights to select next speaker and self-select as next speaker are almost exclusively the teacher's, and when a pupil speaks, it is usually in answer to the teacher (Edwards, in press; McHoul, 1978). Because all participants collaboratively endorse these asymmetrical rights for turn-taking, teachers retain responsibility, as mentioned in the preceding section, firstly for deciding which topics shall be discussed (hence also for regulating learning) and secondly for arranging nonproblematic transitions from one speaker to the next.

We can see more concretely how this works by looking at some data incorporating the question–answer–evaluation sequences described in the preceding section:

(32) Teacher: Sarah Davis (v) can you tell me another word
                      starting with 'S'?
     Sarah D.:   Spoon
     Teacher: Spoon good girl
                      And the other Sarah (v) you tell me another
     Sarah V.:   Sock
     Teacher: Sock good girl
                      Betty (v) can you tell me another?
     Betty: Sailor

Teacher: A sailor good girl
          That's a very good word
                    (Betty, School Recording, 5 years, 7 months)

By prefacing her questions with address terms which nominate specific children, the teacher forestalls the potential problems of simultaneous turns. Also, in each instance, the pupil's turn at talk consists *only* of an answer. Rather than, say, posing a question back to the teacher or another pupil, or elaborating, or introducing a new topic, etc., pupils' turns are characteristically complete on the completion of the answer itself. We can also see from these data that self-selection by other pupils following the answer does not occur: the teacher speaks next, providing both an evaluation of the preceding answer and then another question. She thus bypasses the problems which would arise if all speakers had equal rights to self-select and to select next speaker.

When we consider the home data, we find a more equitable distribution of rights among speakers. This can be seen in the following, not atypical, example:

(33)   [Mother and Jonathan are doing
                              housework together]

Mother: I think it's a bit smeary
Jonathan: Why do you think it's a bit smeary?
Mother: Because you put far too much polish on
           . .
           Right now you can put the things back on there and
           I'll put the carpet sweeper over the room
           . .
Jonathan: Well why can't I put the carpet sweeper over the
           room?
Mother: Because that is my job O.K.?
Jonathan: What is my job?
Mother: You've done your job you've polished your
           furniture
           In a minute I'm going in my bedroom and you can
           polish my furniture if you like.
Jonathan: Yes
           . . .

Don't need that

. .

We need that on there don't we?

. . . .

We need – don't we?

Mother: Now that one goes over there doesn't it?

. .

Jonathan: We need the Mister man here don't we?

. .

This we must draw   this I –

I don't know the name of that one so I –

Mother: It's our onion isn't it?

Jonathan: So it must be –   I don't know the name

It must be Mister Wooden the name must be

Mother: Oh all right

                                    (Jonathan, 3 years, 6 months)

If we compare this example with the school conversations we can note several differences: the asymmetry of participant rights to initiate question–answer sequences is not in play, as the child contributes both questions and answers; in these question–answer sequences the three-part structure is not displayed, and therefore the child's contributions are not inevitably framed by an adult utterance immediately before and after his turn; the child's turns at talk are not tied to a minimal length; and the utterance types in general are more varied than the question-answer types and variants of these which occur most frequently in the class discussions.

Turning again to the school data, in example (32) we pointed out that one of the ways in which the teacher avoids overlap in selecting next speaker is by nomination (although a variety of other means – e.g. pointing and nodding are also used). There are, however, other methods, where potential answerers are not just selected at random. Rather, the teacher uses a set of strategies designed to establish a *pool* of potential contributors before posing a question. One of these strategies was exemplified in (29), where a prefatory question was addressed to the class as a whole, soliciting a response from more than one pupil. Additional examples of such question prefaces occur in the following:

(34) Teacher: . . . they took a long time to grow and they're just
                now beginning to peep through the soil
           ⎡   Do they look as pretty as those?
           │ Child 1: But they're –
           │ Children: No   [Many voices including Child 2]
           ⎣ Teacher: Why not?
              Child 2: They haven't come up very well yet
                          (Betty, School Recording, 5 years, 7 months)
(35) Teacher: Well yesterday was Tuesday but of course we
                weren't here were we?
           ⎡   [T scans class. Many voices
           │   including Claire's]
           ⎣ Children: No
              Teacher: No Claire (v) why weren't we here?
                        Why didn't we come to school yesterday?
              Claire: ⟨∗∗∗∗∗⟩
                          (Betty, School Recording, 5 years, 7 months)

In these instances, *each* of the pupils, by answering the first question,
makes visible to the teacher the fact that he or she has available the
relevant knowledge to answer the next question. The teacher is thus
able to diminish the risk of selecting pupils who are unable or
unwilling to answer.

These prefatory yes/no questions are not, however, the only ways
in which teachers set up pools of respondents. Hand-raising is also
elicited for this purpose, as in the following:

(36) ⎡Teacher: Did anyone give his snowman any clothes
     │   [T scans class]
     │ Child 1: I gave him a hat   [T does not hear/respond]
     ⎣   [Short pause while hands go up,
                                  including Nicola's]
        Teacher: You did Nicola (v)   [T fixes gaze on Nicola]
                  What did you give your snowman?
        Nicola   A scarf
                          (Betty, School Recording, 5 years, 7 months)
(37) Teacher: Erm right
     ⎡   Who else made a snowman in their garden?
     │   [Short pause while hands go up,
     ⎣   including Richard's]

> [T scans class and fixes gaze on
> Richard]
Teacher: Richard (v) what did you give your snowman?
Richard: I gave him two buttons for his eyes.
> (Betty, School Recording, 5 years, 7 months)

As with the former examples, the teacher's first turn establishes a pool of respondents, but here the response is nonverbal. This method, unlike the former, additionally allows the pool to be *sustained* over extended sequences of talk. This tends to happen in those instances where the teacher goes on to ask a question requiring several children to add successively to a list of items as answers (e.g. 'What do we buy at the greengrocer's shop?')

Interestingly, question prefaces which elicit hand-raising tend to draw on a restricted range of interrogative structures of the type 'How many of you . . . ?', 'Did any of you . . . ?', 'Which ones of you . . . ?', 'Who . . . ?', 'Who else . . . ?' (cf. (36) and (37)). And indeed such utterances are used to elicit hand-raising much more frequently than explicit directives to put up hands. The latter are largely restricted to two types of conversational environment. Firstly, they are used to restore order when overparticipation has occurred and, secondly, they are used when an interrogative type utterance such as those in (36) and (37) does not elicit hand-raising unproblematically:

(38) Teacher: Can anyone tell me WHY the bed's called a
                four-poster?
     Child 1:   ⟨Because it's cold⟩ [Child 1 raises hand and
                                     simultaneously replies]
     Teacher: Put up – wait a minute
                Put your hands up and I'll ask you
                    [Hands are raised, including Ian's.
                    T. fixes gaze on Ian]
                Ian (v)
     Ian: Because it's got four posts
                (Stella, School Recording, 4 years, 10 months)

It would seem, then, that teachers for the most part attempt to establish pools of candidate answerers by means of syntactically interrogative prefatory utterances which share many features in common with both the question prefaces we looked at earlier and with the general conversational strategy of pre-sequencing. It tends to be only in the event of this strategy failing that they use directives to raise hands which have an imperative form.

In summary, then, we might suggest that although participation in conversation which involves such large numbers of participants may be a new experience for most children entering the infant school, the formal devices by which orderly participation is managed – question and answer exchanges, pre-sequences and directives – are unlikely to be unfamiliar to them. In common with the other areas of interaction we have examined across the two settings, we again find the idea of children having problems with classroom discourse requirements somewhat difficult to entertain.

Conclusion

From this limited and partial analysis of home and school interaction it is possible to draw certain tentative conclusions. Although much further study is needed before anything even approaching a final statement can be made, it is possible to draw certain tentative conclusions from this limited analysis of home and school interaction. Bringing together the points made in the preceding sections, we can make the following observations.

Perhaps most importantly, there is *much* continuity in the nature of the interaction occurring in each setting, despite differences in situation, purpose, participant groups, etc. From the point of view of the child participants, from whatever social background, there is little in the nature of the interactional demands which will be made of them in school that they will not already have become familiar with at home, at the level of conversational structure. It is possible, however, to identify areas where home and school differ, but these do not lie in the types of conversational structures occurring in each setting. Rather, they consist, firstly, in the relative frequency of types in the two settings, secondly in an *asymmetry* of the participants' contributions to the interactions, and lastly in the *interactional* significance which certain structures 'carry' in the school as opposed to the home. In each case the differences can be traced firstly to the pedagogic motivation which underlies much of the talk in schools (as opposed to the much wider and more diffuse purposes for which talk occurs at home), and secondly (though of course these two dimensions are interlocking) to the special requirements for the maintenance of order in conversations involving large numbers of participants.

At least by attending to these two dimensions of conversation, then, further study may provide additional areas of difference between talk at home and at school.

The social and educational significance of such differences would, of course, be a further question and, as we argued at the outset, the extrapolation from features of language to wider social and political concerns is a dangerous proceeding, especially when it is done on the basis of scant empirical evidence. Even when such 'evidence' is finally assembled, however, it is hardly likely to provide the final solution to the social and educational problems in the ways often envisaged. For, ultimately, it seems to us unlikely than any educational policy is going to succeed in its aim, which is based on the view that, say, class-related patterns of educational or occupational achievement are reducible to differences in language use. In fact, we would go further than this in suggesting that the preoccupation with language which has characterised the educational problem-solving strain of research over recent years has had some rather undesirable political consequences. Essentially, we would maintain that the concern with class-related distributions of linguistic variables has deflected attention away from the glaring material and economic factors involved in the persistent underachievement of working class children. To illustrate what we mean by this, we shall merely draw attention to two events in the recent history of educational research.

The first of these concerns the fact that when research into 'linguistic deprivation' was in its hey-day, the British Government Commission on Secondary Schooling, headed by John Newsom, reported that 79 per cent of state secondary schools in inner city areas were badly impoverished both in terms of learning materials and of experienced staff (Newsom, 1963). The second relates to the publication some time later of a breakdown of the higher status professions in terms of the educational backgrounds of their occupants, carried out by David Boyd. This demonstrated unequivocally that the massive overrepresentation of ex-public school boys at this level in the occupation structure had, for most professions, either remained stable or actually increased over the last thirty years (Boyd,

1974). Despite findings such as these, some educational researchers remain confirmed in their belief that the roots of inequality in our society are linguistic. We hope, in the preceding pages, to have given some grounds for rejecting this belief.

7

Language, literacy and education

GORDON WELLS

'The faculty of language stands at the centre of our conception of mankind: speech makes us human and literacy makes us civilized.' (Olson, 1977)

In the child's linguistic development, there are three major phases.[1] The first is characterised by the discovery of language, as patterns of sound take on meaning and purpose in the repetitive activities that play so large a part in the infant's interaction with his parents and other primary caregivers. In this phase, during which the infant simultaneously discovers his own separate identity and his ability to bring about changes in the people and objects that make up his environment, language functions first and foremost as a means for the regulation of activity and interaction. Then, as objects and events in his environment, and his own and other people's activities within this environment, are made the focus of conversational attention, he gradually discovers a further important function of language – that of representing, or standing for, the objects and events that make up his experience.

The second phase is one of consolidation and diversification. Through his participation in the talk that directs and interprets the variety of events that constitute everyday life, the child gradually takes over the language of his community and, in the process, absorbs the cultural values and working assumptions that are

---

[1] This chapter is a revised and expanded version of a paper which originally appeared in *New Education* 1.2 (1979) under the title 'Language, literacy and educational success'.

encoded in that particular community's use of language. He also begins to gain control of a variety of different language registers, as he learns to adjust his style of speaking and listening to the requirements of the social context – the participants, the setting and the task in hand. Thus, by the time he goes to school, the child has made substantial progress towards mastering the resources of the spoken language and can draw upon those resources appropriately to achieve a wide range of interactional objectives in the familiar contexts of everyday activities.

However, while the first two phases of development are characterised by the close interrelatedness of language, action and social context, the third phase sees a loosening of these links, as the child becomes conscious of his own mental states and capable of reflecting on his experience. As thought and action become separable, the function that language performs of representing the objects and events of experience is drawn upon to provide a 'tool for thinking' and a means for communicating to others the results of the thinking process. As a result, there is a development in the child's use of language towards the expression of more individually differentiated meaning, and towards the detachment of language from its context of immediate experience. From being restricted to the received opinions and attitudes embodied in the conversation of his immediate social group, he begins to acquire the means to arrive at his own interpretation of experience and, ultimately, to influence the interpretations of others.

The preceding chapters have been chiefly concerned with the first two phases of development and have stressed the embeddedness of early language in its context of practical activity. In this final chapter we shall be concerned with the third phase and with the ways in which the freeing of language and thinking from the context of immediate experience is facilitated by formal schooling and, more particularly, by the acquisition of literacy.

In literate cultures such as ours, however, it is difficult to separate out the specific contribution of literacy from the more general effects of schooling. In the course of this chapter, therefore, we shall review some of the evidence from studies of less literate cultures which are relevant to this issue and we shall also examine the role of literacy in the different levels of educational attainment characteristic of different social groups within our own culture. Finally, we shall consider

the implication of the results of our enquiry for the teaching of
literacy in the early stages of education.

Literacy and the facilitation of cognitive skills

Various claims have been made for the importance of literacy in the
development of civilisations past and present. Of these, the most
fundamental is the practical advantage of being able to extend
communication across time and space. With this comes easy access
to the skills and knowledge built up by previous generations and to
current developments in the sciences, technology and politics and in
many other fields of practical activity. Written language also serves
the very important function of an external memory, whether it be as
a record of public events and current debate – the material from
which history is eventually made – or merely in the form of notes and
instructions to oneself or one's immediate associates. On another
dimension, written literature – novels, poetry and drama – opens up
a whole realm of vicarious experience through which the reader –
and the writer – can extend his understanding of other people's
motives and feelings and at the same time gain more insight into his
own.

Important though these benefits are, however, there is another
potential consequence of literacy which has been seen by many
writers to have an even greater significance, and that is the increased
level of cognitive functioning which is encouraged by the more
detached and critical attitude to experience that use of the written
language promotes. Goody & Watt (1968), for example, in a historical discussion of the effects of literacy, attach great significance to the
contribution of the first alphabetic writing system to the emergence
of Greek political and intellectual culture. They emphasise the spur
to critical thinking that came from the recognition of discrepancy
between written records and personal experience, and they stress the
important role played by an efficient writing system in the development of the ability to abstract linguistic expressions from the particular content and contexts to which they initially referred. As a result of
the cognitive activities encouraged by the use of a written language,
they argue:

'it does not seem to be merely a matter of ethnocentric
prejudice to say that in two areas at least the Greeks developed

intellectual techniques that were historically unique, and that possessed intrinsic empirical advantages which led to their widespread adoption by most subsequent literate cultures: the first area is epistemological, where the Greeks developed a new kind of logical method; and the second area is that of taxonomy, where the Greeks established our accepted categories in the fields of knowledge – theology, physics, biology and so forth.' (p. 52)

What was true for the intellectual pioneers of Western culture, Plato, Aristotle, Herodotus and others, it has been argued, is also potentially true for each individual who grows up in a literate society. With the acquisition of literacy comes a more detached and reflective attitude to experience and this, in turn, promotes higher levels of cognitive functioning than are readily available in cultures that are restricted to purely oral communication. It is for this reason that, in the article from which the opening quotation is taken, Olson claims a 'civilising' function for literacy. Since such a claim, if correct, has important implications for educational practice, we shall examine the arguments in greater detail.

Olson's claim is based on the belief that, compared with speech, written language leads to a different orientation to meaning on the part of those who use it – a difference that stems from the relationship between sender, receiver and situational context characteristic of the conditions in which the two media are used. In characteristically oral communication, the meaning attributed to an utterance is to be found in an interaction between the speaker, the expectations of the listener, the actual speech signal, and relevant information in the situation. In written language, on the other hand, and particularly in scientific and philosophical writing, the meaning is to a much greater extent to be found in the text alone. Whereas the typical situation in which speech occurs, that of face-to-face interaction, requires the participants to devote a considerable portion of their attention to the management of the interpersonal relationship in order to monitor and sustain mutual understanding, the typical situation in which a written message is produced or received lacks the co-presence of the participants and the shared situation, with the result that, without the requirement for attention to the interpersonal axis, attention can be devoted exclusively to the formulation of the message. For the same reason, Olson argues, the meaning has to be located in the text, because there is nowhere else where it can be found.

Of course, meaning can never reside wholly in the text. As we saw in chapter 1, even with the most fully and explicitly formulated message, understanding is only possible if the reader brings to the text a store of cultural and personal knowledge, assumptions and values similar to those of the writer, on which he can draw in interpreting the meaning encoded in the text. As Austin (1962) and other **speech act** theorists have argued, even the meaning of 'standard descriptive sentences' is only fully interpretable by reference to their use in context; furthermore, such descriptions are never fully explicit and determinate, since it is simply not possible to provide a description which does not rest upon implicit assumptions which themselves are capable of further explication (Waismann, 1953). Thus interpretive judgments about the meaning of a sentence must always be made with respect to a particular context.

For these reasons, it must be insisted that *all* linguistic communications require an interaction between sender, receiver and context. In this respect, varieties of spoken and written language differ only in the *extent* to which they attempt to achieve autonomous and explicit representation of meaning in the form of the message alone. In fact, Olson goes some way towards recognising this when he notes (1977: 275) that explicitness of meaning may be better thought of as a goal rather than as an achievement, and one relevant only to rather specialised uses of written language.

Nevertheless, he is surely right in arguing that the consequences of setting this goal for even some uses of written language have been far-reaching. On the historical dimension, we have already seen how the new orientation to meaning encouraged by the invention of a fully alphabetic writing system led to the development of many branches of Western thought. Olson develops this argument for more recent times, and shows how concentration on the meaning contained in the text led to the renaissance of the philosophical tradition in the sixteenth and seventeenth centuries and later to the growth of deductive, empirical science. On the dimension of individual writers and readers also, he argues that the attempt to make the organisation of the written text act as the autonomous and explicit representation of intended meaning leads to the development of a greater awareness of the abstract relationship between language and experience and a greater willingness to exploit the symbolic possibilities inherent in language. The acquisition of literacy, he argues, thus provides a tool for, and the spur to, higher levels of analytic thinking and formal reasoning – skills which are amongst the chief forces in the development of civilisation, both in whole cultures and in its individual members.

In more recent work, the psychological consequences of the acquisition of literacy have been studied experimentally, and support has been found for the arguments advanced above both from experiments comparing adult and child members of our literate culture and from experiments involving children at various stages in the acquisition of literacy (Olson & Hildyard, in press). Similar results have also been reported by Rawson (1978) who found that an experimental programme of reading instruction given to under-achieving 10-year-olds was effective in facilitating the development of certain cognitive operations.

A cross-cultural perspective
However, where learning to read and write are only part – albeit a major part – of a broader programme of systematic instruction, as they are in Western societies, it is difficult to disentangle the consequences of the acquisition of literacy from those of the more general intellectual training that is the aim of most of the school curriculum. To assess the contribution of literacy alone, it would seem to be necessary to study it out of the context of schooling. And here the investigations of Scribner & Cole (1978) into the effects of literacy amongst the Vai people of Liberia are of particular relevance.

Unlike most of the other indigenous traditional societies of Liberia, the Vai have a syllabic writing system which was invented some 150 years ago, and which is used most commonly for letters between relatives and business associates. The mastery of this script is not acquired through formal schooling and, although the ability to read and write is socially valued, these activities are not separated off from the rest of everyday life by, for example, surrounding them with a body of ritual or making them the preserve of a special caste of scribes. The question that Scribner & Cole set out to investigate was whether skill in the use of this script, as opposed to the more general skills acquired through formal schooling, was associated with higher levels of performance on a variety of cognitive and metalinguistic tasks than those achieved by nonliterate, uneducated members of the same culture. The results of this comparison were clear-cut; whereas level of performance on the cognitive tasks was associated with length of formal schooling, it was not associated with literacy in the Vai script; literates and nonliterates did not differ significantly on any of the tasks investigated. However, when tasks, such as explaining a new type of board game, were presented, requiring skills more closely related to those involved in the activities for which the Vai script is commonly used, they found that men literate in the Vai script were far superior to nonliterates in both a face-to-face and a 'dictated letter' condition. They were also superior on a task which involved repeating and comprehending sentences which were read slowly syllable by syllable.

The increased intellectual skills produced by literacy in the Vai script were thus those that are closely associated with the activities involved in the use of this particular script; there was no increase in generalised competences such as abstraction, verbal reasoning or metalinguistic ability.[2] However, there was another important finding that applied across all tasks: in every case there were some nonliterates who also achieved high scores or displayed the same skills as Vai literates.

Scribner & Cole (1978: 11) interpret these results as evidence against the generalised facilitation of 'higher order' intellectual skills that is frequently claimed to result from the acquisition of literacy; they argue instead that the skills that are facilitated depend upon the way in which literacy is socially organised and used within particular cultures. In some societies, such as that of the Vai, literacy serves a practical but limited function. The intellectual skills that are facilitated, therefore, are restricted to those that are closely related to the uses to which reading and writing are put. In other cultures, where literacy is central to a more general system of formal education, generalised cognitive skills are facilitated, because schooling provides people with a great deal of practice in treating individual learning problems as instances of classes of problems 'of the same type'.

---

[2] A feature of Vai script which may be relevant to their results, although not discussed in this context by Scribner & Cole, is its syllabic base. Olson (1977) stresses that it is the independence from remembered speech, made possible only by a phonetic alphabet, that facilitates the explicit rendering of meaning in text.

Further evidence which bears on the issue as to whether it is schooling rather than literacy which acts as a spur to cognitive development comes from a series of studies carried out by Bruner and his associates (Bruner, 1964; Bruner, Olver & Greenfield, 1966), and it is to a review of these that we now turn.

Culture, language and cognition

In very general terms, Bruner sees the development of the characteristically human cognitive capacities for recognising and solving problems to have resulted from the internalisation of 'amplification systems', which are culturally transmitted from one generation to the next. In the history of the human race, he argues, there have been a number of highly significant technological advances, which have given man increased control over his environment. In the life history of each human being, these technologies shape the cultural environment in which he grows up and make available techniques for enhancing the intellectual potential with which he is biologically endowed.

In 'The growth of mind' (Bruner, 1972) he states the argument as follows:

'What a culture does to assist the development of the powers of mind of its members is, in effect, to provide amplification systems to which human beings, equipped with appropriate skills, can link themselves. There are, first, the amplifiers of action – hammers, levers, digging sticks, wheels – but more important the programmes of action into which such implements can be substituted. Second, there are amplifiers of the senses, ways of looking and noticing that can take advantage of devices ranging from smoke signals and hailers to diagrams and pictures that stop the action or microscopes that enlarge it. Finally and most powerfully, there are amplifiers of the thought processes, ways of thinking that employ language and formation of explanation, and later use such languages as mathematics and logic and even find automatic servants to crank out of the consequences. A culture is, then, a deviser, a repository and a transmitter of amplification systems and of the devices that fit into such systems.' (pp. 68–9)

The significance of these amplifiers for the development of the individual's cognitive capacities is that they provide powerful systems for the internal organisation and shaping of experience. Elsewhere, Bruner (1964) refers to them as the enactive, ikonic and symbolic modes of representation, and he suggests that their acquisition is both sequential and cumulative. In the context of the present discussion it is the symbolic mode which is of greatest importance, for when it is harnessed to thinking, in what Vygotsky (1962) calls 'verbal thought', it can provide an extremely powerful amplifier of cognitive capacity.

However, although the exploitation of the language-based symbolic mode of representation is seen by Bruner as the final stage of cognitive development, it is not a stage that is inevitably reached in all cultures. In order for the individual to learn to make use of the symbolic power of language in the performance of cognitive tasks, a degree of deliberate tuition is required, which is typically provided by formal schooling. However, as we have already seen, the provision of formal schooling only occurs in societies that have come to value the effects of literacy.

One of the studies that Bruner and his colleagues report was carried out in Senegal by Patricia Greenfield. Here, the varying degrees to which French culture had penetrated the colony allowed a natural experimental comparison to be made between three groups of school-age children, all members of the Wolof tribe. The first group consisted of rural children who had not attended school; the second group also consisted of rural children, but the members of this group were attending one of the local village schools; the third group were school-children from the country's capital, Dakar. The tasks, which involved conservation and grouping pictures of objects according to shared attributes, were presented in Wolof; the language of school instruction, however, was French.

It would not be appropriate to attempt to report the results of the experiments in detail here. However, the general finding was that, on both tasks, the children attending school performed better at each age than those not attending school and, within the groups of school children, those with a greater command of French performed better than the less effectively bilingual children.

Interpreting these results, Bruner & Greenfield (1972) attribute them to a fundamental difference in world view between the two cultures into which these groups of children had been differentially assimilated, and this in turn resulted from the range of technological amplifiers available within the two cultures. The indigenous Wolof culture, based on a subsistence economy in which there is little control over the inanimate world, is characterised by a 'collective' orientation, which gives little value to individualistic self-consciousness. By contrast, in the European culture, which is associated with the use of the French language and based on a more powerful and differentiated economy, high value is given to the individual's acquisition of skilled control of objects and to self-conscious awareness of his psychological processes.

The set towards a collective or an individualistic orientation is established very early, Bruner suggests, in the way in which the child's actions are typically interpreted by his caregivers. In a collective culture, actions are given a social interpretation: they are treated as signifying a desire on the part of the child in relation to other persons. In an individualistic culture, on the other hand, actions are interpreted in terms of the 'motoric competence' that is manifested independently of the actor's motive, and the foundations are laid for the later development of conscious awareness of the separation between psychological states and physical events, and between the verbal formulations in which thoughts are expressed and the objects and events to which those formulations apply.

The failure of the unschooled monolingual Wolof children to supply justifications for their judgments on the conservation task, or to use superordinate categories on the picture-grouping task, is thus seen to stem from a general cultural orientation towards a social interpretation of experience which does not encourage a reflective consideration of how things might be other than they appear. Significantly however, the children who had attended school were not so limited in their responses to the tasks. 'It appears', Bruner & Greenfield remark,

'that school tends to give them something akin to Western self-consciousness, for they can answer questions implying a distinction between their psychological reaction and external events; and, as they advance in school, they become increasingly capable of categorizing the same stimuli, according to several different criteria or "points of view".' (1972: 41)

Literacy and symbolic representation

Cultural differences in world view of the magnitude that we have been considering may seem rather far removed from questions of language use and, more specifically, from the role of literacy in cognitive development. Clearly, as in the case of the difference between the Greeks and their less civilised neighbours, the emergence of a self-conscious rational orientation to experience was not due entirely to the invention and widespread adoption of an alphabetic writing system. Political and economic factors were also of importance. But, as was argued above, the experience for the reader or writer of the separation between what is meant and what is encoded in the text is a powerful spur to the self-conscious reflectiveness which Bruner sees to be such an important difference between collective and individualistic cultures, as described above. So, although it was schooling which was found to be instrumental in the move towards a more individualistic, Western-style orientation to experience in the bilingual Wolof children, we should not under-estimate the underlying influence of literacy, both in creating conditions where schooling is thought to be necessary for cultural continuity and in determining the content and mode of presentation of the school curriculum.

Something akin to the distinction Olson (1977) makes between the characteristic orientations to meaning associated with spoken and written language also seems called for by the general account of cognitive development that Bruner offers in terms of the successive mastery of the three modes of representation, enactive, ikonic and symbolic. For, as we have just seen, although members of all cultures learn a mother tongue and use it effectively for the purposes of social and practical interaction, it is not the case that, in all cultures, the power inherent in language for symbolic representation is fully exploited in cognitive activity. And even in those cultures where such skills are developed, they are not acquired until some considerable time after the language itself has largely been mastered.

For example, consider the relationship between two propositions conveyed by the connective 'if'. There is hardly a 4-year-old who does not understand correctly what his father means when he says: 'If you don't eat up your cabbage, you will have to go to bed without any pudding.' And almost all the children in the Bristol study were themselves producing similar utterances before they started school.

Yet it is several years later before they are able to solve problems posed in terms such as the following: 'In a game where the players have to collect plastic chips of as many different shapes as possible, there is a rule: If the colour on the dice is not black, the player must pick up a square chip. John and Mary are playing the game and John has just picked a triangle. Which of these colours did he throw: red, black or blue?' In both cases the relationship that the child has to comprehend concerns the consequence of a failure to fulfil a necessary condition. However, the lack of contextual support for general statements, such as this rule of a game, or for instructions to place three coloured bricks 'red in front of blue but behind green', quoted in chapter 5, makes them much more intellectually demanding than specific requests or statements arising out of the immediate context, such as the father's threat referred to above. Children are not able to understand and act upon the more general type of statement or request simply by knowing the words and sentence structures.

If an individual has learned to talk, and talking involves the use of a symbolic system, why is it that the symbolic mode of representation is not immediately available as an instrument of thought? The cross-cultural evidence that we have considered makes it clear that the mere mastery of a language for everyday communication is not sufficient to guarantee that it will be exploited to any significant extent in the organisation and manipulation of the experience that it encodes. This discrepancy between the potential cognitive power of language and the habitual uses to which it is put was memorably characterised by Sapir many years ago:

> 'It does not follow . . . that the use to which language is put is always, or even mainly, conceptual. We are not in ordinary life so much concerned with concepts as with concrete particularities and specific relations. When I say, for instance, "I had a good breakfast this morning", it is clear that I am not in the throes of laborious thought, that what I have to transmit is hardly more than a pleasurable memory symbolically rendered in the grooves of habitual expression. Each element in the sentence defines a separate concept or conceptual relation, or both combined, but the sentence as a whole has no conceptual significance whatever. It is somewhat as though a dynamo capable of generating enough power to

run an elevator were operated almost exclusively to feed an
electric doorbell.' (1921: 14)

However, although the habitual use of language may not involve
much conceptual significance, it is clear that a certain level of symbolic representation of experience is required in order to acquire the
language in the first place. But there also seems to be a second level of
symbolic representation – or at least a second level of ability to
exploit the organisation of the symbolic system – which is required
to manipulate the experience that the symbols represent. To achieve
this second level it is necessary, in Bruner's words, 'to bring the world
of experience under the control of principles of organization that are
in some degree isomorphic with the structural principles of syntax'
(Bruner et al. 1966: 47) – and one might also add, 'of semantics'.
What the child has to develop, therefore, is an enhanced awareness
of the *symbolic* properties of linguistic representations: the realisation that the meaning and implications of a message depend upon the
precise linguistic formulation of that message and upon the internal
relations and consistency between its constituent parts, rather than
upon any necessary correspondence between the message and the
perception or memories of the extralinguistic context(s) to which the
message might apply. In the case of the plastic chip game, for
example, the child has to be able to solve the problem solely in terms
of his understanding of the verbal formulation of the rules, rather
than depending on having seen people actually play the game. In
other words, the child has to learn, as Donaldson (1978) puts it, to
'disembed' his thinking from the supportive context of actual experience and to bring it under the control of the meanings that are
encoded in the linguistic message alone.

Such a change in orientation to linguistic meaning, and hence of
level of cognitive functioning, is precisely what Olson (1977) claims
to result from the acquisition of literacy and, in particular, from
learning to meet the demands of prose text. Bruner also – although
he does not place the same emphasis on literacy – concludes that, in
order to reach this level of cognitive and symbolic functioning, some
special training is required. Typically, in fully literate cultures, this
takes the form of a systematic education that is separated from the
context of immediately relevant activity and which, by virtue of that
separation, is heavily dependent for the representation and manipu-

lation of experience on the explicit symbolisation which is most characteristically found in written language.

It seems, therefore, that there are strong reasons for believing that literacy does contribute significantly to the development of higher levels of cognitive functioning. Historically, we have seen that the emergence of a broad-based literacy played a considerable part in the development of Western rational thought in Greek times and in its renaissance in the sixteenth and seventeenth centuries. Similarly, there are grounds for believing that, in the case of individual members of a literate society, the acquisition of literacy *can* be associated with the important facilitating effects on cognitive development that Olson describes. However, in the case of individual development, it is necessary to make a number of qualifications.

Clearly, literacy is not an all-or-nothing ability. There is a basic level of literacy that almost all pupils achieve, which may not go much beyond the ability to read material which is already familiar from other sources, and to write about particular first-hand experience. This seems to correspond fairly closely to the level of literacy attained by the Vai, as reported by Scribner & Cole (1978). At this level, although there may be consequences for cognitive functioning, they are likely to be rather limited and of restricted significance. For the effects of literacy to generalise across the full range of an individual's intellectual activities with the sort of cognitive consequences that Olson claims, a much higher level of literacy is required, which is only likely to result from working with unfamiliar as well as with familiar material and from the attempt to organise and reorganise that material to meet the demands of particular problems and tasks.

At this level, a further distinction needs to be made between reading and writing. Use of the term 'literacy' implies that the two activities are equivalent in their consequences for cognitive functioning. But this is hardly likely to be so. Reading requires one to be attentive to the precise organisation of an already created text, recognising the meaning of the individual components and combining them in a way that is guided by the context of the surrounding text. As already argued above (p. 244, the reader's reconstruction of the intended message always involves some contribution from his own experience, both to give substance to the conceptual categories symbolised in the text, and to supply the organising principles and information that the writer assumes his audience will have by virtue of their common interest in the topic with which the text is concerned. He may also approach the same text with one of a variety of purposes, and these, too, influence the nature of the interaction between the writer's message and the reader's contribution (Gibson & Levin, 1975). Skill in reading thus involves recalling, adding to and reshaping stored experience, as guided by the meanings conveyed in the text, but also with a balance between the various processes appropriate to the task in hand.

Demanding though this complex process is, it is nevertheless strongly supported by the structure of meaning and expression already present in the text. The *creation* of written text, on the other hand, lacks the support of a pre-existing structure; it thus places even greater demands on the cognitive and linguistic skills of the writer. There are at least three conceptually distinct processes involved in writing of almost any kind (cf. chapter 1, p. 55): (a) assembling the relevant meanings and organising them in a structure appropriate to the particular narrative, argument, description, etc. which is the purpose of the writing; (b) shaping the material so that it is oriented to the expectations and information which it can be assumed the intended reader will bring to the text; (c) encoding it in words and syntactic structures which coherently, explicitly and elegantly express the intended message. In practice, of course, the three processes interact in a complex way that involves thinking, writing, reviewing and rewriting, over an extended period of time, as the created text gradually approaches the original conception and, at the same time, subtly modifies and develops it.

Rather little is known in detail about these processes and their interrelationship but, in the context of the present discussion of the cognitive consequences of literacy, it is clear that it is particularly in the *creation* of written text that the individual is made most aware of the symbolising function of language, and of the power that it has to capture experience so that it may be considered, questioned and modified in the interests of increased understanding and future applications. If, as Bruner and Olson suggest, it is a self-conscious and reflective attitude to experience that encourages the development of higher-level cognitive skills, this is surely most strongly promoted by the dialogue with oneself – or at least with the internalised other (Mead, 1934), who is the idealised reader of what is written – that any extended act of writing involves.

There is one final, but important, qualification. Although higher levels of cognitive functioning may be strongly associated with the symbolic manipulation of meaning encoded in linguistic representations, such a use of language is not confined to the written mode. Very precisely formulated reasoning can also occur in speech, as is frequently the case in, for example, cross-examinations of witnesses, spontaneous contributions to seminars, diagnoses of illness, or of machine malfunction, etc., and such uses of language can be found in nonliterate as well as in literate cultures. Nor, on the other hand, does communication in the written mode necessarily require a level of conceptualisation or reasoning that is at a significantly higher level than that which is required by much everyday conversation. For example, the level of thinking that is called upon when reading many newspaper articles or advertisements, or the average romance or detective story, is not very different from that which is required when listening to an orally presented narrative. Similarly, most letters written between friends do not require of the writer intellectual skills that go much beyond those required to give a coherent account of events in conversation, and many business letters or memos convey information or directives that could be dealt with equally effectively in face-to-face encounters or by the use of the telephone.

It is not literacy, as such, therefore, that is of such significance, but rather the symbolic manipulation of experience through the sort of language which is *most characteristic* of written text. Spoken communication can also display the same analytic orientation to meaning, particularly amongst those who are fully literate, and it is probably in this mode that the cognitive consequences for everyday life are most fully realised. Furthermore, as Scribner & Cole suggest, much depends on the range of uses and topics with which these symbolising skills are associated. Where they are restricted to very specific tasks, such as ordering goods or making inventories of gifts at weddings, as with the use of the Vai script, or to a highly compartmentalised body of knowledge, as can too easily happen when they are associated *only* with the abstract curricular content of formal schooling, the psychological effects will not generalise across the full range of an individual's intellectual activities, as they may when the more reflective and analytic orientation to meaning which characterises the extended use of expository writing permeates a much greater part of an individual's daily activities.

Subcultural differences in language and cognition

In our attempts to evaluate the importance of literacy for intellectual development we have looked, so far, only at differences between cultures, where these cultures have been globally characterised as literate or nonliterate. But within cultures such as our own, in which universal literacy has almost been achieved, there are still important subcultural differences in the average level of performance on the sort of abstract reasoning tasks that have been used in the cross-cultural comparisons. Can these, too, be attributed to the effects of literacy, or is some other sort of explanation required?

If the acquisition of literacy does have the facilitating effects on cognitive development that Olson and others suggest, there should be a close relationship between level of cognitive functioning and degree of mastery of the written language, whatever the social background of the individuals concerned. However, this is not altogether the case. Differences between working and middle class samples, whether of adolescents or adults, are too frequently reported (e.g. as reviewed by Morrison & McIntyre, 1971) for there to be much doubt that there are significant differences between the two groups in their average level of performance, even though the vast majority of members of our culture achieve functional literacy in the primary stage of education and continue to receive several more years of compulsory education, in which written language plays an increasingly important part. Furthermore, such class-associated differences in performance on cognitive tasks are already found at the time of entry to school, before children have learned to read at all, and rather than being reduced by formal schooling, they tend to persist and even increase in magnitude, in spite of the common emphasis on literacy in the education of all children.

It was to explain such differences in levels of educational attainment that Bernstein developed his theory of the role of the two linguistic **codes** in the socialisation of members of working and middle class subcultures. According to one of the fullest formulations of his theory (Bernstein, 1971), different types of family organisation, either positional or personal, lead to qualitative differences in the styles of speech adopted in a wide range of contexts of interaction, these differences springing from, and serving to transmit, fundamentally different orientations to meaning, which Bernstein associates with the 'restricted' and 'elaborated' codes. The meanings emphasised by a restricted code, he claims, are dependent upon particular contexts and lacking in explicitness and individual differentiation of meaning; by contrast, the meanings emphasised by an elaborated code are more general and context-independent, and are realised in a more verbally explicit form. It is socialisation through, and into, an elaborated code that accounts, in Bernstein's view, for the typical superiority of middle class subjects on higher-order cognitive tasks, since success in such tasks requires the kind of orientation to meaning that distinguishes an elaborated from a restricted code.

Attractive though this theory is, in its bold linking of social structure, language use and educational attainment, it has not been well supported by empirical investigation (cf. Edwards (1976a) and Robinson (1978) for a detailed review of the empirical studies carried out to test the theory). In the present context it would be inappropriate to rehearse in detail the arguments that have been raised by these and other critics against the class–code–attainment theory, but a number of general suggestions will be made as to why it fails to account for the observable facts.

In the first place, in spite of the discussion of the codes as if there were two, and only two, discrete codes or groups of codes, the many and various parameters that are used to distinguish them (e.g. the occurrence of uncommon adjectives or complex verbal groups, or of expressions of tentativeness such as 'I think', as opposed to 'socio-centric' tags such as 'you know') are almost all continuous, implying that we are dealing with a greater or lesser frequency of the features in question, rather than with a binary distinction between presence and absence. Put in more everyday terms, all styles of speaking draw upon the grammar and lexicon of the same language; the differences in frequency of particular classes of item or structure, or in length and type of pausing, are only relative. The identification of two, and only two, codes is thus a somewhat arbitrary dichotomising of the many dimensions on which styles of speaking vary.

Secondly, if the sharp distinction between the codes disappears, so too does the force of arguments, based on this distinction, about the psychological consequences of access to one rather than the other of the postulated codes. Differences in level of cognitive functioning most probably *are* related to habitual language use – as we saw in the previous section – but not in the sharply dichotomised manner suggested by Bernstein or by Tough (1977), who makes similar claims about the cognitive effects of differences in language use. For, in this respect too, when a representative sample of the population is studied, continuous variation, rather than a simple polarisation, is found on all the dimensions that have been investigated (Wells, 1977, in press a).

Thirdly, there is an oversimplification introduced by the division of the population into middle and (lower) working class. (Bernstein is, in fact, inconsistent on the question of whether all the working class or only the semi-skilled and unskilled lower working class are predominantly oriented to a restricted code.) But in either case, as Rosen (1972) has argued, it is too crude a distinction to do justice to the social structure of our society, even in terms of relative status, and it completely ignores the nature of the varied social relationships into which people enter at work and in their leisure activities. However, it is precisely such differences in what parents talk about to whom and for what purposes, in their dealings with other people outside the home, that might be expected to have a fairly direct influence upon the language that they use within the home in communicating with their children.

That there are differences between children in their experience of linguistic interaction in their early years at home has been clearly demonstrated in a number of recent investigations (cf. chapter 2, pp. 114–15), including the Bristol longitudinal study. Evidence from this also shows that there is a clear association between the quality of the adults' contributions to conversation and their children's rate of oral language development in the pre-school years (Ellis & Wells, 1980; Wells, in press b). However, differences in adult speech and in children's rate of oral language development are much less clearly associated with social class, and there are no obvious differences in style of child or adult speech that would lend support to the theory of strongly class-associated differences in code (Wells, 1979a).

There is no disagreement with Bernstein and other commentators, however, about the tendency for subsequent attainment in school and performance on cognitive tasks to be related to social class, with children from professional middle class backgrounds, on average, scoring more highly than their peers from unskilled and semi-skilled backgrounds. Such a class-associated variation in performance is already apparent in the data from the Bristol study as soon as the children start going to school – in spite of the lack of any similar association with respect to variation in spontaneous oral language performance and rate of development. The problem is thus to discover what it is that differentiates the pre-school experience of children from different types of social background in such a way as to lead to the pattern of differential performance so frequently observed during the course of formal education.

In the previous paragraphs reasons have been given for disagreeing with the explanation offered by Bernstein in terms of the class–code theory. Nevertheless, I believe there is an important insight in what I take to be the core of his theory. Essentially, what he is suggesting is that the way in which each individual child constructs his model of the world, and discovers his place and power of control within it, is most strongly influenced by the values and orientations that are encoded and transmitted in the everyday conversations he has with his parents and other adults in his immediate environment. And, of particular importance for his subsequent educational achievement, is the extent to which this conversational experience helps him to develop an awareness of the way in which language allows particular situations, problems and predicaments to be represented in symbolic categories and relations, which can be communicated about and acted upon independently of their particular contexts of origin – that is to say, the extent to which he learns from his experience to use language as a means of 'disembedded thinking'.

Where Bernstein and those who accept his theory are wrong, I believe, is in considering such linguistic experiences to be determined by social class and to be manifest in differential use of two sharply distinguished codes. In the following section I wish to develop an alternative explanation which, whilst still appealing to linguistic experience as one important influence on educational achievement, attributes this influence to the place and value of literacy in the child's early experience. And this, although associated with social class, is not determined by it in any simple way.

The role of literacy in pre-school development
The starting point for the argument that I wish to develop is the finding of Scribner & Cole (1978) that the unschooled members of the Vai culture who had acquired literacy in the Vai script did not have any superiority in generalised intellectual competences, but that

they did show increased intellectual skills on tasks closely associated with the use of this particular script. They interpret this finding as evidence that, in considering the facilitation of higher-level cognitive skills, what matters is the range of uses to which literacy skills are put, rather than their mere acquisition. In the Vai culture, it will be remembered, the main use of literacy was in the writing of letters between trading associates or between relatives. For this reason, and also because of the ambiguity of its syllabic characters, it was closely linked only to particular practical activities and the contexts in which these occurred. It was not used, in Sapir's words, to power the elevator of conceptual thought – to gain detachment from and to reflect upon experience. Not surprisingly, therefore, it did not have important generalised consequences for the level of cognitive functioning of those who used the script.

Even in a fully literate society, however, there are considerable differences between individuals in the uses they make of their ability to read and write. At one extreme, there are those whose profession involves the 'constant wrestle with words and meanings' (Eliot, 1944) in order to create new understanding, whether through the 'raids on the inarticulate' of the poet or the novelist, or the construction of chains of evidence and logical reasoning by the scientist or philosopher. At the other extreme are those whose reading consists mainly of the headlines of the daily paper and the ubiquitous shop signs and advertisements that beset the urban dweller on every side; typically their only uses of writing are shopping lists, the occasional postcard when on holiday and official forms to be completed for various state and commercial organisations. Between these extremes, however, there are many degrees of involvement with literacy and many kinds of activity in which reading and writing play a part.

There is thus no simple dichotomy between literate and non-literate but, instead, many varieties and degrees of literacy, depending on the range of uses to which the skills of literacy are put. If literacy has cognitive consequences, as we have argued, these will therefore also be a matter of degree and not simply an all-or-nothing effect. For those whose uses of literacy are highly restricted, the consequences are likely to be of limited generality; on the other hand, those who have frequent and varied demands made of them to achieve precision of meaning in the written form are likely to carry this habit over to their spoken communication, when this is appropriate, and to employ symbolically mediated skills of abstraction and reasoning in structuring and solving the various problems they confront in their everyday lives. Thus, whilst the initial acquisition of literacy at school is likely to facilitate the cognitive development of all members of a literate culture to some degree, even more important is the extent to which the continued use of these skills is encouraged outside the school context in which they are originally acquired and, subsequently, at work and in the many other activities of adult life.

If it is then argued that the role of literacy in adult life is likely to be related to occupation – and thus to social class – this must be conceded. But there is no necessary connection, as a survey currently being conducted in Bristol shows. For, whilst the uses made of the skills of reading and writing by the majority of adults can be quite well predicted by the demands of their particular occupations, there are also manual workers who, in their leisure time, write poems, keep the minutes of meetings of social clubs, read novels and biographies, just as there are professional workers who rarely read, except occasionally to consult a technical manual, and never write if alternative means of communication can be used instead. Even these examples, however, suggest a simple class-based division to which there are occasional exceptions, whereas it would be more accurate to reject any such dichotomisation and to recognise the very great variety of patterns that actually occur and the many influences besides occupation that lead to their occurrence.

Having briefly considered the role of literacy in adult life, let us now return to the children with whom this discussion began, and re-examine the differences in pre-school experiences that might be expected to facilitate their initial educational progress, and particularly the acquisition of the skills of literacy on which so much of their subsequent education will be based. It was suggested earlier that Bernstein's general theory of cultural transmission gave a helpful insight into the way in which the values and practices of one generation are taken over by the next in the exchange of meanings that constitute everyday conversation. He also offered an account of differences between social groups in terms of orientation to different orders of meaning within such conversations. What is being proposed here is that this general theoretical account is probably cor-

rect, but that what chiefly accounts for the different orders of meaning to which different children are oriented is the sorts of skills that
their parents and other caregivers make use of in their own social and
occupational activities, and particularly those involving the symbolic potential of language, which is most fully exploited in activities
involving sustained writing and reading.

It seems likely for example that, by virtue of the interests and
involvements of their parents, some children will be more oriented
towards practical and social skills relevant to the unfolding of everyday activities in the particular contexts with which they are familiar
– carrying out household routines, visits to the shops or park,
polishing the car, and so forth. Other children – by virtue of somewhat different parental activities – will, in addition, become familiar
with situations in which, before action is taken, a phase of more specifically linguistic interaction intervenes, in which the practical or
social situation is discussed with some degree of detachment and
embryonic analysis, with a view to the recognition and formulation
of principles of some degree of generality, for example, planning the
route for a holiday, identifying birds or leaves seen during a walk,
deciding between competing ways of spending pocket money, and so
on. There are no doubt also other patterns in which aesthetic and
moral values are considered, such as discussing the reasons for other
people's behaviour; but sufficient has been said to indicate how
differences between children relevant to their subsequent learning at
school may originate and become established as a result of their
parents' personal interests and activities.

Although little attention has so far been given to the detailed
exploration of the effects on children's early cognitive development
of the different activities which their parents engage in outside the
home, this is surely a topic that would repay investigation since, as
already argued above, these are far more varied than is often recognised. Moreover, it is these, rather than simple occupational status,
that are likely to determine both what parents talk about with their
children and the way in which they interpret and direct their children's behaviour.

Concerning the effects of parental interest and involvement in
literacy within the home, there is rather more information. In many
studies, differences in pupils' progress in learning to read have been
found to be related to the number of books in the home, the range of

books and other reading matter read by the parents and the frequency with which they read to their children (e.g. Douglas, 1964; Durkin, 1966). When we investigated the antecedents of the early progress in reading made by a subsample of the Bristol children, we found that the best single predictor of attainment in literacy after two years of schooling was the extent of the children's own understanding of the purposes and mechanics of literacy at the time when they started school. This, in turn, was strongly associated with the interest in literacy that their parents had shared with them in the preceding years through reading to them and looking at books, magazines and mail-order catalogues together, and through drawing and 'writing'. It was also associated with the quality of the parents' responses to their conversational initiations and to the extent to which, when appropriate, the causes of inadequate communication had been given explicit attention (Moon & Wells, 1979; Raban, in preparation). Thus, whilst part of the facilitating experience of the more successful children involved the shared activities of being read to, and looking at and talking about books, equally important was the way in which everyday events were picked up in talk, and meanings developed and made more coherent through extended conversation.

One of the important dimensions on which these children differed, therefore, was in the extent to which their early experience was influenced by reading and writing, and by the sort of spoken language that is congruent with the books that they would soon be starting to read themselves. We might also reasonably surmise that the difference between parents in the extent to which they provided such experiences was related in part to their own education and to their understanding of their role as the child's first teachers. However, it is very probable that the extent to which, in their own daily lives, they continued to find enjoyment and utility in the exercise of the skills that Olson and others associate with literacy was equally important in influencing their behaviour. Greenfield (1972) describes such homes as those in which people 'speak a written language', and if by that, we understand that meanings are made explicit, when occasion demands, and general conclusions drawn on the basis of overt reasoning, then this is a helpful characterisation. Such an account also comes quite close to some of Bernstein's characterisations of homes which are oriented to an elaborated code. But, whereas for him the determining factor was social class, here the major source of this style of interaction is attributed to the pervading role of literacy in everyday life.

Literacy in school

All the writers we have considered so far are agreed upon the importance of schooling for the development of those cognitive skills that are associated with symbolic activities, though they differ in the extent to which they attribute this development exclusively to the acquisition of literacy. However, all recognise its importance. We might therefore expect that, in those cultures where there is compulsory formal schooling with a strong emphasis on the acquisition and use of literacy, all children would show an increase in ability to engage successfully in higher-level cognitive and symbolic activities, independent of their social background. Yet this has been shown to be very far from the case, as was noted on page 256 above. Differences between social groups that are quite small on entry to school typically increase as the years of schooling progress. Indeed, many pupils, particularly those from families at the lower end of the social scale, leave school hardly more competent with respect to such activities than adolescents in other cultures who have not attended school at all (Deutsch, 1965). Clearly, in such cases, the acquisition of literacy has not led to the cognitive development that is argued to be associated with the processing of written text.

On the basis of such evidence it would be possible to conclude that the consequences of learning to use a written language have been greatly exaggerated. Before taking this step, however, we should consider whether there may be other explanations for the serious underachievement of so many children – particularly those from a lower social class background – who have, nevertheless, learned to read and write.

One possible contributory factor has already been touched upon – the example and support provided by the home. Where the skills associated with the representation of meaning in written language are not used or valued by the parents and other adults in the home environment, children will be less likely to accept the school's valuation of them, or to receive encouragement to persist with tasks that they may initially find difficult or lacking in meaning. However, even with lack of home support, it should be possible for a child to make progress commensurate with his intellectual potential, if appropriate opportunities are provided at school. This, after all, must be the case for many children in non-Western cultures, whose parents have little understanding of schools or of reading and writing.

But are the opportunities at school appropriate for children who come from homes where little value is given to literacy and the uses to which it may be put? Is the teaching of reading and writing meaningful to such children at every stage, and do they understand the tasks they are asked to perform? The knowledge that forms the content of the curriculum and the subject matter about which children are expected to read and write is to some extent unfamiliar to all children, as is the requirement that operations upon that knowledge should be 'disembedded' from particular, familiar situations. But for such children it is of particular importance that, as Barnes (1976) puts it, 'school' knowledge should be converted into 'action' knowledge. A critical question, therefore, is whether sufficient efforts are made, through pupil-initiated tasks, fieldwork and open-ended discussion, to bridge the gap between the relatively abstract formulations of knowledge in the classroom and the children's first-hand experience of the world of 'real' activities outside. The value of a formal education for intellectual development may, as Bruner suggests (p. 252 above), lie in the fact that it is separated from the context of immediately relevant activity, but that does not mean that it should lose touch with its base in such activity. Indeed, without such a base to provide its material, and as a proving-ground in which to test out the conclusions reached through symbolic operations, there is a real danger that classroom learning can become an empty formalism with no impact at all on pupils' general intellectual functioning.

Evidence of this sort of thing happening can be found, for example, in King's (1978) account of three infant schools, where he observed children being given maths cards to complete, although the teachers were well aware that some of the children were unable to read the instructions correctly and so were having to work in partial ignorance of the nature of the tasks. At later stages, too, numerous examples could be cited of pupils copying material into notebooks from blackboard or reference books, although many of the terms used are devoid of meaning for them and their understanding of the principles underlying the material remains at best sketchy and at worst nonexistent. If such situations of 'symbolic violence' (Bourdieu & Passeron, 1977) are at all frequent in pupils' experience, it can hardly be surprising if they fail to appreciate the power for solving 'real' problems that is inherent in the language they are being asked to read and write.

Most important of all, and a question which applies to *all* pupils, regardless of home experience: Are they encouraged to adopt an independent, enquiring and critical attitude to the information that is presented to them and the problems they are given to solve? This, it will be recalled, was the characteristic most responsible for the intellectual development that accompanied the Greeks' discovery of a fully autonomous writing system. Until it is also a characteristic of the way in which reading and writing function in the school experience of all pupils, it would be unwise to reject the arguments that have been put forward for the enhancement of cognitive skills being associated with the practice of literacy. Though, of course, it must be emphasised that what is meant by literacy here is the full exploitation of the meanings encoded in language, whether spoken or written, and not the mere unthinking performance of routine activities of reading and writing.

Unfortunately, where these conditions do not obtain, it is just those children whose parents do not value and encourage the skills of literacy presupposed by formal education who will have most difficulty in understanding and internalising the purpose of many classroom activities. Perhaps this is one of the reasons why so many pupils, discouraged by their lack of success, become bored and uncooperative and eventually reject all invitations to engage in activities which they perceive as 'academic' and associated with the purposes of the school.

At the same time, however, we should not ignore the influences that impinge on pupils and their parents from the wider society outside the school. Clearly the extent of parents' understanding of, and concurrence with, the aims of education cannot be separated from the limited control over their personal lives and their employment opportunities experienced by many members of our hierarchically organised society. Nor can awareness of their parents' and neighbours' experience fail to have an effect, in turn, on the children's level of aspiration and their willingness to engage in academic activities which have no apparent practical pay-off. Large social and material inequalities such as these are undoubtedly a major influence on pupils' school achievement, and any attempt to improve children's opportunities for intellectual development must tackle the sources of inequality as well as their resulting manifestations in school.

Nevertheless, since one way to break out of the cycle of oppression is to acquire and make full use of the skills of literacy (Freire, 1970), it is still important that schools do everything they can to ensure that each pupil discovers the power that control of these skills can bring – whatever the degree of support and encouragement provided by the home. So it is to a consideration of the classroom implications of the argument developed in this chapter that we turn in the final section.

Implications for the classroom

In the introduction to this chapter it was suggested that there are three broad phases in language development, with the acquisition of literacy being intimately connected with the third. Vygotsky (1962), too, refers to three stages in the development of any psychological function in somewhat parallel terms. In the first stage, he argues, a function is acquired in an undifferentiated form and then, in the second stage, it is gradually differentiated. Only in the third stage, however, does it become available for conscious exploitation. One of the main arguments of this chapter has been that it is in and through the acquisition of the skills of literacy that the individual's command of language reaches the stage where it is available for deliberate and conscious exploitation. However, reading and writing are themselves functions which go through the same stages of development and this should be borne in mind in planning the language curriculum.

As we have seen above, Bruner considers that the higher levels of symbolic functioning are only attained as a result of systematic training, and it is to provide such training, amongst other things, that systems of formal education have been instituted. Acquisition of the ability to read and write are also usually seen as requiring systematic instruction, and in this the acquisition of literacy is seen to contrast with spontaneous untaught, acquisition of speech. However, whilst it is probably true that most children would not learn to read and write if left entirely to their own devices, the contrast has been much exaggerated. Parents, whether deliberately or spontaneously, do frequently act and speak in ways which help their children to learn to talk. Teachers, on the other hand, although typically much more systematic and didactic in their interaction with young children, do not always teach in ways which promote their pupils' learning. The point, of course, is that learning and teaching are not related to each other in any simple reciprocal relationship: much that we are taught we fail to learn and much that we learn is learned without teaching.

A very important distinction needs to be made, in fact, between teaching that is directed by a concern to provide optimum conditions for individual children to learn, and teaching that is directed by a predetermined structure that is mainly for the teacher's benefit. The reason for the continuing popularity of complete reading schemes, for example, seems to owe as much to teachers' need of reassurance that pupils are 'progressing' systematically, as it does to their considered belief that such material best meets the needs of each individual child. This is not, of course, to argue that deliberate instruction is never appropriate, nor that systematically organised materials are not useful as a resource to draw upon (cf. Moon & Raban, 1980), but simply to suggest that the decision as to when and how to use them should be based on the particular current needs of individual children and not on the dictates of some abstract curriculum.

As Walkerdine and Sinha argue in chapter 5, a child will find it much easier to take on the curricular goals and orientations to knowledge of the classroom, and make them his own, if continuity of learning can be maintained as far as possible between home and school. Most of the child's early learning at home occurs as a result of recognising and attempting to solve problems which arise in the course of practical activities that are frequently initiated by the child himself. The adult role that seems to be most helpful is chiefly one of giving encouragement to sustain motivation and providing a resource of information and skill from which the child can take according to his own purposes.

With the transition to school there must inevitably be changes in the relationship between child learner and adult 'helper', since one of the chief aims of schooling is to help the child to transcend the limitations of thinking which is tied to the context of immediate practical activity. The teacher will thus wish to channel the child's interests and encourage him to engage in tasks which require him to master new skills for obtaining, organising and utilising information, and to become more reflective in his approach to problem-solving. However, there is still an important place for child-initiated practical activities, as these can provide both the starting point and the motivation for the more abstract learning which it is wished to encourage.

The extract in table 7.1 from a recording made in a junior class-

Table 7.1. *Excerpt from the dialogue in a junior classroom**

T: Colin, are you having a problem?

C: Just trying to – think out – something
Just trying to think out how high I want the pole

T: Could you work there a while, I'll just help Colin. [to another child]
[Teacher joins Colin, who is using a metre stick, extending it with a small ruler. He is reading off the measurement he needs for the height of the tripod he is planning to make]

C: One metre and –

T: Can you imagine for a minute that you're taking a photograph. How high would be comfortable?

C: Er, this is what I done – trying to find that out. I put this like that and held it and just pretend that I was looking through and I thought I'd have it about that high cos that could include the camera on top and that's how far I want it – one metre and 13 – [Counts on small ruler]
One metre and thirteen centimetres

T: Is that going to be the height of your tripod?

C: Yes – of the pole.

T: Is each pole going to be that height?

C: I'm only going to have three um – yes. The other 2 are going to be a bit longer.

T: Can you show me how you're going to do your plan?

C: I've got –

T: Sit yourself down.

C: I've got a ⟨lump⟩ of wood

Table 7.1. *Excerpt from the dialogue in a junior classroom** [cont.]

T: Pardon
    I've got some wood, – and that's what its
    going to look like. It's going to have those
    bits so I can put something around it to
    hold the camera on and – I'm going to try
    and get something that can – a round hole
    – but that could hold on – on legs which is
    going to be rather hard.

T: Have you looked in the camera book to see if
    it shows a diagram that would help you?

C: – er I have looked in one

T: Did you notice that there was another one
    there today?

C: No – Yes there is

T: Perhaps in a moment you'd like to look at
    that – that might be helpful.

C: Yes

T: What else will you need?

C: Um yes. – A sharp tool that I can make the
    ends of them – rather sharp so they can dig
    in the ground – or I could have blunt ones
    that just stand out to keep it steady.

T: And how will you set your tripod up?

C: It's going to always be set up (laughs) – just
    all you have to do is just take it outside to
    something – like that.

T: How do you think that's going to improve
    your photography?

C: It's going to keep it much stiller and the
    picture will be much better – cos they
    won't go blurry through movement.

T: Will you have a look at that book with me?

C: Yes

[Colin settles and looks
through book]

---

* From part of an ETV programme (McKenzie, 1980) recorded in a first-year junior
class in a London school. I am grateful to Moira McKenzie for bringing it to my
attention and allowing me to reproduce it.

room gives an example of how this can occur. Colin (aged 7 years) has used the school camera and is interested to find out more about how it works. In this extract he is planning how he is going to make a tripod for the model camera that he is constructing, and is thinking through in advance the problems he is likely to encounter. By engaging him in discussion about his plan, the teacher helps him to represent it symbolically in language and to reflect upon the implications of what he has said. The extract also illustrates how, in order to carry out the demanding task he has set himself, Colin is led quite naturally to consult reference books and to represent his proposed solution in another symbolic form – that of the plan that he is drawing.

Colin, of course, can already read – and write – with some fluency, and is at the stage of putting these skills to use. He has already begun to discover the value of literacy. For many children, however, this discovery takes much longer to achieve, as they struggle with the unfamiliar medium of written or printed text. As already mentioned, progress is much more rapid if children already have some familiarity with the purposes and conventions of written language when they come to school. But even then there is a great deal that is new and unfamiliar about the written representation of language that has to be mastered in order to become a fluent reader (cf. Perera (1979) for a helpful discussion of the similarities and differences between speech and writing).

It would not be appropriate here to embark on a full discussion of the relative merits of the various approaches to the teaching of reading and, in any case, the subject has been excellently treated by others (e.g. Clay, 1972; Holdaway, 1972; Mackay et al., 1970; Smith, 1978). However, some of the points discussed in earlier sections have a bearing on this issue and are worth considering a little further.

In the paper by Olson (1977) referred to earlier, the claim is made that in written language the meaning is in the text and that, in comprehending (or constructing) such texts, dependence on presupposed, commonsense, knowledge of the world should be reduced to a minimum. Although, as we have seen, this is a goal that can only be approximated, the path towards this goal is one that teachers should be concerned with from the beginning. Ideally, from this point of view, the 'decoding' approach to reading would seem best able to assist the child to grasp the text-centred organisation of meaning in written language, since it focuses attention upon the text as text from the beginning. However, as Olson himself recognises, this approach could only be successful if the child were already familiar with this use of language in spoken form and, in addition, had no difficulties with the conventions of written language. However, since this is rarely the case, we should not take Olson's characterisation of written language as a justification for adopting a wholesale decoding approach.

On the other hand, complete reliance on context as a strategy for obtaining meaning from text, which might seem to be advocated by Goodman (1968), for example, is not going to be successful either, in the long run, in promoting an analytic approach to the encoded meaning, since it merely perpetuates the strategies evolved for comprehending conversationally situated speech. This can be very helpful for the beginning reader, but to become fully literate requires the development of the ability to treat the text as the primary locus of meaning. A competent reader does not merely use the text as a cue to guessing the meaning intended by the writer; he also uses it to determine what that meaning is.

There are, it seems to me, a number of ways out of this dilemma; ways which are, in fact, adopted by successful teachers. The first of these involves the recognition that initial mastery of the skills of decoding is best achieved in the context of reconstructing meanings from texts that are interesting in themselves. But such texts must also be sufficiently close in content and form to the spoken utterances with which the child is familiar for him to be able to adopt strategies already developed for the comprehension of speech. Then, as fluency is gradually achieved, emphasis can begin to be focused more precisely on the meanings and implications conveyed by the specific form of the written text. Alongside this runs a two-fold emphasis on possibilities inherent in spoken language, both of which prepare the child to cope with meaning in written text, but both of which are valuable in their own right. The first involves frequent reading aloud to children from a wide variety of written texts, so that they become increasingly familiar with 'the language of books' and better able to recognise the characteristic patterns of written text in the books that they read for themselves. The second involves encouraging children to formulate their questions, instructions and statements in such a way that intended meaning is made more fully explicit. In this way the children develop a more reflective awareness of the precise meaning of what is said and begin to discover the power of symbolic representation for posing and resolving problems of many different kinds.

Equally important in the practice of the successful teacher is the provision of opportunities to engage in activities which vary the demands made on children's growing language skills. As has already been argued, different curricular goals call for different styles of linguistic interaction (cf. Brown, 1978; Wells, 1978), and it is an important part of a teacher's skill to be able to induct children into appropriate ways of speaking for different purposes and in different contexts. Using the children's own interests as the starting point for activities is particularly valuable in this respect. For, where the child is the originator of the task in hand, he is likely to have a much greater commitment to it and to take much greater responsibility for formulating his ideas in a manner which is clear and explicit enough for others to understand. Explaining his ideas to a critical but interested group of fellow pupils, as well as to the teacher, is particularly beneficial from this point of view.

A similar approach to the skills of written language is also necessary, as Scribner & Cole (1978) make clear. Activities that are intended to develop analytic reasoning skills need to be distinguished from those intended to encourage clear reporting and summarising of facts. Similarly, children's attention needs to be drawn to the various purposes that are served by the different kinds of relationships between words and phrases: for example, the emotive associations that express feeling and evoke mood, on the one hand, and, on the other, the logical relations that link the steps in an argument or exposition. Naturally, these differentiated uses of written language can only be introduced gradually, and whenever possible they should be linked to the children's first-hand experiences so that they will be perceived as having meaning for them. However, the wider the range of activities that can be realistically engaged in, the more likely it is that the skills of literacy developed in school will be valued and utilised beyond the confines of the classroom.

The final point I wish to make concerns the importance of writing. Many discussions of literacy, particularly of the early stages, give most of their attention to reading. But it is in the process of composition – in 'wrestling with words and meanings' – whether to render

subtleties of feeling, to convey precise observation of objects, or to
develop a coherent line of reasoning, that one ultimately becomes
most fully aware of the power – and limitations – of the written
language (cf. Britton et al. 1975). It is also through writing in various
modes that one is most called upon to develop those skills of literacy
which are associated with higher levels of cognitive activity. In my
view, therefore, the common practice of waiting until children are
already quite fluent readers before encouraging them to compose
written texts is to miss one of the most effective means of introducing
them to the possibilities that this new medium of communication
makes available.

The reason usually given for this separation of receptive and
productive activities is the difficulty children have in mastering the
skills of handwriting. But this need not be a deterrent for a resourceful teacher. One possibility is for children to 'write aloud' their
stories, notices, observations and so on, which the teacher can either
take down on the spot or recover from a recorded tape later in the
day. The 'Breakthrough sentence-maker' (Mackay et al. 1970) and
other similar devices offer another possibility. Whatever method
adopted, teachers who encourage 'composition' from the beginning
of the literacy programme testify to the important contribution that
this makes to their pupils' growing understanding of the forms and
functions characteristic of written language.

In the following examples we see some of these particular characteristics of written language beginning to emerge in the free writing
of two girls, both nearly 6 years old. The first two examples come
from a book about things which interested her, compiled, complete
with index, during an absence from school (Collerson, 1978). The
first piece concerns everyday objects and, in the choice of the
superordinate term 'pottery' to include 'a dish' and 'a cup' and in the
use of the timeless present tense and the impersonal pronoun 'you',
represents the first steps towards abstract generalisation.

Pottery

Pottery is useful because you can drink and
eat out of it. You eat off a dish and drink out
of a cup. Pottery goes in cupboards.

The second piece is also an observation, but although it also uses the present tense to express the timelessness of the statements being made, in its use of metaphor – the moon 'watching the sun' – and the repeated antithesis of 'stars' and 'moon', it moves towards the sort of shaping of experience that is more characteristic of poetry.

Stars and the Moon

There are lots of stars in the sky. Stars are important,
so is the moon. Stars twinkle; the moon shines at night.
You can see them. Sometimes the moon is up at daytime
watching the sun.

The final example comes from writing done in class and, in its simple narrative pattern, it is quite typical of the sort of 'stories' that children produce at this stage. However, what is particularly interesting about this piece is that, in making up a story about the letters in her name, Melanie demonstrates her awareness of the arbitrariness of linguistic form and of the separation between form and the objects and events to which they normally refer. Here we see, then, another aspect of the development of a reflective attitude to experience that can be encouraged by learning to write.

One day there was a M and the M
played with the e and the e played with the l
and the l played with the a and the a played with n
and the n played with the i and the i played
with the e and the e played with nobody
and the e was very sad. (from Raban, forthcoming)

In these examples we see only the very early stages of writing, but already there is an indication of how, in engaging in the attempt to capture and arrange meanings in a form which has objective existence in a permanent text on the page, these writers are discovering something of the creative and intellectual satisfaction of writing. Of the developmental processes that lead from these beginnings to the full integration of aesthetic, intellectual and social skills with command of the language system itself we are still extremely ignorant (but cf. Bereiter, 1979; Clay, 1975). However, if the arguments of this chapter are essentially correct, it is through helping each individual child to master and use these skills that schools make one of their most important contributions to children's development. For it is in learning, through writing, to become reflectively aware of both the uniqueness and the universality of human experience and of their own and other people's responses to that experience, that children can most fully take possession of the heritage of a literate civilisation, and contribute to its further development.

Appendix

Bristol language development study: transcripts

Conventions and layout of transcripts
The speech of the child being studied is set out in the left-hand column. The speech of all other participants is set out in the centre column, with identifying initials were necessary. Each new utterance starts on a new line.

Contextual information is enclosed in square brackets [ ] and set out in the right-hand column.

Interpretations of utterances and descriptions of tone of voice, where applicable, are enclosed in round brackets ( ) and included immediately after the utterance to which they apply.

Utterances, or parts of utterances, about which there is doubt are enclosed in angular brackets ⟨ ⟩; where two interpretations are possible they are both given, separated by an oblique stroke.

Symbols of the International Phonetic Alphabet are used for utterances, or parts of utterances, which cannot be interpreted with certainty. Phonetic symbols are always enclosed by square brackets. Except where there is doubt about the speaker's intended meaning, the speech is transcribed in Standard English orthography.

The following is a list of additional symbols used, with an explanation of their significance (stops and commas are not used as in normal punctuation).

?	used at end of any utterance where an interrogative meaning is considered to have been intended
!	used at the end of an utterance considered to have exclamatory intention
'	apostrophe: used as normal for contractions and elision of syllables
*	used to indicate unintelligibility, for whatever reason. The number of asterisks corresponds as nearly as possible to the number of words judged to have been uttered
. . .	stops are used to indicate pauses. One stop is used for a very short

	pause. Thereafter, the number of stops used corresponds to the estimated length of the pause in seconds. Pauses over 5 seconds in length are shown with the figure for the length of the pause, e.g. . . 8 . .
———	where utterances overlap because both speakers speak at once, the overlapping portions are underlined
" "	inverted commas are used to enclose utterances considered to be 'speech for self'
+	indicates unbroken intonation contour where a pause or clause boundary might otherwise indicate the end of an utterance
–	indicates a hiatus, either because the utterance is incomplete or because the speaker makes a fresh start at the word or utterance
(v)	indicates that the preceding word was used as a vocative, to call or hold the attention of the addressee

Intonation

Some of the transcripts include a representation of intonation, in which case the following additional conventions apply:

/	tone unit boundary. Where an utterance consists of only one tone unit, no boundaries are marked

'	this symbol immediately precedes both prominent and tonic syllables
	    Prominent syllables[1] take a single digit before the symbol to indicate their relative pitch height
	    Tonic syllables[2] take two or more digits before the symbol to indicate the onset level, range and direction of significant pitch movement (see 'Pitch height' below)

↑ ↓	shift of pitch range relatively higher or lower than that normal for the speaker
↑↑ ↓↓	shift to extra high or extra low pitch
:	lengthened syllable. The symbol follows the syllable to which it applies

Pitch height. The height, direction and range of significant pitch movement is represented by a set of digits corresponding to points on a scale. The pitch range of a speaker is divided into five notional intervals, numbered 1–5 from high to low, thus:

---

[1] Prominent syllables are salient with respect to combinations of pitch, duration and intensity.

[2] Tonic syllables carry at least the onset of significant pitch movement. Significant pitch movement in its entirety may, of course, occur on a single syllable or be spread over a number of syllables.

The following information is retrievable from this coding:

Direction of movement	Halliday (1967) Tones
Falling: (e.g. 13, 25)	Tone 1
Rising: (e.g. 31, 43)	Tone 2
Level: (e.g. 33)	Tone 3
Fall–Rise: (e.g. 343) or (e.g. 342)	Tone 4 or Tone 2[3]
Rise–Fall: (e.g. 324)	Tone 5

Conversation between a child and his mother (table 1.1) Mark (28 months) and Mother are in the kitchen. Mother has just finished washing up

1	13 'Play Mummy(v)	
2	M: All 232 'right	
3	1 '[ʃɪʃ] wash 32 'up / 21 'Mummy(v)?	
	(=have you finished washing up?)	
4	M: 21 'Pardon?	
5	1 '[ʃɪʃ] wash 31 'up?	
6	M: 44 'Yes	
7	34 'Oh	
8	M: Let me just 24 'dry my hands	
9	343 'Alright	
10	23 'In there	[Mark looks for towel]
11	M: 24 'Here	
12	34 '[ɪəa] (= here you are)	[Mark gives towel to Mother]
13	M: 2 'Just a 343 'minute	
14	M: Will you put the 2 'top back on the	
	23 'washing basket / 32 'please	
15	32 'Uh?	
16	31 'Uh?	
17	M: 3 'Put the 32 'top / back on the	
	14 'washing basket	
18	↑ On 13 'there / 32 'Mummy(v)?	
19	On 232 'there?	
20	M: 23 'Yes	

[3] Fall–rise movements may be of two types, corresponding to Halliday's Tone 2 and Tone 4. They are conventionally denoted in the transcripts as follows: Tone 2 is represented with a higher terminal pitch than its onset (e.g. 342), whereas Tone 4 is represented as having a terminal pitch no higher than its onset (e.g. 232, 354).

Conversation between a child and his mother (table 1.1) Mark (28 months) and Mother are in the Kitchen. Mother has just finished washing up [*cont.*]

21		M: No not the 2 'towel in 43 'there	
22		M: The 2 'top of the 24 'basket on it	
23	343 'Alright		
24	On 24 'there		
25	↑ 31 'Uh?		
26	32 'Uh?		
27		M: 2 'Put the 32 'lid / . . on 2 'top of the 24 'basket	
28	On er – on 232 'there?		
29		M: Yes 33 'please	
30	232 'Alright		
31	32 'You / 32 'dry / 42 'hands		
32		M: I've 23 'dried my hands now	
33	Put towel in 34 'there		
34		M: 13 'No / it's 2 'not 32 'dirty	
35	342 'Tis		
36		M: No it 32 'isn't	
37	342 'Tis		
38	32 'Mummy(v) / 24 'play		
39	23 'Play Mummy(v)		
40		M: Well I 13 'will play / if you put the 2 'top on the 32 'basket	
41	342 'Alright		
42	24 'There		[Mark puts top on basket]
43	34 'There		
44	14 'Play Mummy(v)		
45	23 'Mummy(v) / come 24 'on		

Conversation between a child and his mother (table 2.3) Mark (23 months) is in the kitchen with Mother and sister Helen (9 months)

1	232 'Mummy(v)		[Mark is looking in a
2	13 'Mummy		mirror and sees
3		M 23 'What?	reflections of himself
4	24 'There / there 34 'Mark		and his mother]
5		M: Is that 232 'Mark?	
6	231 'Mummy		
7		M: 231 'Mm	
8	231 'Mummy		
9		M: 231 'Yes / that's 231 'Mummy	
10	453*		

Conversation between a child and his mother (table 2.3) Mark (23 months) is in the kitchen with Mother and sister Helen (9 months) [*cont.*]

11	24 'Mummy
12	232 'Mummy(v)
13	M: 231 'Mm
14	24 'There / 231 'Mummy
	. . .
15	232 'Mummy (v)
16	13 'There / Mark 24 'there
17	M: 2 'Look at 24 'Helen
18	M: She's going to 13 'sleep
	(30 seconds' pause)
19	13 '[ɛəæ] (= look at that) [Mark can see birds in
20	23 'Birds / 34 'Mummy(v) the garden]
21	M: 213 'Mm
22	23 'Jubs (= birds)
23	M: What are they 34 'doing?
24	Jub 13 'bread
25	M: Oh 213 'look
26	M: They're 343 'eating /the 12 'berries / 14 'aren't they?
27	24 'Yeh
28	M: 2 'That's their 213 'food
29	M: They have 343 'berries / for 23 'dinner
30	24 'Oh

Conversation between a child and his mother (table 2.5) Mark (25 months) is in the dining room with Mother. Mark is looking out of the window

---

1	Where 232 'man gone? [Mark has seen a man
2	Where 232 'man gone? working in his
3	M: I don't 13 'know garden]
4	M: I 2 ex'pect he's gone 23 in'side / because it's 34 'snowing
	. . .
5	Where man 231 'gone?
6	M: In the ↑13 'house
7	32 'Uh?
8	M: Into his 34 'house
9	232 'No
10	121 'No

Conversation between a child and his mother (table 2.5) Mark (25 months) is in the dining room with Mother. Mark is looking out of the window [*cont.*]

11	Gone to 23'shop / 33 'Mummy(v)	[The local shop is close
12		M: Gone 342 'where? to Mark's house]
13	Gone 24 'shop	
14		M: To the 231 'shop?
15	23 'Yeh	
16		M: 2 'What's he going to 34 'buy?
17	44 Er – / 231 'biscuits	
18		M: 232 'Biscuits / 343 'mm
19	32 'Uh?	
20		M: 343 'Mm
21		M: What 34 'else?
22	44 Er – / 231 'meat	
23		M: 33 'Mm
24	342 'Meat	
25	33 Er – / 231 'sweeties	
26	Buy a 23 'big / 34 'bag / 45 'sweets	
27		M: Buy 232 'sweets?
28	24 'Yeh	
29	M – er – buy – man / the 23 'man / 23 'buy / 34 'sweets	
30		M: 32 'Will he?
31	23 'Yeh	
32	Daddy buy 232 'sweets	
33	Daddy buy 342 'sweets	
34		M: 24 'Why?
35	23 'Oh / er – [ə] 23 'shop	
36	Mark do buy 32 'some – / 32 'sweet – / 43 'sweeties	
37	Mark buy 32 'some – / 32 'um –	
38	Mark buy 32 'some – / 32 'um –	
39	I 342 'did	

References

Anglin, J. M. (1977) *Word, Object and Conceptual Development*. New York: Norton Press.

Argyle, M. (1969) *Social Interaction*. London: Methuen.

Atkinson, J. M. & Drew, P. (1979) *Order in Court*. London: Macmillan.

Austin, J. L. (1962) *How to do Things with Words*. Oxford University Press.

Baldie, B. J. (1976) The acquisition of the passive voice. *Journal of Child Language* 3: 331–48.

Barnes, D. (1969) *Language, the Learner and the School*. Harmondsworth, Middx: Penguin.

(1976) *From Communication to Curriculum*. Harmondsworth, Middx: Penguin.

Bates, E., Camaioni, L. & Volterra, V. (1975) The acquisition of performatives prior to speech. *Merrill-Palmer Quarterly* 21.3: 205–26.

Bem, S. (1970) The role of comprehension in children's problem solving. *Developmental Psychology* 2: 351–8.

Benedict, H. (1978) Language comprehension in 9–15 month old children. In Campbell, R. N. & Smith, P. T. (eds) *Recent Advances in the Psychology of Language: language development and mother–child interaction*. New York: Plenum Press.

Bennett, J. (1976) *Linguistic Behaviour*. Cambridge University Press.

Bereiter, C. (1979) Development in writing. In Gregg, L. W. & Steinberg, E. (eds) *Cognitive Processes in Writing*. Hillsdale, NJ: Erlbaum.

Berko-Gleason, J. (1977) Talking to children: some notes on feedback. In Snow, C. E. & Ferguson, C. A. (eds) *Talking to Children: language input and acquisition*. Cambridge University Press.

Berko-Gleason, J. & Weintraub, S. (1978) Input language and the acquisition of communicative competence. In Nelson, K. E. (ed.) *Children's Language*, vol. I. New York: Gardner Press.

Bernstein, B. (1971) *Class, Codes and Control*, vol. I. London: Routledge & Kegan Paul.

Bever, T. G. (1970) The cognitive basis for linguistic structures. In Hayes, J. R. (ed.) *Cognition and the Development of Language*. New York: Wiley.

Bierwisch, M. (1970) Semantics. In Lyons, J. (ed.) *New Horizons in Linguistics*. Harmondsworth, Middx: Penguin.

Blank, M. (1973) *Teaching Learning in the Preschool: a dialogue approach*. Columbus, Ohio: Merrill.

Bloom, L. M. (1970) *Language Development: form and function in emerging grammars*. Cambridge, Mass.: MIT Press.

(1973) *One Word at a Time*. The Hague: Mouton.

Bloom, L. M., Lightbown, P. & Hood, L. (1975) *Structure and Variation in Child Language*. Society for Research in Child Development Monographs 40.

Bloom, L. M., Rocissano, L. & Hood, L. (1976) Adult–child discourse: developmental interaction between information processing and linguistic knowledge. *Cognitive Psychology* 8: 527–52.

Blumenthal, A. L. (1970) *Language and Psychology: historical aspects of psycholinguistics*. New York: Wiley.

Bourdieu, P. & Passeron, J. C. (1977) *Reproduction: toward a theory of educational systems*. Beverly Hills, Calif.: Sage.

Bowerman, M. (1973) *Early Syntactic Development: a cross-linguistic study with special reference to Finnish*. Cambridge University Press.

(1978) The acquisition of word meaning: an investigation into some current conflicts. In Waterson, N. & Snow, C. E. (eds) *The Development of Communication*. London: Wiley.

Boyd, D. (1974) *Elites and their Education: the educational and social background of eight elite groups*. Windsor: NFER.

Bransford, J. D. & McCarrell, N. S. (1974) A sketch of a cognitive approach to comprehension: some thoughts about understanding what it means to comprehend. In Weimer, W. B. & Palermo, D. S. (eds) *Cognition and the Symbolic Processes*. Hillsdale, NJ: Erlbaum.

Braunwald, S. R. (1978) Context, word and meaning: towards a communicational analysis of lexical acquisition. In Lock, A. J. (ed.) *Action, Gesture and Symbol: the emergence of language*. London: Academic Press.

Brazil, D. (1975) *Discourse Intonation*. University of Birmingham, English Language Research.

(1978) *Discourse Intonation II*. University of Birmingham, English Language Research.

Bridges, A. (1979) Directing two-year-olds' attention: some clues to understanding. *Journal of Child Language* 6: 211–26.

(1980) SVO comprehension strategies reconsidered: the evidence of individual patterns of response. *Journal of Child Language* 7: 89–104.

Britton, J. (1970) *Language and Learning*. London: Allen Lane.

Britton, J. et al. (1975) *The Development of Writing Abilities*. London: Macmillan.

Broen, P. A. (1972) *The Verbal Environment of the Language Learning Child*. American Speech & Hearing Association Monograph 17.

Brown, G. (1978) Understanding spoken language. *TESOL Quarterly* 12.3: 271–83.

Brown, R. (1958) How shall a thing be called? *Psychological Review* 65: 14–21.

(1973) *A First Language: the early stages*. London: Allen & Unwin.

(1977) Introduction. In Snow, C. E. & Ferguson, C. A. (eds) *Talking to Children: language input and acquisition*. Cambridge University Press.

Brown, R., Cazden, C. & Bellugi, U. (1969) The child's grammar from I to III. In Hill, J. P. (ed.) *The Second Annual Minnesota Symposium on Child Psychology*. Minneapolis: University of Minnesota Press.

Bruner, J. S. (1964) The course of cognitive growth. *American Psychologist* 19: 1–15.

(1972) *The Relevance of Education*. Harmondsworth, Middx: Penguin Education.

(1974) *Beyond the Information Given: studies in the psychology of knowing*. London: Allen & Unwin.

(1975a) The ontogenesis of speech acts. *Journal of Child Language* 2: 1–19.

(1975b) From communication to language: a psychological perspective. *Cognition* 3: 255–87. Reprinted in Lee, V. (ed.) *Language Development*. London: Croom Helm, 1979.

(1977) The role of dialogue in language acquisition. Paper given at the Conference on the Child's Conception of Language, Nijmegen, May 1977.

(1978) Learning how to do things with words. In Bruner, J. S. & Garton, A. (eds) *Human Growth and Development*. Oxford University Press.

Bruner, J. S. & Greenfield, P. M. (1972) Culture and cognitive growth. In Bruner, J. S. *The Relevance of Education*. Harmondsworth, Middx: Penguin Education.

Bruner, J. S., Olver, R. & Greenfield, P. M. (1966) *Studies in Cognitive Growth*. New York: Wiley.

Campbell, R. & Wales, R. (1970) On the study of language acquisition. In Lyons, J. (ed.) *New Horizons in Linguistics*. Harmondsworth, Middx: Penguin.

Carter, A. (1974) The development of communication in the sensori-motor period: a case study. Unpublished PhD dissertation, University of California, Berkeley.

(1979) Prespeech meaning relations: an outline of one infant's sensorimotor morpheme development. In Fletcher, P. & Garman, M. (eds) *Language Acquisition*. Cambridge University Press.

Chafe, W. L. (1970) *Meaning and the Structure of Language*. University of Chicago Press.

(1974) Conversation with Wallace Chafe. In Parret, H., *Discussing Language*. The Hague: Mouton.

(1977) Creativity in verbalisation and its implications for the nature of stored knowledge. In Freedle, R. O. (ed.) *Discourse Production and Comprehension*. Norwood, NJ: Ablex Publishing Corp.

Chapman, R. S. (1974) Discussion summary: developmental relationship between receptive and expressive language. In Schiefelbusch, R. L. & Lloyd, L. L. (eds) *Language Perspectives: acquisition, retardation and intervention*. Cambridge, Mass.: MIT Press.

(1978) Comprehension strategies in children. In Kavanagh, J. F. & Strange, W. (eds) *Speech and Language in Laboratory, School and Clinic*. Cambridge, Mass.: MIT Press.

Chapman, R. S. & Kohn, L. L. (1977) Comprehension strategies in two and three year olds: animate agents or probable events? Paper presented to the Stanford Child Language Research Forum, Stanford University, California.

Chomsky, C. (1969) *The Acquisition of Syntax in Children from 5–10*. Cambridge, Mass.: MIT Press.

Chomsky, N. A. (1957) *Syntactic Structures*. The Hague: Mouton.

(1959) Review of 'Verbal Behaviour' by B. F. Skinner. *Language* 35: 26–58.

(1964) Discussion of Miller and Ervin's paper. In Bellugi, U. & Brown, R. (eds) *The Acquisition of Language*. Society for Research in Child Development Monographs 29.1.

(1965) *Aspects of the Theory of Syntax*. Cambridge, Mass.: MIT Press.

(1968) *Language and Mind*. New York: Harcourt, Brace & World.

(1976) *Reflections on Language*. London: Temple Smith (in assoc. with Fontana Books).

Cicourel, A. V. (1973) *Cognitive Sociology*. Harmondsworth, Middx: Penguin.

Clark, E. V. (1973a) What's in a word? On the child's acquisition of semantics in his first language. In Moore, T. E. (ed.) *Cognitive Development and the Acquisition of Language*. New York: Academic Press.

(1973b) Non-linguistic strategies and the acquisition of word meanings. *Cognition* 2: 161–82.

(1977) Strategies and the mapping problem in first language acquisition. In Macnamara, J. (ed.) *Language Learning and Thought*. New York: Academic Press.

Clark, H. H. (1978) Inferring what is meant. In Levelt, W. J. M. & Flores d'Arcais, G. B. (eds) *Studies in Perception of Language*. New York: Wiley.

Clark, H. H. & Clark, E. V. (1977) *Language and Psychology*. New York: Harcourt, Brace Jovanovich.

Clark, H. H. & Haviland, S. E. (1977) Comprehension and the given–new contract. In Freedle, R. O. (ed.) *Discourse Production and Comprehension*. Norwood, NJ: Ablex Publishing Corp.

Clay, M. M. (1972) *Reading: the patterning of complex behaviour*. London: Heinemann Educational.

(1975) *What Did I Write?* Auckland: Heinemann Educational Books (N.Z.).

Coghill, V. (1978) Infant school reasoning. Unpublished papers, Teachers' Research Group, University of London Institute of Education.

Collerson, J. W. (1978) *The Development of Children's Writing*. Working Paper 1, Milperra College of Advanced Education, New South Wales.

Cromer, R. (1974) The development of language and cognition: the cognition hypothesis. In Foss, B. M. (ed.) *New Perspectives in Child Development*. Harmondsworth, Middx: Penguin.

(1976) Developmental strategies for language. In Hamilton, V. & Vernon, M. D. (eds) *The Development of Cognitive Processes*. New York: Academic Press.

Cross, T. G. (1977) Mothers' speech adjustments: the contribution of selected child listener variables. In Snow, C. E. & Ferguson, C. A. (eds) *Talking to Children: language input and acquisition*. Cambridge University Press.

(1978) Mothers' speech and its association with rate of linguistic development in young children. In Waterson, N. & Snow, C. E. (eds) *The Development of Communication*. Chichester: Wiley.

Crystal, D., Fletcher, P. & Garman, M. (1976) *The Grammatical Analysis of Language Disability: a procedure for assessment and remediation*. London: Edward Arnold.

Davies, E. C. (1979) *On the Semantics of Syntax*. London: Croom Helm.

Derwing, B. L. (1973) *Transformational Grammar as a Theory of Language Acquisition*. Cambridge University Press.

Deutsch, M. (1965) The role of social class in language development and cognition. *American Journal of Orthopsychiatry* 35.1: 78–88.

de Villiers, J. G. & de Villiers, P. A. (1973) The development of the use of word order in comprehension. *Journal of Psycholinguistic Research* 1.4: 331–41.

(1974) Competence and performance in child language: are children really competent to judge? *Journal of Child Language* 1: 11–22.

Dewart, M. H. (1975) A psychological investigation of sentence comprehension by children. Unpublished PhD thesis, University College, London.

Donaldson, M. (1978) *Children's Minds*. London: Fontana.

Dore, J. (1975) Holophrases, speech acts and language universals. *Journal of Child Language* 2: 21–40.

(1979) Conversation and preschool language development. In Fletcher, P. & Garman, M. (eds) *Language Acquisition*. Cambridge University Press.

Douglas, J. W. B. (1964) *The Home and the School: study of ability and attainment in the primary schools*. London: MacGibbon & Kee.

Drew, P. (1978) Accusations: the occasioned use of members' knowledge of 'religious geography' in describing events. *Sociology* 12.1: 1–22.

(in press) The organisation and management of corrections in 'instructional' talk: a response to Wells and Montgomery. In French, P. & MacLure, M. (eds) *Adult–Child Conversation: studies in structure and process*. London: Croom Helm.

Durkin, D. (1966) *Children Who Read Early*. New York: Teachers' College Press.

Edwards, A. D. (1976a) *Language in Culture and Class*. London: Heinemann Educational.

(1976b) Speech codes and speech variants: social-class and task differences in children's speech. *Journal of Child Language* 3: 247–66.

(in press) Analysing classroom talk. In French, P. & MacLure, M. (eds) *Adult–Child Conversation: studies in structure and process*. London: Croom Helm.

Edwards, A. D. & Furlong, V. T. (1978) *The Language of Teaching: meaning in classroom interaction*. London: Heinemann Educational.

Edwards, D. (1978) Social relations and early language. In Lock, A. J. (ed.) *Action, Gesture and Symbol: the emergence of language*. London: Academic Press.

Eimas, P. D., Siqueland, E. R., Jusczyk, P. & Vigorito, J. (1971) Speech perception in infants. *Science* 171: 303–6.

Eliot, T. S. (1944) *Four Quartets*. London: Faber & Faber.

Ellis, R. & Wells, C. G. (1980) Enabling factors in adult–child discourse. *First Language* 1: 46–62.

Ervin-Tripp, S. M. (1976) Is Sybil there? The structure of some American-English directives. *Language in Society* 5: 25–66.

(1977a) Wait for me, Roller-skate. In Ervin-Tripp, S. M. & Mitchell-Kernan, C. (eds) *Child Discourse*. New York: Academic Press.

(1977b) Some features of early adult–child dialogues. Unpublished paper.

(in press) Speech acts, social meaning and social learning. In Giles, H., Robinson, W. P. & Smith, P. M. (eds) *Language: social psychological perspectives*. Oxford: Pergamon.

Ervin-Tripp, S. M. & Miller, W. (1977) Early discourse: some questions about questions. In Lewis, M. & Rosenblum, L. A. (eds) *Interaction, Conversation, and the Development of Language*. New York: Wiley.

Ervin-Tripp, S. M. & Mitchell-Kernan, C. (eds) (1977) *Child Discourse*. New York: Academic Press.

Ferguson, C. A. (1964) Baby talk in six languages. *American Anthropologist* 66: 103–14.

Ferrier, L. J. (1978) Some observations of error in context. In Waterson, N. & Snow, C. E. (eds) *The Development of Communication*. Chichester: Wiley.

Fillmore, C. J. (1968) The case for case. In Bach, E. & Harms, R. T. (eds) *Universals in Linguistic Theory*. New York: Holt, Rinehart.

Flanders, N. H. (1970) *Analyzing Teacher Behaviour*. Reading, Mass.: Addison-Wesley.

Fodor, J. A., Bever, T. G. & Garrett, M. F. (1974) *The Psychology of Language: an introduction to psycholinguistics and generative grammar*. New York: McGraw Hill.

Fraser, C., Bellugi, U. & Brown, R. (1963) Control of grammar in imitation, comprehension and production. *Journal of Verbal Learning and Verbal Behaviour* 2: 121–35.

Freeman, N. H., Lloyd, S. & Sinha, C. G. (in press) Infant search tasks reveal early concepts of containment and canonical usage of objects. *Cognition*.

Frege, G. (1892) Über Sinn und Bedeutung. *Zeitschrift für Philosophie und philosophische Kritik* 100: 25–50.

Freire, P. (1970) *Pedagogy of the Oppressed*. New York: Seabury.

French, P. (1980) Getting round the rules: on children's strategies for circumventing conversational restrictions. Paper delivered to Annual Conference of the Association for Child Psychology and Psychiatry, Tavistock Clinic, London, June 1980.

French, P. & MacLure, M. (1979) Getting the right answer and getting the answer right. *Research in Education* 22: 1–23.

Fromkin, V. (ed.) (1973) *Speech Errors as Linguistic Evidence*. The Hague: Mouton.

Garfinkel, H. & Sacks, H. (1970) On formal structures of practical actions. In McKinney, J. C. & Tiryakian, E. A. (eds) *Theoretical Sociology*. New York: Appleton-Century-Crofts.

Garnica, O. K. (1977) Some prosodic and paralinguistic features of speech to young children. In Snow, C. E. & Ferguson, C. A. (eds) *Talking to Children: language input and acquisition*. Cambridge University Press.

Garvey, C. (1975) Requests and responses in children's speech. *Journal of Child Language* 2: 41–63.

  (1977) The contingent query: a dependent act in conversation. In Lewis, M. & Rosenblum, L. A. (eds) *Interaction, Conversation, and the Development of Language*. New York: Wiley.

Gelman, R. & Shatz, M. (1977) Appropriate speech adjustments: the operation of conversational constraints on talk to two year olds. In Lewis, M. & Rosenblum, L. A. (eds) *Interaction, Conversation, and the Development of Language*. New York: Wiley.

Gibson, E. J. & Levin, H. (1975) *The Psychology of Reading*. Cambridge, Mass.: MIT Press.

Glucksberg, S., Hay, A. & Danks, J. (1976) Words in utterance contexts: young children do not confuse the meaning of 'same' and 'different'. *Child Development* 47: 737–41.

Goodman, K. S. (ed.) (1968) *The Psycholinguistic Nature of the Reading Process*. Detroit: Wayne State University Press.

Goody, J. & Watt, I. (1968) The consequences of literacy. In Goody, J. (ed.) *Literacy in Traditional Societies*. Cambridge University Press.

Greenfield, P. H. (1972) Oral or written language: the consequences for cognitive development in Africa, the United States and England. *Language and Speech* 15.2: 169–78.

Greenfield, P. H. & Smith, J. H. (1976) *The Structure of Communication in Early Language Development*. New York: Academic Press.

Grice, H. P. (1957) Meaning. *Philosophical Review* 66: 377–88.

(1975) Logic and conversation. In Cole, P. & Morgan, J. L. (eds) *Syntax and Semantics*, vol. III. New York: Academic Press.

Griffiths, P. (1979) Speech acts and early sentences. In Fletcher, P. & Garman, M. (eds) *Language Acquisition*. Cambridge University Press.

Habermas, J. (1970) On systematically distorted communication. *Inquiry* 13: 205–18.

Halliday, M. A. K. (1967a) *Intonation and Grammar in British English*. The Hague: Mouton.

(1967b) Notes on transitivity and theme in English Part 2. *Journal of Linguistics* 3: 199–244.

(1970) Language structure and language function. In Lyons, J. (ed.) *New Horizons in Linguistics*. Harmondsworth, Middx: Penguin.

(1975) *Learning How to Mean*. London: Edward Arnold.

(1977) Language as code and language as behaviour: a systemic–functional interpretation of the nature and ontogenesis of dialogue. To appear in Lamb, S. M. & Makkai, A. (eds) *Semiotics of Culture and Language*.

Halliday, M. A. K. & Hasan, R. (1976) *Cohesion in English*. London: Longman.

Halliday, M. A. K., Mackintosh, A. & Strevens, P. (1964) *The Linguistic Sciences and Language Teaching*. London: Longman.

Hammersley, M. (1974) The organisation of pupil participation. *Sociological Review* 22: 355–68.

(1977) School learning: the cultural resources required by pupils to answer a teacher's question. In Woods, P. & Hammersley, M. (eds) *School Experience: explorations in the sociology of education*. London: Croom Helm.

Heatlie, S. & Ramsey, E. (1971) An investigation into alternative methods of assessing the readability of books used in schools. *Proceedings of the Seventh Annual Study Conference of U.K.R.A.* London: Ward Lock.

Heritage, J. C. & Watson, D. R. (1979) Formulations as conversational objects. In Psathas, G. (ed.) *Everyday Language: studies in ethnomethodology*. New York: Irvington.

Holdaway, D. (1972) *Independence in Reading*. Auckland, N.Z.: Ashton Scholastic.

Hustler, D. (in press) Clarification requests: a response to Langford. In French, P. & MacLure, M. (eds) *Adult–Child Conversation: studies in structure and process*. London: Croom Helm.

Huttenlocher, J. (1974) The origins of language comprehension. In Solso, R. L. (ed.) *Theories of Cognitive Psychology*. Potomac, Md: Erlbaum.

Hymes, D. (1972) On communicative competence. In Pride, J. B. & Holmes, J. (eds) *Sociolinguistics*. Harmondsworth, Middx: Penguin.

Johnston, J. R. & Slobin, D. I. (1979) The development of locative expressions in English, Italian, Serbo-Croation and Turkish. *Journal of Child
Language* 6: 529–46.

Kamin, L. J. (1974) *The Science and Politics of I.Q.* New York: Erlbaum.

Keenan, E. O. (1974) Conversational competence in children. *Journal of
Child Language* 1: 163–83.

(1977) Making it last: repetition in children's discourse. In Ervin-Tripp,
S. M. & Mitchell-Kernan, C. (eds) *Child Discourse*. New York:
Academic Press.

Kernan, K. T. (1969) The acquisition of language by Samoan children.
Unpublished PhD dissertation, University of California, Berkeley.

King, R. (1978) *All Things Bright and Beautiful*. Chichester: Wiley.

Klima, E. S. & Bellugi, U. (1966) Syntactic regularities in the speech of
children. In Lyons, J. & Wales, R. J. (eds) *Psycholinguistics Papers*.
Edinburgh University Press.

Kobashigawa, B. (1969) Repetitions in a mother's speech to her child. In
Language, Society and the Child. Working paper 13, Language
Research Laboratory, University of California, Berkeley.

Labov, W. (1970) The logic of non-standard English. In Williams, F. (ed.)
Language and Poverty. Chicago: Markham Publishing Co.

Labov, W. & Fanshel, D. (1977) *Therapeutic Discourse: psychotherapy as
conversation*. New York: Academic Press.

Lenneberg, E. H. (1967) *Biological Foundations of Language*. New York:
Wiley.

(1975) The Concept of language differentiation. In O'Connor, N. (ed.)
Language, Cognitive Deficits and Retardation. London: Butterworth.

Leopold, W. F. (1939) *Speech Development of a Bilingual Child*, vol. I.
Evanston, Ill.: Northwestern University Press.

Levelt, W. J. M. (1978) A survey of studies in sentence perception:
1970–1976. In Levelt, W. J. M. & Flores d'Arcais, G. B. (eds) *Studies in
Perception and Language*. New York: Wiley.

Lewis, M. (1963) *Language, Thought and Personality*. London: Harrap.

Lewis, M. & Rosenblum, L. A. (eds) (1977) *Interaction, Conversation, and
the Development of Language*. New York: Wiley.

Lowe, M. (1975) Trends in the development of representational play in
infants from one to three years – an observational study. *Journal of
Child Psychology and Psychiatry* 16: 33–47.

Lyons, J. (1968) *Introduction to Theoretical Linguistics*. Cambridge
University Press.

(1977) *Semantics*. Cambridge University Press.

McCarthy, D. (1954) Language development in children. In Carmichael, L.
(ed.) *Manual of Child Psychology*. New York: Wiley.

McGarrigle, J. & Donaldson, M. (1975) Conservation accidents. *Cognition*
3.4: 341–50.

McHoul, A. (1978) The organisation of turns at formal talk in the classroom. *Language in Society* 7: 183–213.

Mackay, D. et al. (1970) *Breakthrough to Literacy: teachers' manual.* London: Longman (for Schools Council).

McKenzie, M. (1980) *Extending Literacy.* London: ILEA Centre for Language in Primary Education.

MacLure, M. & French, P. (1980) Routes to right answers: on pupils' strategies for answering teachers' questions. In Woods, P. (ed.) *Pupil Strategies.* London: Croom Helm.

Macnamara, J. (1972). Cognitive basis of language learning in infants. *Psychological Review* 79: 1–13.

(1977) On the relation between language learning and thought. In Macnamara, J. (ed.) *Language Learning and Thought.* New York: Academic Press.

McNeill, D. (1966) The creation of language by children. In Lyons, J. & Wales, R. (eds) *Psycholinguistics Papers.* Edinburgh University Press.

(1970) *The Acquisition of Language: the study of developmental psycholinguistics.* New York: Harper & Row.

Marshall, J. (1979) Language acquisition in a biological frame of reference. In Fletcher, P. & Garman, M. (eds) *Language Acquisition.* Cambridge University Press.

Marslen-Wilson, W. D., Tyler, L. K. & Seidenberg, M. (1978) Sentence processing and the clause boundary. In Levelt, W. J. M. & Flores d'Arcais, G. B. (eds) *Studies in the Perception of Language.* New York: Wiley.

Massaro, D. W. (1975) *Experimental Psychology and Information Processing.* Chicago: Rand McNally.

Mead, G. H. (1934) *Mind, Self, and Society.* University of Chicago Press.

Mehan, H. (1978) Structuring school structure. *Harvard Educational Review* 48.1: 32–64.

Miller, G. A., Galanter, E. & Pribram, K. (1960) *Plans and the Structure of Behavior.* New York: Holt, Rinehart.

Miller, G. A. & Johnson-Laird, P. N. (1976) *Language and Perception.* Cambridge University Press.

Miller, W. R. & Ervin, S. M. (1965) The development of grammar in child language. In Bellugi, U. & Brown, R. (eds) *The Acquisition of Language.* Society for Research in Child Development Monographs 29.1.

Mishler, E. (1979) Meaning in context: Is there any other kind? *Harvard Educational Review* 49.1: 1–19.

Moon, C. & Raban, E. B. (1980) *A Question of Reading* (revised edition). Basingstoke: Macmillan Education.

Moon, C. & Wells, C. G. (1979) The influences of the home on learning to read. *Journal of Research in Reading* 2.1: 53–62.

Morrison, A. & McIntyre, D. (1971) *Schools and Socialization.* Harmondsworth, Middx: Penguin.

Morton, J. (1971) What could possibly be innate? In Morton, J. (ed.)

Biological and Social Factors in Psycholinguistics. London: Logos Press.

Nelson, Katherine (1973) *Structure and Strategy in Learning to Talk*. Society for Research in Child Development Monographs 38.1–2.

— (1974) Concept, word and sentence: inter-relations in acquisition and development. *Psychological Review* 81: 267–84.

— (1977) The conceptual basis for naming. In Macnamara, J. (ed.) *Language Learning and Thought*. New York: Academic Press.

— (1979) Individual differences in language development: implications for development and language. Mimeo. Graduate Centre, City University of New York.

Nelson, K. E. (1977) Aspects of language acquisition and use from age two to age twenty. *Journal of the American Academy of Child Psychiatry* 16: 584–607.

Newport, E. L. (1976) Motherese: the speech of mothers to young children. In Castellan, N. J., Pisoni, D. P. & Potts, G. R. (eds) *Cognitive Theory*, vol. II. Hillsdale, NJ: Erlbaum.

Newport, E. L. & Gleitman, H. (1977) Maternal self-repetition and the child's acquisition of language. *Stanford Papers and Reports on Child Language Development* 13.

Newport, E. L., Gleitman, H. & Gleitman, L. (1977) Mother, I'd rather do it myself: some effects and non-effects of maternal speech style. In Snow, C. E. & Ferguson, C. A. (eds) *Talking to Children: language input and acquisition*. Cambridge University Press.

Newsom, J. (1963) *Half our Future: a report of the Central Advisory Council for Education*. London: HMSO.

Newson, J. (1977) An intersubjective approach to the systematic description of mother–infant interaction. In Schaffer, H. R. (eds) *Studies in Mother–Infant Interaction*. London: Academic Press.

Nuffield Mathematics Project (1972) *Checking Up. II*. Edinburgh: Chambers; London: Murray.

Olson, D. (1977) From utterance to text: the bias of language in speech and writing. *Harvard Educational Review* 47.3: 257–81.

Olson, D. & Hildyard, A. (in press) Literacy and the specialization of language: some aspects of the comprehension and thought processes of literate and non-literate children and adults. In Warren, N. (ed.) *Advances in Cross-Cultural Psychology*. London: Academic Press.

Pateman, T. (1975) *Language, Truth and Politics*. Sidmouth: Stroud and Pateman.

Payne, G. & Hustler, D. (1980) Teaching the class: the practical management of a cohort. *British Journal of Sociology of Education* 1.1: 49–66.

Perera, K. (1979) Reading and writing. In Cruttenden, A. *Language in Infancy and Childhood*. Manchester University Press.

Phillips, J. R. (1973) Syntax and vocabulary of mothers' speech to young children, age and sex comparisons. *Child Development* 44: 182–5.

Piaget, J. (1962) *Play, Dreams and Imitation*. London: Routledge & Kegan Paul.

Piaget, J. & Inhelder, B. (1969) *The Psychology of the Child*. London: Routledge & Kegan Paul.

Poussaint, A. F. (1967) A Negro psychiatrist explains the Negro psyche. *New York Times Magazine*, 20 August, p. 52.

Powell, J. (1978) Pupils' meanings and teachers' meanings of words in science. Unpublished papers. Teachers' Research Group, University of London Institute of Education.

Raban, E. B. (in preparation) *Children Learning to Read*. To be published by Cambridge University Press.

Ratner, N. & Bruner, J. S. (1978) Games, social exchange and the acquisition of language. *Journal of Child Language* 5: 391–402.

Rawson, H. (1978) The function of reading in the transition to concrete and formal operations. In Presseusen, B. Z., Goldstein, D. & Appel, M. H. (eds) *Topics in Cognitive Development*, vol. II: *Language and Operational Thought*. London: Plenum Press.

Robinson, W. P. (1978) *Language Management in Education: the Australian context*. Sydney: George Allen & Unwin.

Rosch, E. (1977) Classification of real-word objects: origins and representation in cognition. In Johnson-Laird, P. N. & Wason, P. C. (eds) *Thinking*. Cambridge University Press.

Rose, N. (1979) The psychological complex: mental measurement and social administration. *Ideology and Consciousness* 5.

Rose, S. (1978) *Race, education and intelligence: a teacher's guide*. London: NUT.

Rosen, H. (1972) *Language and Class: a critical look at the theories of Basil Bernstein*. Bristol: Falling Wall Press.

Sachs, J. & Devin, J. (1976) Young children's knowledge of age-appropriate speech styles. *Journal of Child Language* 3: 81–98.

Sachs, J., Brown, R. & Salerno, R. (1976) Adults' speech to children. In von Raffler-Engel, W. & Lebrun, Y. (eds) *Baby Talk and Infant Speech*. Amsterdam: Swets & Zeitlinger.

Sacks, H. (1967) Lecture 8, October 31st. Mimeo. University of California, Irvine.

  (1968) Lecture Notes, April 17. Mimeo. University of California, Irvine.

  (1974) On the analysability of stories by children. In Turner, R. (ed.) *Ethnomethodology*. Harmondsworth, Middx: Penguin.

Sacks, H., Schegloff, E. A. & Jefferson, G. (1974) A simplest systematics for the organization of turn-taking for conversation. *Language* 50: 696–735. Reprinted in Schenkein, J. (ed.) *Studies in the Organisation of Conversational Interaction*. New York: Academic Press, 1978.

Sapir, E. (1921) *Language*. New York: Harcourt Brace.

Savić, S. (1975) Aspects of adult–child communication: the problem of question-acquisition. *Journal of Child Language* 2: 251–60.

Scaife, M. & Bruner, J. S. (1975) The capacity for joint visual attention in the infant. *Nature* 253.5489: 265–6.

Schaerlaekens, A. M. (1973) *The Two-Word Stage in Child Language Development: a study based on evidence provided by Dutch-speaking triplets.* The Hague: Mouton.

Schaffer, H. R. (1971) *The Growth of Sociability.* Harmondsworth, Middx: Penguin.

(ed.) (1977) *Studies in Mother–Infant Interaction.* London: Academic Press.

Schank, R. C. & Abelson, R. P. (1977) *Scripts, Plans, Goals and Understanding: an inquiry into human knowledge structures.* Hillsdale, NJ: Erlbaum.

Schegloff, E., Jefferson, G. & Sacks, H. (1977) The preference for self-correction in the organisation of repair in conversation. *Language* 53: 361–82.

Scribner, S. & Cole, M. (1978) *Literacy without Schooling: testing for intellectual effects.* Vai Literacy Project Working Paper 2. Rockefeller University, Laboratory of Comparative Human Cognition.

Searle, J. R. (1969) *Speech Acts: an essay in the philosophy of language.* Cambridge University Press.

(1975) Indirect speech acts. In Cole, P. & Morgan, J. L. (eds) *Syntax and Semantics,*, vol. III. New York: Academic Press.

(1977) A classification of illocutionary acts. *Language in Society* 5: 1–23.

Shatz, M. (1978a) Children's comprehension of their mothers' question-directives. *Journal of Child Language* 5: 39–46.

(1978b) On the development of communicative understanding: an early strategy for interpreting and responding to messages. *Cognitive Psychology* 10: 271–301.

Shatz, M. & Gelman, R. (1973) *The Development of Communication Skills: modifications in the speech of young children as a function of listener.* Society for Research in Child Development Monographs 38.

Shields, M. (1978) The child as psychologist. In Lock, A. J. (ed.) *Action, Gesture and Symbol: the emergence of language.* London: Academic Press.

Sinclair, H. & Bronckart, J. P. (1972) SVO: a linguistic universal? A study in developmental psycholinguistics. *Journal of Experimental Child Psychology* 14: 329–48.

Sinclair, J. McH. & Coulthard, R. M. (1975) *Towards an Analysis of Discourse: the English used by teachers and pupils.* Oxford University Press.

Sinha, C. & Carabine, B. (in press) Interactions between lexis and discourse in conservation and comprehension tasks. *Journal of Child Language.*

Sinha, C. & Walkerdine, V. (1978) Conservation, a problem in language, culture and thought. In Waterson, N. & Snow, C. E. (eds) *The Development of Communication.* London: Wiley.

Skinner, B. F. (1957) *Verbal Behavior.* New York: Appleton.

Slobin, D. I. (1973) Cognitive prerequisites for the development of grammar. In Ferguson, C. A. & Slobin, D. I. (eds) *Studies in Child Language Development*. New York: Holt, Rinehart.

(1979) *The Role of Language in Language Acquisition*. Mimeo. University of California, Berkeley.

Slobin, D. I., Antinucci, F., Wells, C. G. et al. (1972) *Semantics of Child Speech: coding manual*. Institute of Human Learning, University of California, Berkeley.

Smith, F. (1975) *Comprehension and Learning*. London: Holt, Rinehart.

(1978) *Reading*. Cambridge University Press.

Snow, C. E. (1972) Mothers' speech to children learning language. *Child Development* 43: 549–65.

(1977) Mothers' speech research: from input to interaction. In Snow, C. E. & Ferguson, C. A. (eds) *Talking to Children: language input and acquisition*. Cambridge University Press.

(1978) Social interaction and language acquisition. To appear in the Proceedings of the First International Congress for the study of Child Language, Tokyo, 1978.

Snow, C. E. & Ferguson, C. A. (eds) (1977) *Talking to Children: language input and acquisition*. Cambridge University Press.

Speier, M. (1976) The child as conversationalist: some culture-contact features of conversational interactions between adults and children. In Hammersley, M. & Woods, P. (eds) *The Process of Schooling: a sociological perspective*. London: Routledge & Kegan Paul.

Stanford, G. S. (1978) The role of language in mathematics. Unpublished papers. Teachers' Research Group, University of London Institute of Education.

Stern, D. N. (1974) Mother and infant at play: the dyadic interaction involving facial, vocal and gaze behaviours. In Lewis, M. & Rosenblum, L. A. (eds) *The Effect of the Infant on its Caregiver*. New York: Wiley.

(1977) *The First Relationship: infant and mother*. London: Open Books.

Strohner, H. & Nelson, K. (1974) The young child's development of sentence comprehension: the influence of event probability, non-verbal context, syntactic form and strategies. *Child Development* 45: 567–76.

Stubbs, M. (1976) *Language, Schools and Classrooms: contemporary sociology of the school*. London: Methuen.

Sylvester-Bradley, B. & Trevarthen, C. (1978) Baby talk as an adaptation to the infant's communication. In Waterson, N. & Snow, C. E. (eds) *The Development of Communication*. London: Wiley.

Templin, M. C. (1957) *Certain Language Skills in Children*. Minneapolis: University of Minnesota Press.

Tough, J. (1973) The language of young children: implications for the education of the young disadvantaged child. In Chazan, M. (ed.) *Education in the Early Years*. Faculty of Education, University College of Swansea.

(1977) *The Development of Meaning*. London: Unwin Education Books,

Trevarthen, C. (1974) Conversations with a two-month-old. *New Scientist* 2, May 1974, p. 230.

Trevarthen, C. & Hubley, P. (1978) Secondary intersubjectivity: confidence, confiding and acts of meaning in the first year. In Lock, A. J. (ed.) *Action, Gesture and Symbol: the emergence of language*. London: Academic Press.

Trevarthen, C., Hubley, P. & Sheeran, L. (1975) Psychological actions in early infancy. *La Recherche* 6.56: 447–58.

Vorster, J. (1974) *Mother Speech to Children: some methodological considerations*. Institute for General Linguistics, University of Amsterdam.

Vygotsky, L. S. (1962) *Thought and Language*. Cambridge, Mass.: MIT Press.

(1978) *Mind in Society*. Cambridge, Mass.: Harvard University Press.

Waismann, F. (1953) Language strata. In Flew, A. G. N. (ed.) *Logic and Language* (second series). Oxford: Blackwell.

Walkerdine, V. (1975) Spatial and temporal relational terms in the linguistic and cognitive development of young children. Unpublished PhD thesis, University of Bristol.

Walkerdine, V. & Corran, G. (1977) Cognitive development and educational practice: pupil progress in primary school mathematics. Paper presented to British Psychological Society Developmental Section Annual Conference. Cambridge.

Walkerdine, V. & Sinha, C. (1978) The internal triangle: language, reasoning and the social context. In Markova, I. (ed.) *The Social Context of Language*. Chichester: Wiley.

Wells, C. G. (1973) *Coding Manual for the Description of Child Speech in its Conversational Context*. University of Bristol School of Education. Revised edition, 1975.

(1974a) Learning to code experience through language. *Journal of Child Language* 1: 243–69.

(1974b) Communication through language. Paper given to Pre-school section of the Annual Conference of the National Association for the Teaching of English, York, April 1974.

(1975) Interpersonal communication and the development of language. Paper given at Third International Symposium on First Language Acquisition, London, September 1975.

(1976) Comprehension: what it means to understand. *English in Education* 10.2: 24–37.

(1977) Language use and educational success: an empirical response to Joan Tough's 'The Development of Meaning' (1977). *Research in Education* 18: 9–34.

(1978) Talking with children, the complementary roles of parents and teachers. *English in Education* 12.2: 15–38.

(1979a) Variation in child language. In Fletcher, P. & Garman, M. (eds)

Language Acquisition. Cambridge University Press. Reprinted in Lee, V. (ed.) *Language Development*. London: Croom Helm, 1979.

(1979b) Learning and using the auxiliary verb in English. In Lee, V. (ed.) *Language Development*. London: Croom Helm.

(in press a) Influences of the home on language development. In Davies, A. (ed.) *Language and Learning at School and Home*. London: SSRC/Heinemann.

(in press b) Adjustments in adult–child conversation: some effects of interaction. In Giles, H., Robinson, W. P. & Smith, P. M. (eds) *Language: social and psychological perspectives*. Oxford: Pergamon.

(in press c) Apprenticeship in meaning. In Nelson, K. E. (ed.) *Children's Language*, vol. II. New York: Gardner Press.

Wells, C. G. & Montgomery, M. (in press) Adult–child discourse at home and at school. In French, P. & MacLure, M. (eds) *Adult–Child Conversation: studies in structure and process*. London: Croom Helm.

Wells, C. G. & Robinson, W. P. (in press) The role of adult speech in language development. In Fraser, C. & Scherer, K. (eds) *The Social Psychology of Language*. Cambridge University Press.

Wells, C. G. & Woll, B. (1979) The development of meaning relations in children's speech. Paper given at Child Language Seminar, Reading, April 1979.

Wells, C. G., Barnes, S. B. & Satterly, D. (in preparation) Characteristics of adult speech which predict children's language development.

Wells, C. G., MacLure, M. & Montgomery, M. (1979) Some strategies for sustaining conversation. Paper given at Sixth LACUS Forum. To appear in Werth, P. (ed.) *The Development of Conversation and Discourse*. London: Croom Helm, in press.

Wells, C. G., Montgomery, M. & MacLure, M. (1979) Adult–child discourse: outline of a model of analysis. *Journal of Pragmatics* 3: 337–80.

Werth, P. (forthcoming) *Focus in Generative Grammar*. To be published by Croom Helm.

Widdowson, H. (1979) Rules and procedures in discourse analysis. In Myers, T. (ed.) *The Development of Conversation and Discourse*. Edinburgh University Press.

Wittgenstein, L. (1953) *Philosophical Investigations*. Oxford: Blackwell.

Woll, B. (1979) Sex as a variable in child language development. *Bristol Working Papers in Language* 1: 71–86.

Wootton, A. (1975) *Dilemmas of Discourse*. London: Allen & Unwin.

(in press) On children's use of address terms. In French, P. & MacLure, M. (eds) *Adult–Child Conversation: studies in structure and process*. London: Croom Helm.

Index

acknowledge 32–5, 45, 209, 213; *see also* discourse; exchange; give; solicit
adjacency pairs 28–9, 180; *see also* turn
anaphora 58, 104
aspect 57
asymmetry, interactional 168, 169–82, 221, 227, 232–4, 237
attitude 51–2, 54–5, 57, 61, 69

behaviour, verbal/nonverbal 17, 35–6, 66, 70–1, 83, 125
Bristol language development study 2–15, 114–15, 167, 183, 187, 192–3, 195–6, 250, 258, 261, 263, 277–82

case grammar 3, 84–5
categories 50, 70–2, 110, 144, 161
children's 14, 17, 183–92, 194, 196–8, 201, 214–16, 249, 259
see also concept
clarification 130–1, 163, 172, 174
clues, nature of 131–4
code, linguistic 4, 72, 113–14, 256–9, 263
cognition hypothesis 84–8, 94–5, 110
cognitive development 189–91, 198–201
and literacy 20, 242–9, 250–6, 260–4
and primary school 79–88, 94–5, 183, 186–7, 194–9, 204, 264, 273–4
and social background 256–9
cohesion 30–1, 57–8, 104; *see also* discourse; exchange

cohort, class as 229
communication 1–2, 16–17, 23, 36, 50–5, 63, 66–8, 72, 73, 91, 103, 108, 116–17, 122–5, 158, 175, 185, 242
adult–child 76–7, 96–101, 104–6, 114, 203, 263
attitude 51–2, 54–5, 57, 61, 69
interpersonal function of 49, 90–1, 94, 96, 112, 244
oral 242–3
pathological 117–18
purpose of 48–9, 51–2, 54–5, 57, 66, 69, 93, 115
topic of 49–52, 54–7, 60, 66, 69, 88, 103–4, 115
triangle of 46–8, 54
see also competence, communicative; comprehension; context
communicative development 96–101, 108, 120, 168, 175, 181–2
competence 12, 55, 75–6, 158, 168, 175, 216, 264
communicative 56, 181–2
intellectual 259–60
componential analysis 136–7, 139, 142
comprehension 63–8, 271–2
development of 17, 91–3, 116–56, 193–201
process of 117–22
of syntax 147–54
see also concept; context; meaning; understanding
concept 49–50
conceptual development 17, 81–2, 134, 138–40, 143–5, 185, 187, 251–3, 260

concept – *cont.*
extension/intension of 137–8, 140–2
object 91–2, 144–6, 240–1
referential 147
relational 145–6, 259
see also functional core concept
theory; instantiation rules
conservation tasks 191–4, 248–9
constitutive view of language 157–8,
161–2, 181
context:
and comprehension 116–17,
119–21, 125, 129, 133–4, 152–6,
186–96, 202–3
conversational 57, 64, 72, 108, 179
home 205–39
influence of 15–16, 52, 77, 183
interactive 116, 157, 169
and meaning 17–19, 137–8, 146–7,
157–68, 181, 200, 244, 253,
256–7, 272
school 196–204, 205–39
situational 3–4, 7, 12, 23–4, 43, 47,
53–4, 57, 62, 64–5, 68–70, 81,
83, 98–100, 109, 157, 184, 241,
243, 259
see also cue, contextual;
relationships, social; socialisation
contract, given–new 53, 135
contrast 31, 58; *see also* discourse;
exchange
conversation:
adult–adult 36, 118, 224–5
development of 12–13, 101–9
and development of meaning 162–3,
166, 181
organisation of 23–37, 43–4, 46–8,
51–3, 67–8, 73, 120, 208–9,
228–37
parent–child 4–17, 112, 115, 116,
126, 128–9, 162, 166–82, 208,
258–9, 263
purpose of 67, 132
sequential structure of 13, 26, 36,
37, 100, 174–5, 181, 209–13,
216–19, 221–2, 224–8, 237
sustaining 104, 107–8, 123, 125
see also meaning, negotiation of;
proto-conversation; turn
cooperative principle of discourse 30,
54, 68, 71, 117–18, 120
corrections 163, 217–22
other correction 217–20
self-correction 61, 163, 218–20
cue 17, 43, 47, 66–8, 109, 119, 151,
153

contextual 188, 196
culture and language 247–9, 250, 252,
256, 261, 264

discourse 13, 62, 69, 74, 135–6, 192,
199–200, 216, 237
organising 32–47, 51–2
repressive 117
sequential structure of 26–9, 35–6,
37, 45, 48
sustaining 29–32
see also cooperative principle;
exchange; paradigmatic
dimension; speech acts; syntagmic
dimension; turn

education 2, 18–19
and literacy 20–1, 243–8, 250,
252–3, 255–8, 261–2, 264–76
see also intervention in language
development; school
ellipsis 58, 166
emphasis 58–9
exchange 29–36, 59, 72, 97, 100,
122–3, 126, 128, 133, 171, 228
initiation 29–35, 40
linking 30–6, 45
see also discourse; pre-sequence
experience, internal representation of
49–50, 52, 54, 63, 73, 76, 79, 86,
94
expressive intention 111–12; *see also*
vocabulary

feedback 61–3, 76, 94–5, 109, 132–3,
162, 164, 166
form, linguistic 16, 56, 62, 74, 79,
86–7, 106–11, 118, 152–3, 275
and function 40–5, 109, 116, 128–9
formulation 164–7, 181
function 12, 20, 37, 71, 92, 112,
167–8, 240–1
and form 40–5, 109, 116, 128–9
interpersonal 49, 89–91, 112
functional core concept theory
139–45; *see also* concept

gaze 27, 51, 64, 67, 95, 132
gesture 27, 36, 55, 64, 67, 69, 73, 76,
90–1, 93–8, 100, 108, 185
give 32–4, 45; *see also* acknowledge;
discourse; exchange; solicit
grammar 12, 23, 49, 63, 71, 73, 91,
109, 165
acquisition of 3, 94, 207
see also case grammar;

transformational-generative grammar
greeting 27, 209

hearer 17, 26–8, 40–1, 43–5, 47, 52–8, 60, 63–5, 68, 73, 93, 117, 121–2
home:
  language use in 9, 11, 16, 19, 34, 205–39, 258, 264–5, 268
  participation in conversation 228, 230, 233–4

implicatures 30, 53, 57
informational content of utterance 17, 52–4, 57–9, 61, 63–6, 73, 90–1, 106, 108, 119, 121–2, 130–1, 151, 159; *see also* clues, nature of
instantiation rules 143
intelligence, *see* thought and language
intention, communicative 23–5, 47–8, 55–6, 94–5, 99, 105, 108, 116
  meaning intention 55–63, 64, 66–9, 70, 72, 73, 83, 109, 119–20, 159, 185, 244, 272–3
  semantic 83
  see also expressive intention; referential intention
interaction 2, 11, 15–21, 22–72, 76, 157–8, 208–9, 226–7, 244
  child–parent 1, 76–7, 90, 93–101, 109, 112, 162–3, 168–9, 170–5, 181, 184, 240
  at home 205–6, 208–13, 216, 220–2, 226–8, 230, 233, 237, 258
  initiation of 11, 103–4, 185
  and intersubjectivity 94–101
  parent–child 4, 24–5, 68, 96–7, 104–5, 109, 114–15, 116, 124–5, 133, 164, 167, 170–2, 206–7
  relations in 117
  at school 9, 205–16, 219, 221–2, 226–37
  skills 157–8
  styles of 114–15
  see also asymmetry, interactional; communication; variables of interaction
intersubjectivity 47, 68, 94–101, 119
  intersubjective attention 53–4, 97, 108
intervention in language development 200–4; *see also* education; school
intonation 12–13, 26, 33, 45, 57–60,

63, 69, 103–4, 111, 278; *see also* pitch; tone

language ability 2, 7, 113, 175; *see also* competence
language acquisition 16–17, 24, 50, 72, 74–8, 86, 110, 147, 167, 188, 191, 245, 252
  rate of 112–13
language acquisition device (LAD) 76–8
language development 2, 74–5, 78–9, 116, 167
  cognitive basis 79–88, 94–5, 198–201; *see also* cognitive development
  pre-school children 2–8, 15–18, 72, 73–7, 79–85, 88–93, 96–101, 116, 122, 143, 157, 181, 240–1, 258–9
  and primary school 183–4, 186, 192, 194, 204, 267, 275
  and role of literacy 259–64
  scale of 13–15
  variation 13, 74, 109–15, 155, 259
language use 23–4, 68, 70–1, 113, 116, 118, 134, 238, 241, 250–2, 255, 257–60, 265, 272–3
  and context 12, 157, 161–2, 167, 205–39, 241
  patterns of 1–2
  by pre-school children 4, 12
  see also home; school
lexicon 17, 74, 134–5
lexis 55–7, 60–1, 65, 69, 71, 73, 94, 109, 154, 165, 181, 207
literacy 20–1, 241
  and cognitive development 20, 242–7, 250–6, 260–1
  and education 243
  and pre-school development 259–64
  and school 264–76
  and social background 256–9, 261–2
  and symbolic representation 250–5
  teaching of 242
locative orientation test 187–91

meaning 20, 41, 56, 62, 74, 79, 98, 109–10, 121, 153, 157–68, 243–4, 252–5, 261–3
  attribution of 134
  communication of 23, 47, 50, 54, 64, 87–8
  construction of 46, 115
  contrast 56–60
  'core' meaning 138–9

meaning – *cont.*
  and early development 3–4, 13, 16,
    80–5, 184–5, 187, 204, 241,
    261–2
  ideational/referential 91, 108, 112,
    134–6, 143
  intention 55–63, 64, 66–9, 70, 72,
    73, 83, 109, 119–20, 159, 185,
    244, 272–3
  negotiation of 15, 23–6, 68, 71–2,
    82, 106, 108, 115
  orientation to 4, 113, 243–4, 250,
    252, 255–7, 261–2
  pragmatic dimension 3, 88–94, 103,
    112
  relational 82–5, 88, 103–4, 135–40,
    142, 145–6
  of sentence 167
  word 80–5, 92, 100, 103, 117,
    134–47, 155, 187
  see also context; reference; sense
message, communication of 16–18,
    48–55, 57–61, 63–9, 73, 87–8,
    109, 116–19, 244, 252–4
  modification of 122–5, 131–3
  see also communication; orientation
mismatch theories 9–10, 19, 129, 205–
    206, 227
mood 45, 56–7, 59–61
morphophonology 74, 79
motherese 123–5; *see also*
    conversation, parent–child
move, conversational 29–37, 45–6,
    51–2, 59, 133, 162
  initiate 29–35, 103–4, 126–30, 227
  respond 29–35, 126–30
  return 35
  see also acknowledge; exchange;
    give; prospectiveness; solicit;
    speech acts

Newsom Report on Secondary
    Schooling 238

object constancy 145; *see also* concept
orientation 52–4, 57–8, 60–1, 69, 73,
    94, 103, 117, 120, 249, 259, 268;
    see also meaning; message
overextension 81–2, 141, 143–4, 186
overlap 141–2, 186

paradigmatic dimension of discourse
    27–8, 32–6, 45
parents, role of 6, 8, 9, 18, 96–8, 101,
    104–6, 108, 112, 114–15, 123,
    162–6, 168–74, 176, 180–2,
    219–21, 225, 262–3, 266–8; *see*

    also conversation, parent–child;
    home; motherese
partial semantics hypothesis 142; *see*
    also semantic feature hypothesis
participation 228–37, 238
  overparticipation 228, 230–1, 236
  see also turn
performance 2, 55–6, 76, 255
  and social background 256–9,
    264–7
phonology 23, 61, 65, 71, 73, 121,
    207, 227
pitch 33–4, 45, 59–61, 104, 278–9;
    see also intonation
plan 48, 50, 54, 61, 63–4, 69
possession, expression of 88, 167
pre-invitation 225
pre-sequence 35, 126–8, 130–1,
    224–8, 237
production 48–53, 55, 61–5, 68, 71,
    93–4, 108, 116, 140, 162
pronoun/pronominal 30–1, 58, 111
prospectiveness 33; *see also* exchange;
    linking
proto-conversation 97, 108
proto-language 90, 93, 103, 110
prototypes 138–9, 144–5
purpose of utterance 16, 20, 48–9,
    51–2, 54–5, 57, 66, 69, 115, 119,
    160, 171, 226, 237

question 27–8, 39–40, 106–7, 129–30,
    171–6, 178, 217
  corrections 217–22, 226–7
  'pseudo-questions' 211–12, 216
  question prefaces 222–6, 234–7
  in school/home 19, 209–28, 230–6

reading 8–9, 245, 253–4, 260–7, 271;
    see also literacy
reference 112, 134–5; *see also*
    meaning; sense
referential intention 111–12; *see also*
    vocabulary
relationships, social 18–19, 157–8,
    167–8, 180–1
  parent–child 168–9
  see also context
repetition 30, 123
  lexical 104
request 28, 40–1, 42–5, 60, 124, 180,
    209
  for action 126–31
response/answer 27–8, 40, 59, 104,
    106–7, 126–8, 130, 150–5, 164,
    172–4, 180

'child-as-agent' 148, 154
intransitive 148, 154
primitive 147–8, 154
school/home 209–28, 232–7
rules 143
  of grammar 2, 23, 46, 56, 74–6

school:
  and cognitive development 183,
    186–7, 194–201
  and language development 183–4,
    186, 192, 258–9
  language use in 9–12, 16, 18–20,
    155–6, 198–200, 205–39
  and literacy 264–76
  participation in conversation
    228–37
  see also context; education;
    intervention
semantic feature hypothesis 142–4,
  188
semantics 64, 74, 79–86, 88, 103,
  110, 115, 142, 167–8, 252
  development of 17, 187–8
  relations 121, 207
  semantic fields 104, 135–7
  see also partial semantics hypothesis
sense 135; *see also* meaning; reference
sensorimotor intelligence 84–8, 94,
  139, 145
sentence 16, 23, 48, 55, 74–5, 207
  interpretation of 1, 153–4
  meaning of 167
  'standard descriptive sentence' 244
significance, levels of 41–2
signification 193–6, 198–200
skills:
  cognitive 183, 191, 242–5, 254–5,
    259–62, 264, 266
  communicative 133
  interactive 157–8, 162
  language 15, 133, 183, 191, 196–7,
    200, 254, 262, 273
  perception 8
social background, influence of 1, 4,
  9–10, 19–20, 113–14, 205–7,
  237–8, 256
  and language and cognition 256–9,
    261–4
socialisation, role of language in 3–4;
  see also context, situational
solicit 32–6, 45, 52, 130, 174–6, 178,
  234; *see also* acknowledge;
  discourse; exchange; give
speakers 1, 17, 38–41, 43–4, 47–8,
  50–6, 61–5, 68, 73, 93, 117, 119,

121–2, 165; *see also* language
  use; speech
speech 1, 17–18, 61, 63, 75, 98, 243,
  255, 267, 272
  adult–child 122–31
  child 9, 14
  see also speakers
speech acts 48, 55, 90, 126, 244
  categories 70–1
  form and function of 40–5, 129
  repertoire of 36–41, 52
  see also discourse
story-prefaces 175–8
strategies:
  for comprehension 93, 116–17, 122,
    144, 147–55, 197–200, 272
  developing 14, 183–204
  engagement 172–8
  interactional 18–19, 67, 106, 108–9,
    114, 168–82
  probable-event strategies 148–52,
    154
  and school performance 197–200,
    201, 203–4, 211–12, 214–16
  word-order strategies 149–52, 154
stress 67
structure of language 110, 155, 168
  deep 74
  surface 74–5, 121, 151
substitution 58
symbolic representation 248, 250–5,
  259, 262, 264, 267, 271, 273; *see
  also* literacy
syntagmic dimension of discourse
  27–32, 45
syntax 55–7, 65, 69, 74, 86, 110, 117,
  121, 165–8, 181, 207, 227, 252
  comprehension of 147–55
  simplification 123–5, 133
  syntactic development 74–9, 147,
    149

tense 57
tests 9, 202–4
  cognition 191, 245–6, 248–9
  comprehension 7–8, 67, 125–34,
    152–4, 187–96, 201
  IQ 201–2
  linguistic 4, 7–8
  see also conservation tasks; locative
    orientation test
thought and language 84–8, 240–1,
  244–5, 247–9, 260; *see also*
  cognitive development
tone 45, 59–60, 67, 104–5, 277
  tone units 58–61, 67, 278

tone—*contd*
  see also intonation
topic 54–7, 60, 66, 69, 88, 106, 115,
    125–7, 171–2, 174, 179–80, 227,
    229–30, 232
  construction of 49–52
  continuity of 29–31, 103–4, 108
transformational-generative grammar
    3, 16, 23, 55–6, 74–5
turn 12, 16, 25–31, 35, 96, 100, 103,
    105, 169, 174–5, 180, 219–21,
    228–37
  allocation 213, 228–9, 231–4, 236
  see also adjacency pairs;
    participation

underextension 81–2, 141–2, 186
understanding 122–31, 133–4,
    137–47, 201–4; *see also*
    comprehension
utterance 7, 12, 14, 27–8, 46–7,
    57–62, 68, 70, 72, 76, 85, 88,
    98–100, 104, 109, 118–19, 124,
    135, 175–8, 208–9, 213, 277
  and context 121, 134, 153, 157–62,
    164–6, 175, 179–80, 203, 233–6

early 82–3, 88–94, 101–3, 106–7,
    111, 115, 181, 186
  form of 41–5, 53–4, 86, 128–9
  functions of 16, 37, 39–40, 71, 105,
    128–9
  mean length of utterance (MLU)
    82–4, 111–13
  processing 65–8, 71, 116–17,
    121–2, 146–7, 155
  production of 48–53, 55, 61–5, 68,
    71, 93–4, 116, 140, 162
  see also discourse; informational
    content of utterance; message

Vai culture 245–6, 253, 255, 259–60
variables of interaction 208
vocabulary 12, 49, 63
  child 82, 91–2, 111–12, 114, 147,
    155, 207
vocalisation 96, 98, 100, 184

Wolof tribe 248–50
word order 83, 149–52, 154
written language, importance of 1,
    8–9, 20, 242, 253–5, 260–7,
    271–5